A PHENOMENOLOGY OF INSTITUTIONS

To a degree insufficiently captured by the term governance, the present age is one of institutional complexity. China is a case in point. An amalgam of socialist, capitalist, corporatist, and pluralist characteristics, China's systems of governance defy classification using extant categories in the institutionalist literature. What, after all, is a socialist market system?

A Phenomenology of Institutions begins with the problem of describing emergent institutional phenomena using conventional typologies. Constructing a new descriptive framework for rendering new, hybrid, and flexible institutional designs, Raul Lejano, Jia Guo, Hongping Lian, and Bo Yin propose new descriptors, involving concepts of autopoiesis, textuality, and relationality, that might better describe new and emergent models of governance. The authors illustrate the utility of this framework with a number of case studies, each dealing with a different aspect of Chinese legal and civic institutions and comparing these with "Western" models.

This book will be a valuable resource for institutional scholars in the fields of public policy, political science, organization studies, public administration, and international development, studying new and emergent forms of governance.

Raul Lejano is a professor in the Steinhardt School at New York University. He is the author of *Frameworks for Policy Analysis* (Routledge), translated into Chinese as 政策分析框架 – 融合文本与语境 (Tsinghua Press), and co-author of *The Power of Narrative in Environmental Networks* (MIT Press). He has also taught at the Massachusetts Institute of Technology, University of California, Irvine, and the University of Hong Kong.

Jia Guo is an associate professor in the School of Government at Beijing Normal University. Her main research interests are public policy (environmental policy), non-profit organizations, and comparative public administration. She obtained her PhD from the University of Hong Kong. Her work on environmental nongovernmental organizations in China demonstrates how a nuanced form of civil society actor is emerging, combining aspects of traditional nongovernmental institutions and more corporatist forms of civic engagement.

Hongping Lian is an associate professor in the School of Government at Beijing Normal University, and Vice Dean of the Academy of Government at Beijing Normal University, China. She obtained her PhD in sociology from the University of Aberdeen, UK, and did postdoctoral research on housing studies in the Department of Public Policy in City University of Hong Kong with Ray Forrest. Her primary areas of scholarship are land policy and housing policy.

Bo Yin is an associate professor in the College for Criminal Law Science at Beijing Normal University. He received his PhD in law from University of Aberdeen, UK. His primary areas are criminal justice, criminal procedure and legal theory. He has published a monograph titled *Criminal Procedural Consequences Stemming from Criminal Procedural Deficiencies*, as well as about 20 articles in English and Chinese.

'This is a must-read book for those interested in the study of institutional diversity and for those who are interested in the evolution of institutions in developing countries particularly China.'

Eduardo Araral, *Associate Professor,*
National University of Singapore

'Lejano, Guo, Lian, and Yin recognize the deficiencies of existing conceptions of institutions, as evidenced by the rapid growth of "democracy with adjectives" scholarship, and rectify this by constructing a framework for new, hybrid, and evolving institutional designs. This framework for analyzing new and emergent models of governance relies on the concept of relationality, rather than rationality in a Weberian tradition, and explains why so many formal institutional designs are only partly specified and the rest is constituted through interactions between networks of policy actors. This is an important and innovative book for institutional scholars to read, as well as those who study Chinese governance.'

Jessica C. Teets, *Associate Professor,*
Middlebury College

A PHENOMENOLOGY OF INSTITUTIONS

Relationality and Governance in China and Beyond

Raul Lejano, Jia Guo, Hongping Lian and Bo Yin

Routledge
Taylor & Francis Group

NEW YORK AND LONDON

First published 2019
by Routledge
711 Third Avenue, New York, NY 10017

and by Routledge
2 Park Square, Milton Park, Abingdon, Oxon OX14 4RN

Routledge is an imprint of the Taylor & Francis Group, an informa business

© 2019 Taylor & Francis

The right of Raul Lejano, Jia Guo, Hongping Lian, and Bo Yin to be identified as authors of this work has been asserted by them in accordance with sections 77 and 78 of the Copyright, Designs and Patents Act 1988.

All rights reserved. No part of this book may be reprinted or reproduced or utilised in any form or by any electronic, mechanical, or other means, now known or hereafter invented, including photocopying and recording, or in any information storage or retrieval system, without permission in writing from the publishers.

Trademark notice: Product or corporate names may be trademarks or registered trademarks, and are used only for identification and explanation without intent to infringe.

Library of Congress Cataloging-in-Publication Data
Names: Lejano, Raul P., 1961- author.
Title: A phenomenology of institutions: relationality and governance in China and beyond / Raul Lejano, Jia Guo, Hongping Lian, and Bo Yin.
Description: New York, NY : Routledge, 2018. | Includes bibliographical references and index.
Identifiers: LCCN 2018012958| ISBN 9781138667358 (hardback) | ISBN 9781138667365 (pbk.) | ISBN 9781317212423 (epub) | ISBN 9781317212416 (mobipocket/kindle)
Subjects: LCSH: Administrative agencies--China. | Public administration--China. | Political culture--China. | China--Politics and government--Philosophy.
Classification: LCC JQ1511 .L47 2018 | DDC 306.20951--dc23
LC record available at https://lccn.loc.gov/2018012958

ISBN: 978-1-138-66735-8 (hbk)
ISBN: 978-1-138-66736-5 (pbk)
ISBN: 978-1-315-61893-7 (ebk)

Typeset in Bembo
by Taylor & Francis Books

CONTENTS

List of illustrations	*vi*
Acknowledgements	*vii*
Glossary of Terms	*viii*
Preface	*ix*

1 Introduction: The Phenomenology of Institutional Innovation   1

2 Developing New Modes of Institutional Description   13

3 Governing by Metaphor: The Intertextuality of Institutional Life in China   34

4 Relationality in Rural Property Regimes   48

5 Relational Institutions and ENGOs in China: From Nu River to Changzhou   78

6 Multiple Legal Traditions, Legal Pluralism and Institutional Innovation: The Chinese Criminal Procedure System in Contrast   94

7 Conclusion: China, the Looking-Glass   139

Index   *148*

ILLUSTRATIONS

Figures

2.1	Markets in Autopoietic and Sociopoietic Systems	17
2.2	Contrasting Institutional Models	19
2.3	Dialectic Between Text and Context	24
3.1	Intertextual Model of Institutions	38

Tables

2.1	Types of Goods: Expanded Classification System	21
4.1	Types of Goods: Expanded Classification System	71

ACKNOWLEDGEMENTS

Portions of Chapter 1 first appeared as a conference paper, entitled "East vs. West: Distinguishing Institutional Types," presented at the Annual Conference of the International Political Science Association in Madrid, Spain, on July 10, 2012.

Portions of Chapter 3 first appeared as a working paper, entitled "Governing by Metaphor: Rhetoric and Institutions in China," prepared for the Institute of Water Policy at the National University of Singapore, November 2017. This work was partially supported by a WRG grant from the Institute of Water Policy at the National University of Singapore (R-603-000-219-490).

Portions of Chapter 4 first appeared as a working paper, entitled "Institutional Innovation and Rural Land Reform in China: The Case of Chengdu," submitted in June 2017 to the Lincoln Institute of Land Policy.

The bulk of the empirical research for the different case study chapters were done by the following authors: Lejano (with assistance from Li Li and Benjamin Dong Wei) for Chapter 3, Lian and Lejano for Chapter 4, Guo for Chapter 5, and Yin for Chapter 6.

GLOSSARY OF TERMS

English	Chinese	Pinyin
Agricultural exchange center	农交所	nong jiao suo
Central city area	中心城区	zhong xin cheng qu
Comprehensive land consolidation	土地综合整治	tu di zong he zheng zhi
Construction land	建设用地	jian she yong di
Construction Land Quota	建设用地指标	jian she yong di zhi biao
Construction Land Ticket	建设用地票	jian she yong di piao
Deliberation panel	评审小组	ping shen xiao zu
Deliberative mechanism	议事机制	yi shi ji zhi
Guiding price	指导价	zhi dao jia
Household registration	户口	hukou
Land ticket	地票	di paio
Link	挂钩	gua gou
Permit for access	持证准入	chi zheng zhun ru
Permit of use	持证准用	chi zheng zhun yong
Property rights	产权	chan quan
Quota Transaction	指标交易	zhi biao jiao yi
Second-circle	二圈层	er quan ceng
Social investors	社会投资人	she hui tou zi ren
Supervisory committee	监督委员会	jian du wei yuan hui
Village committee	村民委员会	cun min wei yuan hui
Village council	村民议事会	cun min yi shi hui

PREFACE

The book project began in 2016 when Raul Lejano was invited to Beijing Normal University to give a series of lectures on policy analysis. The four co-authors began exchanging notes on their respective research endeavors and found commonalities in the broad themes that they were each pursuing. It became apparent that, observing various case studies in China (and elsewhere), each was looking at modes of governance that were not exactly as the literature might portray them. Hongping Lian was examining property rights reforms where the new rules were neither collective nor private nor common-pool resource property regimes. Jia Guo was looking at nongovernmental organizations (NGOs) that were not exactly like the civil society model many scholars describe in the literature. Bo Yin was looking at legal reforms that were not easily described. Such was the complexity of the cases they were examining.

But the idea for the book began years earlier, in 2006, when Lejano published his first book, *Frameworks for Policy Analysis* (Routledge, also available as a Chinese-language edition, entitled 政策分析框架 融合文本与语境, through Tsinghua University Press). The book began making the case that the reason scholars had difficulty achieving "thickly" described institutional accounts was because of the paucity of descriptive concepts available. Studying resource conservation and other community-based systems, he realized that what characterized them was not always (sometimes, never) the set of rules (à la North or Ostrom) or lines of authority, but the relational way that the pattern of actions evolved in response to the daily interchange among policy actors. It is relationality, not as much rationality in a Weberian (or even von Neumann – Morgenstern) sense, that characterized some of the institutions that were constructed by policymakers, both centralized and on the ground. And, somehow, the word, governance (and the literature that grew around it) did not provide many new routes to describing unique and emerging institutional forms.

As the title suggests, our approach draws some of its spirit from the phenomenological attitude, especially its openness to how things are in the raw, as they are experienced. The goal of such an approach is to describe emerging institutions in a way most faithful to their everyday nature. In other words, how is the institution experienced by different actors in a certain context, as well as by the analysts themselves? Rather than force the institutional phenomena into a predetermined classification scheme, we choose to open up the latter to new modes of classification so as to better capture the reality of institutional life.

The book is about China, as a detour, but it really is about the richness of institutional life, on the one hand, and the sparsity of our means for describing the same, on the other, in other country contexts as well. China just happens to be intriguing and rich with illustrative case studies. The spirit of the book is to go beyond the conventionally typological and examine systems of governance with a fresh eye. It is a little ironic that this leads us to new descriptives that ultimately become (semi-) typological themselves. As will be discussed later, it is inescapable, at least in institutional work, that we move from phenomenology to interpretation.

The theoretical framework was developed in parallel with examination of a number of case studies. In reality, there was no systematic sequencing of research activities, as is common in work that is partly grounded and partly theoretical. We were fairly eclectic with our research methods, in keeping with the multiple disciplinary backgrounds of the authors and the deliberate intention to be fairly open to new and combined approaches and ideas. The book brings together an assortment of research projects, each different from the other but linked by a common desire to uncover what is new and noteworthy about emerging institutional experiments in China. One chapter uses Lian and Lejano's work on rural land reform in Chengdu. Another is based on Guo's research on environmental NGOs in Yunnan and Jiangsu provinces. Later in the book, Yin describes his investigation of legal reforms in particular areas of jurisprudence.

Our work attempts new ways of describing and interpreting emerging institutional designs. To do this, we bracket or set aside strong pre-packaged notions of what institutions are. This also means setting aside normative questions about what they should be and whether or not new institutional designs work well or not. These other questions are best left to future work. More importantly, discussions of how institutions should be always bring in ideological lenses that strongly constrain how institutions are described. At this moment, our interest is in seeking out new forms of description.

Neither is this book about foreseeing the future. We do not know where the institutional experiments, great and small, ongoing in China (and elsewhere) are ultimately headed. Perhaps this is better left to journalists, politicians, and bloggers to speculate over. Our task is working out new ways of discerning what institutional changes are emerging. But we do recognize that this is a time of change for China. There are questions about whether its remarkable period of growth has come to an end or, rather, is settling into a more moderate equilibrium. As this book is going to press, the Central Committee of the Communist Party is moving to remove the term limits for the president and vice-president, there are signs of a new Chinese expansionism (beginning with the so-called Belt and Road initiative), and there are fears of a potential trade war with a protectionist US president. It is in times of uncertainty and change that we need to be better at detecting how institutions are transforming and what they might be transforming into. In short, what is called for is a heightened awareness of, and more faithful modes of describing, such change.

At the same time as we examine emerging institutional changes in China, we confess that our ultimate goal is to deepen the analysis of such changes worldwide, beginning with, but not stopping at, China. Towards the end of the book we will muse on the word "beyond."

The authors would like to thank New York University for partial support, in the way of a Provost's Global Research Initiative grant, for a series of meetings among the researchers. Drs. Lejano and Lian would also like to thank the Lincoln Institute for Land Policy for partial support that funded travel for researchers to Chengdu to gather information for the case study on transferable market instruments for rural property. Dr. Lejano is also grateful to the Institute of Water Policy at the Lee Kuan Yew School of Public Policy at the National University of Singapore for partial funding, in the form of a research grant to study narrative and governance (specifically, the analysis of the use of figures of speech for policy formulation in China). Dr. Lejano would like to thank Beijing Normal University for funding his initial visit to the university, which initiated the book project. Thanks, too, to Kalen Lin for her work on copy editing and fine tuning the text and to Candy Tong for her help with index prepration.

The authors also appreciate the advice and assistance of Natalja Mortensen (senior editor), Maria Landschoot, and Lillian Rand, from Taylor & Francis, as well as several anonymous reviewers of the book proposal and draft manuscript.

1

INTRODUCTION

The Phenomenology of Institutional Innovation

1.1 The Problem of Description

This book is about institutions. More specifically, it is about how they confound us. We feel we have the measure of them – how they are organized, how they work, their form and function. But we have not found the words to say what makes them special and, examined closely enough, invariably unique. The problem we take up in this book is that of institutional description and the difficulty of such given the paucity of descriptives with which we can render new, perhaps innovative, programs.

Take the case of China. The 21st century has, thus far, been its coming-of-age story. Averaging an annual growth rate of 9.5% over the last two decades, China has officially become the largest economy in the world (after adjusting for purchasing power parity).[1] The nation has become the world's largest exporter, since 2009, and the world's largest trading nation, since 2013.[2] Even given a slowdown in its annual growth rate the past few years, China remains an engine for global change.

Change is apace within the nation. At the same time as its economy continues to grow, China has been undergoing an era of profound institutional reform. The process of modernizing its economy meant that the old institutional regime, characterized by massive state-owned enterprises, rural economy, and insularity, needed overhauling if China was to take its place at the helm of the world's developed nations.

Take, for example, the massive process of urbanization that has taken place in China over the last 20 years. It has been a period of unparalleled city building and urban expansion that the world has never seen before – between the years 2000 and 2015, China's urban population grew from 459 million to 780 million, adding an urban population about equal to the size of the US (United Nations, 2015). To generate the capital needed for such an expansion of its urban area, its housing, and industry, the state needed to tap into private capital and direct foreign investment.

2 Introduction

This required institutional change, such as amending the absolute nature of state ownership of urban property in favor of a system allowing usufruct rights for private interests (e.g., land grant contracts allowing use and profit from the land for 50 years for industrial land and 70 years for residential land).

The idea that institutions themselves needed modernization took off during Deng Xiaoping's leadership in the 1980s, and it started a revolutionary process of reform. This continues to this day. In 2014, at the Third Plenum of the ruling party's central committee, the leadership expressed the following commitment:

> The overall goal of deepening the reform comprehensively is to improve and develop socialism with Chinese characteristics, and to promote the modernization of the national governance system and capacity. We must pay more attention to implementing systematic, integrated and coordinated reforms, promoting the development of socialist market economy, democratic politics, advanced culture, a harmonious society and ecological progress.[3]

Notwithstanding the decisive tone of the party's pledge to reform, the fact is that what these reforms mean, in real terms, is an open question. It is unclear what, exactly, a socialist market economy should look like, and how governance is to be modernized while retaining Chinese characteristics (and what these characteristics are is never spelled out). What it suggests, however, is the idea that whatever evolves in this grand institutional experiment, it may have many features unique to its context. The leadership is well aware of the extent and depth of the changes underway, as well as the inescapable need to innovate. As China's current premier and party leader, Xi Jinping, stressed: "We must improve current systems and promote institutional innovation with theoretical innovation based on practice … The basic foundation for building socialism with Chinese characteristics is that China is in the primary stage of socialism."[4]

China's ongoing experiments in governance are an important laboratory from which to learn about institutional design. This is no more evident than in the sectors taken up later in the book (namely, land reform, civil society, jurisprudence), where the scale and pace of such change in China are unprecedented. What is clear is that the present regime is undergoing a period of institutional experimentation. For example, scholars are beginning to study how decentralized policymaking is creating a kind of institutional laboratory (Teets & Hurst, 2014). The Chinese government's longstanding practice of adaptive incrementalism allows us a chance to see a kind of institutional innovation at work. Whether one refers to it, as the policy sciences literature does, as incremental layering or policy patching (Howlett, 2014), China's adaptive process of institutional design allows local experiments around different innovations in governance, which can then be scaled up or outwardly diffused should they prove successful.

Many, perhaps most, Western scholars presume, a priori, that the ultimate goal of institutional modernization is to mimic institutional ideals in the West, where the ideals of free market capitalism and liberal institutions are firmly espoused (though not firmly practiced). But this is too strong an assumption, in the opinion of the authors – even more so since these are mainly institutional "ideals" in the West, not realities. To be sure, many of China's reformers do aim toward these institutional targets (e.g., private property, liberal politics, political pluralism), but only in general terms and not universally, not necessarily coalescing into definitive institutional forms. And there are reasons to think that the forms evolving now are taking on characteristics unique to them, diverging in (as we will discuss) important ways from the idealized Western models. In other words, we may be seeing the evolution of a unique "socialist market system with Chinese characteristics."

The analytical problem is that the modes of institutional description scholars often use are embedded in the forms and language of Western institutional types. These modes of description tend to have strongly dualist frames of reference – i.e., property is either public or private, political agents are either state or nonstate actors, etc. In this introductory chapter, we sketch what we will refer to as a partially phenomenological stance toward institutional description. That is, we bracket away or postpone applying conventional descriptives and attempt to fashion new ones that better capture "the thing itself," a point of view espoused by Edmund Husserl (1901).

The main focus of the book is to find new ways to characterize the "experimentation" underway in China vis-à-vis the design and workings of its institutions. The idea of an "institution" (as a repeatable pattern of actions) is itself phenomenological, allowing us to not talk about legal structures and agencies and classifications, allowing us to bring together otherwise separate fields of law, public administration, and physics or the legislative, executive, and judicial. The idea of an institution has allowed new forms of scholarship, allowing us to focus not just on the formal constitution of government and organizations, but on their practice. In our treatment of institutions, we do not make so much use of structural or functional framings of them, but more as repeatable thought-action complexes. This treatment is not far removed from the idea of discursive institutionalism (Schmidt, 2008), except our treatment is even more phenomenological than this – i.e., institutions can result from precognitive patterns of behavior, where individuals are not consciously aware that they are creating a social construction. Simply, an institution just "is" or, more accurately, is simply "being."

The chapters in this book examine specific areas of governance and closely study how institutions are evolving into what may be unique forms. There is ample evidence that this has been happening for quite some time. Institutional experimentation is deeply embedded in China's system of governance. In a speech on political reform, Xi Jinping described the system in these terms:

> Wading across the river by feeling the stones and top-level design are two component factors of our reform effort … To continue reform and opening up, we need to strengthen our macroscopic thinking and top-level design … At the same time, we must still encourage bold experiments and breakthroughs.[5]

4 Introduction

In so doing, Xi would repeat the same idea originally put forward by Deng Xiaoping two decades ago. This logic of experimentation is not simply what Lindblom (1959) referred to as muddling through, but one of institutional innovation through smaller-scale institutional experiments (Heilmann, 2008; Heilmann & Perry, 2011; Florini, Lai, & Tan, 2012). The goal of the book is to come up with better, deeper ways of describing the institutional innovations that are emerging.

1.2 The Phenomenological Attitude

In this book, we attempt to open up our capacities for observing unique or novel forms of institutional life. In this vein, we take a phenomenological stance toward institutional description, which aspires toward describing phenomena in the most authentic, faithful way possible, which is to bracket away preexisting or dominant conceptual lenses and pay attention "to the things themselves" (Husserl, 1901). Without entering into the epistemological question of whether it is possible to completely bracket away defining concepts, we approach the phenomenological ideal by meeting it halfway and being open to new conceptual lenses by which to describe institutions and, at the same time, attempt to account for our genuine, pre-filtered observations of institutional life as practiced.

While the word "phenomenology" encompasses a wide range of schools of thought and thinkers (e.g., Franz Brentano, Martin Heidegger, Edith Stein, Maurice Merleau-Ponty, and others), we employ key concepts drawn from Husserl, particularly from his treatise, *Logical Investigations* (Husserl, 1901) and *Ideas I* (Husserl, 1913). We begin with moving our focus away from strong notions about what things are to how they appear to us. And this draws from the insight that whatever a thing is, we only know it from our experience of it. That is, things in the world are not objects that we might define or measure, as assumed in the natural sciences, but neither are they completely or wholly sub-jective thoughts or mental construction, as a psychologist might frame it. Rather, they are phenomena, which are the appearances or experiences of things that we focus our consciousness upon.

Being open to the way a thing is experienced or presents itself to us means set-ting aside the tendency to pre-judge what a thing is. For example, if one chooses to frame the world of business, a priori, as a competitive game, then one's under-standing of a business situation might be overly restricted to this conceptual scheme. But perhaps the same situation, if approached from a less rigid perspective, might be experienced in different ways: Experiencing friendship, an artistic act, a cultural rite. Thus, the goal of phenomenology might be understood as "to under-stand and describe phenomena exactly as they appear in an individual's conscious-ness" (Phillipson, 1972, p. 123).

One key idea, in Husserl's phenomenology, is that of epoché, or the bracket-ing of prefiguring conceptual frameworks. In the description of institutional life, this amounts to letting go of a priori forms of institutional classification, especially those derived from "western" (or Weberian) institutional traditions. What modes of description would one then use? In Husserl's method, one turns to authentic descriptions of the experience of the thing – in our case, of pure observation of an institution at work, as well as the accounts of those social actors that enact these institutions.

The phenomenological attitude involves being open to the fresh observation of the everyday workings of institutional life. How might we describe seeing an institution, not as formally designed, but as played out in practice? It is not just the researcher's observation that informs but also the experiences, as recounted, by policy actors themselves who enact an institution. It includes not just the form and specification of institutional rules, but its rhythm, its emotional valence, its cadence. There are many dimensions to the direct observation of institutional life, some of which we will explore. We do not examine every such aspect – for example, while we do not have occasion to analyze it, one notes that institutions are also embodied experiences and the way one physically encounters institutional life matters as much as anything (drawing from Merleau-Ponty, 1945/2012).

Another key idea behind Husserl's phenomenology is that of intentionality, which speaks to how the subject simply does not exist as an autonomous agent but is always intending toward or relating to something else. This suggests that we be open to more relational modes of institutional life, wherein a policy or program is not simply a formal set of rules and roles but a web of relationships that, as they play out, work out what the institution is. We will appreciate how this notion of relationality fits the Chinese context well and provides a depth of insight into institutional life. What we refer to as relationality goes beyond the notion of *guanxi*, or the importance of interpersonal relationships in institutional life, but the idea that formal institutional designs are left underdetermined. They are partly specified by the constituting text, but the rest is left for the network of policy actors to work out as they interact.

The notion of relationality draws from Lejano (2008), which develops the notion that the rules and roles of an institution can be under-determined. Either these formal rules and roles are underspecified or not followed in practice. Why would they be underspecified? In some cases, what an institution really means may be that which is spoken "backstage" as opposed to "frontstage" (Goffman, 1978) – i.e., it cannot be formally acknowledged though it is practiced. To turn toward an American example, right after the tragedy of the terrorist attacks on September 11, 2001, US Congress enacted the Patriot Act which, ostensibly, was meant to deter further acts of terrorism. The aspect of deterrence is not to be doubted, but there were other, unspoken and uncodified, aspects to the Act – e.g., it became the impetus for a massive financial transfer back to the defense industry, which suffered under Bill Clinton's defunding of the military (Joyce & Meyers, 2001). It also became the flashpoint that spurred a sweeping movement to roll back immigration and, in some cases, vilify immigrants.

6 Introduction

In other cases, policies are underspecified perhaps because central government cannot spell out its details, leaving them to more local actors to work out, in adaptive fashion. As we will discuss in later chapters, we can see this adaptive stance at work in many instances of governance in China, beginning with the question of what exactly a socialist market economy is.

What substitutes for the formal and ostensible? It is the established pattern of actions and reactions that correspond to the web of relationships among policy actors. These actions correspond not to any codified text but, instead, to the habituated demands that relationships exert on an actor. If one likens formal institutional rules and roles to a text, then the working and reworking of relationships is part of the larger context in which the program takes place (Lejano, 2006, 2016). We develop these insights into modes of description in the succeeding chapters.

And so, we approach our study of governance in China by simply directly observing its institutional practices. As an example, we might examine the texts by which China's leaders govern the nation and, observing it with fresh eyes, record our impressions of it. We will notice that there is much in the Chinese system of governance that pays respect to words, written and spoken, from its leaders even when they originate in purely ceremonial functions and other non-administrative events. Examining texts from speeches by the current leader, Xi Jinping, one notices, through pure observation, a penchant for using literary expressions (metaphors, aphorisms, euphemisms) often and predictably. Is this simply a matter of rhetorical style? Or perhaps it plays a role in governance in present-day China? Being open to new conceptual lenses, we consider the possibility that perhaps it is a little of both, and these expressions are both rhetorical and strategic.

This brings up a broader question, which is to what extent do policy and legal texts prescribe institutional life in China? Conventionally, rules and regulations can be traced back to an originary text. But, as in the case with literary expressions in speeches, perhaps policy texts have uses other than being simple policy prescriptions. We explore this theme in succeeding chapters.

We made the point of saying that our approach is "halfway" phenomenological. We do not completely bracket away existing, even hegemonic, institutional concepts because part of our approach is comparative. In the succeeding chapters, we will take occasion to, at times, develop new descriptives for institutional life by contrasting these against extant concepts. For example, as discussed in a succeeding chapter, China is presently experimenting with various forms of market instruments for the disposition of rural property. In some (notably Western) literature, there is a presumption that this experiment is tending toward a system of conventional private property rights, just as formally depicted in US and other legal systems. But the outcome of such experimentation is not necessarily a classic private property regime – as we will see, what is evolving may be something altogether unique.

The dialectic approach will prove useful for our analysis. But we are careful not to be espoused to a particular dialectic scheme, since our preference is to set aside strongly structuring analytic concepts in favor of purer description. We maintain such caveats when we have occasion to compare, for example, eastern versus western. There is, after all, no such thing as an "eastern" model of governance, since the signifier "east" is empty. Similarly, "western" means nothing in and of itself. When we utilize these easy dialectic concepts, we do so with caution. And, when we do, our main purpose is to strive to develop alternative modes of description that we arrive at by counterposing them against dominant concepts.

Most generally, we take a hermeneutic approach to studying institutions. That is, an institution is nothing in and of itself outside of how it interacts with other (symbolic, cultural, material, affective) aspects of its environment. Taking the same notion inwards, a policy text is nothing in and of itself outside of its relationship with other texts and with other non-textual elements in the context in which it is embedded. The link between phenomenology and hermeneutics is natural, as it was for Ricoeur. The movement is one from description to interpretation. Ricoeur observed that even as one might attempt pure description, meanings are not given directly but, invariably, are subject to interpretation (Ricoeur, 1981). The feat, then, is flexibility in interpretation, the ability to not reside within a dominant set of interpretive concepts but to explore and discover new ones.

The comparative approach can provide much insight that we might not arrive at otherwise. In the following section, we attempt to sketch out why the comparative approach can be rich ground upon which to build new institutional descriptions. This often begins with a type of deconstruction (a notion from Derrida, 1976), which means bracketing or weakening preformed assumptions and defining concepts.

Unlike Husserl, however, we do not aspire to any kind of essentialism. That is, in working out new modes of describing institutional life, we will never claim to have worked out the essence of the institution or even the experience of it. More in keeping with Dewey, we simply seek out modes of description that prove more effective in practice (Dewey, 1999). But new modes of description are always provisional.

1.3 A Study in Contrasts: Confucius and Weber

Perhaps a good place to start is by recalling the contrast between two socio-political systems, first depicted in such fashion in Weber's tomes, *Economy & Society* and *The Spirit of Capitalism* (1904, 1922). There is, on the one hand, Weber's depiction of the modernist state. In this model, institutions are wrought through and refashioned by a rationalist ethic. Rationalization, in this model, refigures institutions toward means-end rationalities, where specialized systems each move to maximize their individual teleologies. The multiple dimensions and values that make up the life-world split into differing rationalities. This division of labor is

8 Introduction

reflected in the creation of boundaries between different branches of government, between different sectors of the economy, and between areas of civic life. Aesthetic life is now overseen by a foundation of the arts, and art is now to be found in a museum. As Selznick demonstrated, departments of the interior begin acting to maximize the gains of the power sector, to the exclusion of the environment (Selznick, 1949). Nowhere is this more pronounced than in the radical separation between public and private domains. If these spheres intersect, it is in the sense of a mechanical solidarity, where they necessarily have to co-exist in a functional manner. This functional and social division of labor, so the model goes, follows from the need for these rationalized systems to drive toward optimization (whether of utility or power or other measure).

Contrast this with the Confucian ideal of government. Here, the model is not one of individualized, specialized systems that each maximize their respective summum bona; rather, it is one where the goal is similitude or, as March and Olson called it, a logic of appropriateness (March & Olsen, 1989). The ideal government is patterned upon an ideal form, whether as in Taoist terms is to be found in the heavens, or in Confucian terms is located in the family. While we can think about division of labor within a family, the latter is a collective that binds absolutely and where each member of the collective pursues the same end. It is not the division of labor but its integration. The contrast is between the utilitarian ethic (maximizing efficiency) of the Weberian ideal versus the virtue ethic (working like a family) of the Confucian. This is expressed through differing functional differentiation of political life, too. Stereotypically, the Weberian bureaucrat is a narrow means-end specialist; the Confucian bureaucrat is a well-rounded person of letters.

As opposed to an autonomous system, patterned after Weber's zweckrationalitat, the Confucian model corresponds to what Castoriadis called a heteronomy – i.e., a system where institutions derive from an extra-social authority (Castoriadis, 1986). There is no creation of a new institution simply out of a transaction cost-minimizing logic, as Coase or North might describe. In a heteronomy, to some extent, institutions come already pre-divined. Some might say that the ideal of the market, born out of Adam Smith and Friedrich Hayek, has become a heteronomy. After all, especially in the US, the urge to liberalize has taken on religious tones as right-wing ideologues and fiscal conservatives have somehow managed to equate religion with laissez-faire capitalism. But, at its core, the market model justifies itself through the infallible workings of an invisible hand that is not extra-social but, rather, endogenous to the market itself. The market, as designed, creates the invisible hand which then governs the market. In its ideal form, the model is autonomous and autopoietic (a term we will define in Chapter 2), answering to no one, sufficient in and of itself.

Formal institutional designs can be universalizing, applying to all contexts. In contrast, relational systems can result in institutions that evolve differently depending on their context (including time and place), the constellation of policy actors interacting in the policy domain, and the local institutional setting in which it becomes embedded. The liberal model of a democracy is a universal one. So is the ideal of the free market. But, as Clegg suggested, there are as many different markets for bread as there are locales where it is sold (Clegg, 1990; also see Granovetter, 1985). Understood as phenomena, institutions are never universal things.

Throughout most of the book, we deliberately take a descriptive, not normative, lens to institutional design in China. While we are not opposed to evaluating institutional merits and deficiencies, the phenomenological spirit of the inquiry suggests that, at least for now, we bracket away theory-driven evaluation (since extant analytics for evaluation employ conventional modes of description, which we are trying to improve upon). Throughout the succeeding chapters, we strive for richer description, postponing for the meantime the task of evaluation. This allows us to steer beyond strongly hegemonic notions in institutional thought. This includes avoiding the free market triumphalism of laissez-faire economics, capitalism-versus-socialism dogmatism, and refusing to take it on faith that the phrase "socialism with Chinese characteristics" is something actually defined. For our purposes, ideas like capitalism and socialism are neither good nor bad. In fact, as phenomena, these terms mean nothing outside of how they are experienced in practice.

It would seem that our method is primarily inductive, where we first look at the phenomenon at work and then work out how to describe it. But that would be claiming too much. As mentioned, part of our approach might be called "transductive," where we begin conventional concepts from extant theory and, through a dialectic of sorts, develop alternative modes of description, which we then deepen when we begin applying it to the case study. It is, as we admit, a mixed scanning approach, where we alternate between looking at the concept and the case study, in hermeneutic fashion.

We will turn to critique and evaluation toward the end, giving some thought to normative dimensions of institutional life in the final chapter.

1.4 Preview of the Chapters

Let us briefly preview the coming chapters.

In Chapter 2, we sketch some new modes of description that may help in providing a fresh look at China's institutional evolution. It begins with a strategically dialectic conceptual strategy, which is to imagine an antithesis to conventional western institutional models. This temporary dualism helps set the tone for probing into new modes of description that seem to describe the thing as it is. We develop a number of new analytical concepts and modes of description. And, from Chapter 3 onwards, we employ these descriptives, applying them to different institutional situations.

Chapter 3 brackets (or sets aside) strong notions of policy as sets of rules and prescribed roles/authorities and, instead, looks at them as what they are, at face

10 Introduction

value, which is as text. A model of policy as text examines how words (on a page, on a website, in a constitution) are translated into action (especially repeated patterns of action that we refer to as an institution). The chapter takes a look at a novel aspect of governance in China: Rule by metaphor. This pertains to the penchant of the leadership or ruling party to set government policy with a broad brush by, first, using aphorisms, metaphors, or euphemisms to set a basic policy direction in the broadest terms, then allowing more local policy actors to innovate within those broad directives. Perhaps the most relevant metaphor is the one first used by Deng Xiaoping in describing the grand move toward reform, that of "crossing the river by feeling the stones." It sums up the idea of experimentation, adaptive governance, and incrementalist policymaking. However one wants to tease out differences between incrementalism and outright innovation, the model is one of "learning by doing" (Ingram & Fraser, 2006). There are rhetorical reasons for using such figures of speech, of course. The focus of the chapter, however, is on non-rhetorical, strategic uses. A number of case studies will be taken up, including defining the socialist market economy, the South China Sea controversy, and the anti-corruption program.

Chapter 4 focuses on the evolution of property markets. It brackets away preformed notions of property as a bundle of rights and the latter as goods (Penner, 1995). Over the last decade, China has embarked on significant reforms in its system of rural land ownership and management. While the natural inclination of scholars is to characterize this as a step along a path to a full-fledged private property market, a more careful examination suggests that it may not be as simple as this. This chapter argues that what we are seeing is the evolution of institutional designs that are unique in some respects, taking on some elements of a private property market while retaining elements of collectivization. The aim of this book is to better characterize these changes and to describe how the new institutional model may be something more innovative altogether. To do this, we will focus most closely on the pilot program that Chengdu has embarked on around a new form of transferable development rights that links rural farmland to urban development.

Chapter 5 examines the growth and evolution of nongovernmental organizations (NGOs) in China, specifically those working in the environmental arena. In keeping with the phenomenological spirit, the analysis eschews strong definitions of NGOs, which means softening the boundaries between government and civil society, public and private, and other classification schemes. Taking a broad look at these new NGOs, one quickly observes how they diverge from the common notion of the nonstate actor and civil society in western systems. The chapter will examine and describe the less than rigid boundaries between civil society, state, and market as found in these NGOs. Looking more closely, one finds institutional experimentation also occurring in the kind of diversity or polymorphism seen in the differences between one environmental NGO and another.

Chapter 6 examines legal systems and how constitutional and criminal law in China diverges from conventional legal typologies. Looking most broadly, one

Introduction 11

notices how the Chinese constitution functions in a somewhat different manner from, say, the US constitution. Focusing on criminal justice, the chapter will examine current trends and work out unique aspects of this evolving body of law. Chapter 7 sums up what we are learning from China's institutional experiment. We gain new insights into what, possibly, a socialist market economy is beginning to look like. Or what model of civil society is emerging within a strong, one-party system. Or what it means to introduce market instruments in a system where rural land is collectively owned. It also opens up the scholarship to new research questions to be explored. Foremost among these questions is: How can the new analytical descriptives, developed herein, be applied beyond China? In this final chapter, we attempt to sketch some possible answers. We also comment on some fundamental, normative issues that need to be resolved as China's experiment in institutional reform progresses further.

Notes

1 http://data.worldbank.org/data-catalog/GDP-PPP-based-table
2 www.wto.org/english/res_e/statis_e/wts2016_e/wts2016_e.pdf
3 www.china.org.cn/china/third_plenary_session/2014-01/16/content_31212602.htm.
    Decision of the Central Committee of the Communist Party of China on Some Major Issues Concerning Comprehensively Deepening the Reform, Nov. 12, 2013 (downloaded Jan. 8, 2017).
4 Xi Jinping, Study, Disseminate and Implement the Guiding Principles of the 18th CPC National Congress, November 17, 2012. Many of Xi Jinping's speeches can be found in the anthology, Xi Jinping (2014). *The Governance of China*. Beijing: Foreign Languages Press Co.
5 Xi Jinping, Speech at the second group study session of the Political Bureau of the 18th CPC Central Committee, December 31, 2012.

References

Castoriadis, C. (1986). The nature and value of equality, trans. D.A. Curtis. *Philosophy & Social Criticism*, 11(4), 373–390.
Clegg, S.R. (1990). *Modern organisations: Organisation studies in the postmodern world*. London: Sage.
Derrida, J. (1976). *Of grammatology* (p. 141), trans. Gayatri Chakravorty Spivak. Baltimore.
Dewey, J. (1999). *The essential Dewey* (two volumes), ed. L. Hickman & T. Alexander. Bloomington: Indiana University Press.
Florini, A.M., Lai, H., & Tan, Y. (2012). *China experiments: From local innovations to national reform*. Brookings Institution Press.
Goffman, E. (1978). *The presentation of self in everyday life* (p. 56). London: Harmondsworth.
Granovetter, M. (1985). Economic action and social structure: The problem of embeddedness. *American journal of sociology*, 91(3), 481–510.
Heilmann, S. (2008). Policy experimentation in China's economic rise. *Studies in Comparative International Development*, 43(1), 1–26.
Heilmann, S., & Perry, E.J. (Eds.). (2011). *Mao's invisible hand: The political foundations of adaptive governance in China* (p. 320). Cambridge, MA: Harvard University Asia Center.

12 Introduction

Howlett, M. (2014). From the "old" to the "new" policy design: Design thinking beyond markets and collaborative governance. *Policy Sciences*, 47(3), 187–207.

Husserl, E. (1900 [1901/2001]). *Logical investigations*, trans. J.N. Findlay. London.

Husserl, E. (1913). *Ideas: General introduction to pure phenomenology*, trans. B. Gibson. New York: Macmillan.

Ingram, H., & Fraser, L. (2006). *Path dependency and adroit innovation: The case of California water. Punctuated equilibrium and the dynamics of US environmental policy* (pp. 78–109). New Haven, CT: Yale University Press.

Joyce, P.G., & Meyers, R.T. (2001). Budgeting during the Clinton presidency. *Public Budgeting & Finance*, 21(1), 1–21.

Lejano, R.P. (2006). *Frameworks for policy analysis: Merging text and context*. New York: Routledge.

Lejano, R. (2008). The phenomenon of collective action: Modeling institutions as structures of care. *Public Administration Review*, 68(3), 491–504.

Lejano, R. (2016). 政策分析框架 融合文本与语境 (Frameworks for policy analysis: Merging text and context), Chinese translation. Beijing: Tsinghua University Press.

Lejano, R., Wei, D., & Li, L. (2018). *Governing by metaphor: Rhetoric and institutions in China*. Working Paper, Institute for Water Policy, Singapore.

Lindblom, C.E. (1959). The science of "muddling through." *Public Administration Review*, 19(2), 79–88.

March, J.G., & Olsen, J.P. (1989). *Rediscovering institutions*. New York: Simon and Schuster.

Merleau-Ponty, M. (2012). *Phenomenology of perception*, trans. D.A. Landes. London and New York: Routledge. (Prior translation, 1996, *Phenomenology of Perception*, trans. Colin Smith. London and New York: Routledge. From the French original of 1945.)

Penner, J.E. (1995). The bundle of rights picture of property. *UCLA L. rev.*, 43, 711.

Phillipson, M. (1972). Phenomenological philosophy and sociology. In P. Filmer, D. Phillipson, D. Silverman, & D. Walsh (Eds.), *New directions in sociological inquiry* (pp. 119–164). Cambridge: MIT Press.

Ricoeur, P. (1981). *Hermeneutics and the human sciences: Essays on language, action and interpretation*. Cambridge: Cambridge University Press.

Schmidt, V.A. (2008). Discursive institutionalism: The explanatory power of ideas and discourse. *Annual review of political science*, 11.

Selznick, P. (1949). *TVA and the grass roots: A study in the sociology of formal organization* (Vol. 3). University of California Press.

Teets, J.C., & Hurst, W. (Eds.). (2014). *Local governance innovation in China: Experimentation, diffusion, and defiance*. Routledge.

United Nations (2015). *2014 Revision of world urbanization prospects. Population division of the Department of Economic and Social Affairs, (ST/ESA/SER.A/366)*. New York: United Nations.

Weber, M. (1904 [1930]). *The Protestant ethic and the spirit of capitalism*.

Weber, M. (1922). *Economy and society*, ed. and trans. G. Roth & C. Wittick. Berkeley.

2

DEVELOPING NEW MODES OF INSTITUTIONAL DESCRIPTION

In this chapter, we develop several descriptive concepts that will be used throughout the rest of the book. These concepts emerge from both a phenomenological approach, wherein we observe how institutions work in practice (using illustrative cases to develop the ideas) and a dialectic one, wherein we posit alternatives to extant, dominant ideas.

The reader will recognize that quick transition to a mode of analysis that is, simply put, hermeneutic. While we begin our work by establishing our phenomenological sentiments, inevitably, especially for institutional research, we traverse the blurred lines between phenomenology and hermeneutics. This was the case for Ricoeur, and so it is for us. And, so, while Husserl urges us to look to the things themselves (or more precisely, to the experience of them), we realize that these things are, at all times, embedded in a larger environment of other things, people, meaning-systems, and institutions. If we refer, as Ricoeur, to meaningful social activity as text, then invariably, to understand the text, we have to hermeneutically observe their relationship with its larger context. For us, it is not a combination of two modes of examination (phenomenological and hermeneutic), but the same one.

But, first, we describe how institutions can be phenomenal – i.e., things that are uniquely experienced, richly different depending on where they are found, and who enact them. The example used below is that of property markets, but it is meant to be indicative of what we find when examining other sectors of institutional life. We will illustrate how systems, such as real estate markets, are classically conceptualized and inquire into whether and how some systems do not match the canonical descriptions.

14 New Modes of Institutional Description

2.1 Autopoietic versus Sociopoietic Systems

One fundamental way that institutions are normally depicted is to present these as well-circumscribed systems. In this chapter, we weaken this assumption and consider alternative ways to understand an institution. Bracketing, for the moment, the strong notion of a system, we find that this blurs rigid boundaries between what we consider separate domains (e.g., public versus private). We will use the example of the free market ideal to illustrate the phenomenological approach.

Conventionally, markets are separate, self-enclosed systems – by this we mean that buyers and sellers interact in the market and make decisions that are independent of other institutions (government, nonprofits, etc.). Transactions, and values negotiated, emerge from the interaction between buyers and sellers, in a way that is characterized as being endogenous to these interactions. Many recognize that this is an idealized description of a market, but then are unsure how to better describe it. Sometimes, it becomes clearer how we might do so, or what the alternative modes of description might be, as occurs with anomalous situations. Let us begin to deconstruct the model of the autopoietic market.

Picture this scenario. Real estate speculation creates an artificial price bubble. At the same time, easing of credit requirements allows a continued surge in the demand for single family homes. At some point, the market sees total household debt beginning to approach and exceed 100% of the mean household income, thus beginning to outstrip the household's potential income stream. This triggers a cascading series of default, first from homeowners who then faced foreclosure, then from debtors heavily leveraged in securitized mortgage financial instruments. This then triggers a nation-wide recession that initiates a "lost half-decade" for that country.

This, of course, is what actually happened in the US. But what caused it? In the framework that we will construct (Frame-t), it was caused by the maintenance of self-referential, autonomous, autopoietic systems that, by virtue of degree of isolation from other parts of society, then have the potential for runaway crises. This is one way of characterizing the real estate (and financial) system that operated at that time. This, of course, is nothing more than conventional neoclassical economic theory: Value in a market is simply determined by the intersection of supply and demand curves. Nothing else need enter into this dynamic. This system is autopoietic because value is determined completely within this self-enclosed system, without external reference.[1]

What are some of these external references? For one, there is the real earning potential of each individual household – the stream of future income that it conceivably can maintain. And this, in turn, is referenced to the productivity of the household, in real terms (as the material product of their labor), as well as financial. And yet, the real estate market was not referred to this external consideration. If it were, which would have been the case had there been, say, a mortgage cap of 25% of the monthly household income, the system could not have run away like it did.

Another external reference would have been the material (and other) constraints to the sprawling construction of new single-family homes. These constraints have to do with the scarcity of land (in competition with other uses, such as farming, groundwater recharge, open space and conservation, and higher-density housing), which are mainly real material constraints. The real estate market operated purely within the social construction of supply and demand, unhindered by reference to real, material constraints or, alternatively, social-ethical constraints shared among members of a community. And, of course, part of what prolongs the crisis goes back to the autonomy of the system, which brings to mind Milton Friedman's edict that financial crises need only financial solutions (Friedman, 1968).

Autopoiesis requires functional and cognitive separation of a subsystem (the real estate market) from other subsystems (environment, ethics, social convention). It requires depoliticization of the subsystem (i.e., removing government oversight of the market, and by "political" we mean public deliberation). But this essentially traces back to Weber's description of rationalization, as each subsystem pursues its narrow means-end rationality. Autopoiesis takes this logic one step farther and conceives of the autopoietic system as self-creating or self-perpetuating. A market is not created to match demand with supply; rather, demand (and, hence, supply) is created by the market itself. For example, iPads are not created to meet a demand for devices like them; rather, creation of these goods also generates the demand for them. Art is not only created for art's sake; more than this, were there not an art world, there would not be something known as art. A painting of a soup can becomes art only because there is an art domain, a world fueled, in turn, by the soup-can artistry which it defines in the first place. Autopoietic systems are self-contained cycles; as Granovetter (1985) put it, they are "under-socialized" systems. The generation of meaning endogenously and the exchange of values that are completely generated internally in the system is magnified with the creation of securitized mortgages which take the artifice of meaning-values, packages them up as new entities which magnify their symbolic value (and accompanying risk).

The more difficult task is describing its alter, which we might begin by characterizing it as a sociopoietic system. Sociopoietic systems are interlocking subsystems, each mutually referenced to each other. In these systems, subsystem logics are not independent. If Bourdieu describes different fields of social life, he is quick to point out that these fields are not independent of each other and interact (Bourdieu, 1984). Rather, there can be homologies, as Bourdieu described them, that introduce parallel patterns that run across systems (Bourdieu, 1977). For example, Mary Douglas described one such homology, the demarcation of sacred and profane that repeated itself from interior of the home to the world outside (Douglas, 1966). Logics that govern each subsystem are not independent, and meaning, unlike Luhmann's autopoietic systems, can come from an external source.

Consider a counter-example to the runaway real estate market of the US. In 2010, China began experiencing property bubbles, especially in Beijing and

16 New Modes of Institutional Description

Shanghai. Demand certainly looked just like in the US case, and there were enough developers to supply the people with new housing. But there were important differences. First, there was no endlessly inward recursion of meaning, where artificial values began to become more and more removed from the material conditions of everyday life. There were no instruments such as securitized mortgages. Moreover, rather than watch from the sidelines, the Chinese government began acting aggressively to cool down the market: Removing discounts and increasing down payment requirements to 30% for first-time home buyers and to 50% for second-time home buyers.[2] This is not the free market model, and it is not an autopoietic system. Figure 2.1 depicts these contrasting systems. On the right-hand side of Figure 2.1 is a depiction of a sociopoietic system, where the market draws from and feeds back to other subsystems. Note that we can open up the classification scheme even further by blurring the boundaries between subsystems, but that is harder to depict in a diagram.

Whether or not the US-like bubble will have been avoided in China (or whether it has actually already burst), we certainly saw evidence of a differently working system. In this system, government steps in to prevent the runaway escalation of prices and, also, the cascading loss of value after the bubble bursts. And this involves applying an external reference point that seeks to constrain the system to the collective ideal. There are inherent links to the maintenance of the larger social order, including preservation of the limited capital of its aging population – i.e., were the bubble to burst, as in the US, loss of seniors' nest eggs would be too destabilizing to the social order. The dependence of China's senior citizens on these limited forms of capital are, in turn, linked to the previous policy of enforced low fertility rates, limiting the ability of parents to entrust too much of their future on children, and the lack of instruments for long-term investment (such as Individual Retirement Accounts).

2.2 Frame-t and Frame-c

We can generalize the contrast further as that between a condition where there is a high textuality of institutional life and one where institutions evolve hermeneutically.

We posit that an essential difference in these contrasting systems lies in logocentric versus logo-eccentric systems. The main characteristic of the first system is its textuality. That is, in Frame-t meaning and system logic it emerges as a singular text or code. In contrast, the second system, Frame-c, is marked by contextuality, which is the property of meaning emerging from a hermeneutic between text and context. In Frame-t, meaning is completely endogenous to the text itself, while in Frame-c, meaning is a hermeneutic between text and context. This may contradict Gadamer, who thought of all interpretation as a hermeneutic exercise. However, he did distinguish between those modes of interpretation that were consciously hermeneutic, in the sense of deliberately weighing and reflecting upon pre-existing prejudices, versus the unreflective (Gadamer, 1975).

New Modes of Institutional Description 17

It is this hermeneutic that distinguishes institution-making as artifice (i.e., fabrication from scratch) from institution-making as improvisation (i.e., fabrication using things that are ready at hand). In contextualized systems, to some extent, the stuff of institutions is not created but already found in the larger social order. The political order of the US traces back to a single foundational text, the Constitution, that created a new nation. The system still governs itself according to the logic internal to that text. This creation of order out of chaos, as it were, is an act of textuality, where authorship and text are as classically understood – an action of inspired creation. The new text defines "We the People" and becomes the reference point by which the system governs itself. As a text, it has withstood the test of time and is thought to contain whatever ethical or civic foundation the nation needs for self-governance.

But is not the constitution of a nation like China much the same (except that, in this particular case, the constitution defines "We the State"[3])? Yes, except that in contextualist systems, the text does not purport to contain everything needed for interpretation. We might hypothesize that reference to the constitution is not practiced in the same way in China as in the US. Everyday law and discretional decision-making by the authorities are not referenced, legally, in the same juridical way to the constitution, as in the US. Rather, in contextual systems, the text (of the constitution) and the context (the practice of everyday governance, the leadership, the personalities) work together coherently and determine, through this implicit hermeneutic, the institutional reality. Much might be said to be having to be read between the lines in the text in the contextual system, such as how the present-day mixed-capitalist economy functions side by side with the socialist state. These practices are not traceable to the constitution, per se, and in reality do not need to be referenced on an everyday basis. There is no constitutional definition of a mixed-capitalist-socialist state. But that does not mean that there is no coherence.

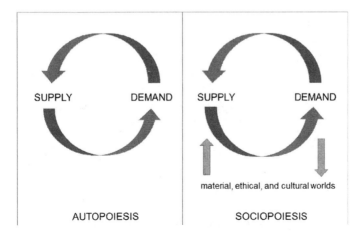

FIGURE 2.1 Markets in Autopoietic and Sociopoietic Systems

18 New Modes of Institutional Description

In other contextual systems, the text may be (or not) a reflection of the institutional life of a nation, but is not a source of meaning. But in highly textualized systems, such as seen in the US constitution, text at least formally is the origin of meaning. There is no institutional life without that text. In contrast, we might reflect on other societies where, for all practical purposes, life goes on without having to reference itself vis-à-vis that text. Everyday institutional life carries on without explicit direction according to these texts.

We might use the terms, self-ostensible versus hermeneutic, to describe these contrasting system types. In the first, meaning is found in the text, which suffices to define an institution. In the second, meaning and institution derives from a dialectic relationship between text, other texts, and other elements of context. The second speaks to nested, sociopoietic, integrated systems. Hermeneutic systems display intertextuality, which, in Kristeva's definition, is the inter-transposability of one system of signs into another (Kristeva, 1980). In US society, the color of one's skin brings in a set of codes, linked to centuries of landed gentry, into everyday political affairs – this is transposition of one set of signs (embedded in racial/ethnic distinctions) into political life, affecting the meaning of other codes, such as formal legal text. Of course, this (the intertextuality of race and institution) is true of other societies as well. But the difference is the ability, and the normative preference, for autonomy of these semiotic systems. In the US, there is a formal code (e.g., Equal Rights Act) ensuring, at least in form, the autonomy of the constitutional system of rights from other symbolic systems. The system, at least ideally, can exist and survive without the intertextual encroachment of racial meaning-systems into the legal. In hermeneutic systems, life proceeds as if the text were, if removed from context, under-determined. Remove the state, and one may find insufficient guidance in interpreting and implementing the constitution. In hermeneutic systems, the text does not suffice. Figure 2.2 depicts these systems schematically.

On one plane, it is the distinction between what Barthes refers to as the readerly versus the writerly text (Barthes, 1974). But, more generally, it is about weakening the notion of textuality itself. If this sounds like post-structuralism, celebrating the play inherent in every text, our thinking goes the other way, moving back to a more originary foundation of institutional life, before text, going back to an organic solidarity where relations, everyday routines, and exchange did not have to be codified to be activated. The modern idea of an institution traces back to the idea of a social contract, that original act of agreeing to be a collective that is thought to underpin all government. The logical consequence of this is to look for texts that codify these social contracts. But if we understand the essence of collective life as not similar to an act of deliberation (whether by individuals or organizations) but as a habituation to place, then we are less likely to seek, and depend on, these original texts, codes, and contracts for meaning. It is not the infinite play of the unbounded text, but Bourdieu's habitus on which these institutions are founded. It is the ability of society to tear itself away from this habitus that characterizes highly textual systems.

On the other hand, highly contextualized systems are often conflated with corruption. The idea of going outside a code evokes those situations where, whatever the rules might say, everything is done with a wink and a nod. While it is easy to understand how people might see this connection between contextualism and unethicality, the association is not a necessary one. The difference, to the authors, between textualized and contextualized systems, is not the prevalence of uncodified behavior, but the basic order being that of going outside the code by necessity. Contextualized systems are where the code does not suffice to establish institutions. While codes are the deliberate product of authorship, context is not authored but explored. So where does context come from, if not authorship? One might suppose nontextual sources of meaning, which goes without saying (geography, genealogy, events). But context also includes the thickly interwoven layers of text upon text – or, perhaps, what Kristeva refers to as intertextuality. Intertextuality precludes a strong notion of authorship, while preserving the agency of texts (Kristeva, 1980).

The figure is a mnemonic for a kind of analysis we can do to examine what makes a particular institution unique. Every institution is a phenomenon that arises from the strong, determinate action of a founding text and the diffuse, improvisational action of its context. For example, the IMF's recipe for structural adjustment is a strongly textual institutional model. In a sense, this text is so unequivocal, it changes entire national landscapes. There is, in the norm, the universal code, that which can be transported from place to place. But there is also the particular, that aspect of an institutional model that necessarily becomes interpreted in place.

Surely there is nothing so codified as the massive bureaucracies of a socialist state. But in some cases, the code for what actions become sustained is not to be wholly found, and sometimes only reflected, in the formal rules as written.

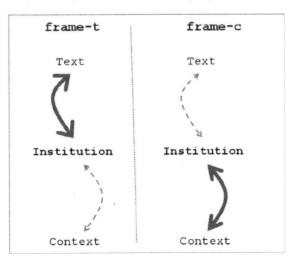

FIGURE 2.2 Contrasting Institutional Models

20 New Modes of Institutional Description

As an ethical theory, the underlying philosophy is not deontological but something more like a virtue ethic, the font of virtue being found in the state (or the party or the people). But the undoing of the strong notion of the state then requires some substitute source of institutional meaning. For the liberal state, that means becoming a textual one. But in a relational system, text is secondary to relationship. What we see evolving in China seems to combine characteristics of both.

2.3 Plenary Goods and Plenary Institutions

Having used the phenomenological strategy of bracketing strong prior assumptions, we now use a more dialectic approach where we imagine alternative concepts that stand in contrast to conventional ones. One conventional classification scheme is to portray things in society as public or private goods. These goods are conventionally understood as rights to use a good – the private good being excludable and rival, and the public good being nonexcludable and nonrival. But we can imagine other properties of these goods, which leads us to alternative forms of goods. Table 2.1 summarizes the properties of different types of goods based on the two aforementioned qualities of excludability and rivalry. It shows, in addition to public and private, two other conventional classes: Club goods and common-pool resources.

In a club good, the "club" has decision-making authority over the resource. Reading into the practice of rural land quotas (see Chapter 4), the state (through its delegate, the municipal government) sponsors the consolidation and quota creation process. It can have a veto power over such proceedings and, more so, needs to guide it and, often, will be the lead proponent of it. This is a kind of shared governance, where authority and responsibility are collocated in multiple bodies at different levels in the network. We feel this is an important quality of an innovative type of institution. We will refer to this property as that of multi-corporality. Because of the joint, all-inclusive nature of authority around quotas, we will refer to these types as plenary goods (Lejano & Del Bianco, 2018), which is found on the far right-hand side of Table 2.1.

This gives us a richer set of characteristics for describing institutional models, as shown in Table 2.1 (where "1" indicates that the characteristic in the leftmost column holds).

The idea of a plenary good may be relevant to related systems in other parts of the world, such as mixed-ownership enterprises (OECD, 2012). But the multi-corporal nature of these goods, as we understand them, pertains not just to ownership but decision-making, implementation, and other aspects of stewardship.

The shared nature of governance around the quotas (discussed in Chapter 4) is an important way of protecting different interests. Individual farmers are not subject to the difficulties of individual negotiation to the extent that the village council and municipality intercede for them. The village, itself, may not be equipped, in terms of technical expertise and staffing, to negotiate and carry out consolidation and quota generation. So being, the process can be managed by the local government or private parties. Rather than being nested institutions, where different actors at different levels act separately, these are conjunctive institutions. Rights and roles are not formally separated from one actor to the other – instead, they are embedded in each other. The actual decisions correspond to mixed rationalities (e.g., not just maximizing return on investment, but other objectives as well).

A classic private market is what we might call an autopoietic system. It is meant to function independently of the state, and decision-making occurs only between private actors. The market transaction is a self-encapsulated thing, where it functions outside the intervention of actors (the State, the Church, society) outside the private parties involved.

In contrast, we can think of an alternative mode of governance as sociopoietic (Lejano & Park, 2015). Going back to the market transaction, in a sociopoietic system the transaction involves the actions and interests of actors other than the two private parties. The transaction does not occur completely independently of these other institutions, such as local government, the party, etc., and prices are not simply endogenous to the private transaction but something influenced by the interaction of all these actors.

Commentators on China's evolving model of governance will sometimes point to the need for greater primacy of "the rule of law." What they mean by this term is that the law, as a text or encoded set of rules, act like an autopoietic system, where decisions and actions stem directly and only from the encoded text. In contrast, in a sociopoietic system, the text is not all of the institution, and other social forces weigh in, in the implementation of the law. Often, the central government will issue directives that are broad guidelines (sometimes using metaphor to describe the policy direction), and it is up to regional or local actors to bring specificity to these through everyday practice.

Sociopoietic systems are relational systems, because the actual institution is determined by the working out of social relationships among policy actors. Describing the relational system goes deeper into this phenomenon by uncovering the nature of the relationships and relating this to how the different policy actors act – this is the micro dimension of relational analysis. There is a macroscopic perspective to characterizing something as a relational system, which is describing

TABLE 2.1 Types of Goods: Expanded Classification System

	private	public	common-pool	club	collective	plenary
excludability	1	0	0	1	1	1
rivalry	1	0	1	0	1	1
divisibility	1	0	0	0	0	0
multicorporality	0	0	0	0	0	1

22 New Modes of Institutional Description

the network arrangement that is the web of relationships that make up the system. Conventional ways of describing systems for collective action separate solutions into state-centered, individual-centered or privatized, or communitarian. Similarly, strategies for development are said to vary depending on whether the strategy revolves around the state (e.g., expert bureaucracies), the individual (e.g. markets), or the community (e.g. nongovernmental organizations and community-based organizations). But what if the actual system involves all these actors working and negotiating jointly? This has been referred to as network governance, but this literature does not really work out what the relationships are between policy actors (simply, that they all act as one group). A relational analysis should be able to delineate how each policy actor acts in the network and to distinguish one kind of network from another.

2.4 Institutional Polymorphism: Specification and Adaptation

Conventional approaches give formal depictions of institutional designs – i.e., describing strong notions of form. Using the analogy of text, these conventional designs are strongly discernible or legible patterns that can be easily copied from place to place, a property referred to as isomorphism. But let us relax (if not bracket) the idea of strongly formal design and begin to consider how designs might blur and adapt to a particular setting. That is, we move from a notion of institutions as textual to that of institutions as contextual.

We now introduce a mode of description that is closely related to, but for practical purposes separate from, the autopoiesis/sociopoiesis continuum. Earlier, we used the example of governance by metaphor to highlight a novel aspect of China's institutional reform: Its tolerance, even promotion of, institutional polymorphism (Lejano & Shankar, 2013). The key idea is the contrast between textualist versus contextualist systems – specifically, the tendency of a system to merely sketch institutional details in its overarching rules (the text) and leave it to actions by actors at lower levels of government in specific jurisdictions (the context) to pin down its details.

Let us clarify some of the concepts we use, beginning with what we mean by contextualism. In their book, *Rediscovering Institutions*, James March and Johan Olsen (1989, p. 3) described a kind of contextualism that subordinated political institutions to the social structures, like class stratification, found in a place. To them, contextualism referred to institutions being epiphenomenal to context – e.g., bureaucratic processes simply reflecting larger social patterns, such as the presence of a ruling elite. We treat institutions as the primary phenomenon, and for us, contextualism means understanding institutions to be continually constructed through the interaction of the originating blueprint with the socio-physical context. Institutions are not determined by context but exist in a dynamic relationship with it.

Often, theorists mean context to be the organizational field (DiMaggio & Powell, 1983), as in a sector of economic activity like finance. In this book, context literally means place and community – the village where a project is conducted, its residents, its streets and alleys, all embedded in a network of relations that make up the institution. We use the term "text" to refer to the formal institutional narrative or blueprint that governs the nature, purpose, and design of a program or policy. Our model of institutional fit posits the institution as constituted by the ongoing dialectic between text and context, as depicted in Figure 2.3.

Figure 2.3 is perhaps a good illustration of the notion of complementary modes of institutional design involving both top-down design and incremental innovation on the ground (i.e., "crossing the river by feeling the stones").

There are two halves to Figure 2.3 (taken from Lejano, 2006). There is the upper half, which is the conventional model of institutional templates being constructed by policy authors, these templates then diffusing outwards and implemented and copied elsewhere. We can refer to this conventional model as depicting policy (or institution) as Text – i.e., something authored and then read, understood, and translated to action. In such a model, policy is constructed by actors who are external to the locale of implementation, such as when legislators craft a policy that is then followed by street-level bureaucrats. Accordingly, Figure 2.3 labels the process depicted in the upper half of the figure as (social) construction.

But street-level bureaucrats can, in fact, adapt a policy to their needs. As proposed, these field agents necessarily interpret the policy and, sometimes, rewrite it (Lipsky, 1971). In such a situation, there is no longer a strong divide between crafters of policy and its implementors. This is depicted in the lower half of Figure 2.3, where the policy or institution is not simply designed and imported into a situation but, instead, grows and transforms within that context. Local policy actors do not simply interpret and implement the policy but are involved in crafting it. If the model depicted in the upper half is more like an alien ship that descends upon a place and acts upon it, the lower half describes something more like a tree that takes root and grows in a place. The thing is in direct relationship with its context and, for this reason, we refer to this model as that of Contextuality and the process as that of Ecology (the latter evoking a type of symbiosis or relationship with context).

Taken together, both upper and lower processes act upon a policy or institution, which is both constructed by crafters of policy and co-designed by local actors and implementors. It can be seen as a kind of hermeneutic, where the back-and-forth exchange between text and context determines meaning (see Ricoeur, 1971; Gadamer, 1975).

There are two processes depicted in Figure 2.3. First, the upper half of the system, depicts how institutions are socially constructed by policy actors that can be external to the locale of implementation. We refer to the generic design of the institution as text, and there exists a constitutive relationship between text and institution. The lower half of the system, on the other hand, focuses not on the initial or generic design of the institution but how it then begins to evolve into a better fit with the locale, which we refer to as context. That is, there exists an ecological relationship between institution and context, where "ecological" simply means that the object of study does not exist autonomously by itself, but in and through relationship with its surroundings. Out of this dialectic between text and context emerges the institution. Figure 2.1 can be understood as a type of hermeneutic, which is a back-and-forth exchange out of which emerges meaning. This is related to what the public administration and policy literatures refer to as top-down and bottom-up schools of implementation (Matland, 1995; Sabatier, 1986). But the focus of Figure 2.3 is different from that of the implementation literature, which focuses primarily on the locus of authority in a system where design and implementation are separate stages in the policy cycle, while our focus is on understanding institutions as phenomena. While previous literature separates into design and implementation, our phenomenological attitude opens us to seeing these as part of multiple, overlapping mechanisms by which the institutions are generated within a constitutive hermeneutic.

The upper half of Figure 2.3, that of institution as constructed, is described in the organizational literature as a process of institutional isomorphis – e.g., DiMaggio and Powell (1983), who describe three mechanisms (coercion, normalization, and mimesis) by which institutions originate from a central locus and, then, diffuse outwards into the field by virtue of legitimation. For example, Lejano and Shankar (2013) discuss the microfinance model of Grameen Bank as something that was created in Bangladesh and subsequently exported elsewhere, to all corners of the globe, including the US. In this case, mimesis involves not just copying the central "text" or design template but also its myriad practices and rituals. The degree to which these influential models transform recipient contexts is a measure of the strength of the process of norm diffusion (Strang & Soule, 1998).

But norm diffusion can be partial. When one examines what has been diffused, one discovers that the policy has actually been translated and transformed

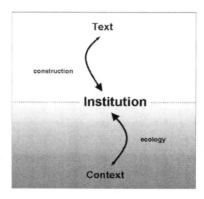

FIGURE 2.3 Dialectic Between Text and Context
(Source: Lejano, 2006)

(Howlett & Rayner, 2008). Another puts it this way: "In the real world, we would never expect a programme to transfer from one government to another without history, culture and institutions being taken into account" (Rose, 1991, p. 21). In the Grameen Bank study mentioned above, it was discovered that when imported to southern India, the model took on many important features determined locally in a process of institutional fitting-into-place (Lejano & Shankar, 2013). This process of fit, which is that depicted in the lower half of Figure 2.3, can come about through different mechanisms. For example, fit may occur because of the need to make the initial design more compatible with features of the new context. Culture can transform an institution, as sometimes one can find that even the mere translation of a policy into a different language can, in fact, modify its meaning. Another way that fit can come about is through resource scarcity. When the new institution requires material or capital to be imported into a place to construct it, but such resources are lacking, then local context can supply the capital, labor, and ideas to build it. The end result can be a new policy or institution, a twist on the original design or an entirely new one. Instead of isomorphism, one finds polymorphism.

When we refer to the lower-half process as an ecology, we evoke the ecological model of institutions (see Hannan & Freeman, 1977). In this work, an organization might be seen as an equilibrium condition with its organizational surroundings. For example, Scott and Meyer (1983) described how organizations in more complex environments develop more elaborate administrative structures. We might note, however, that in this book's open, non-reductive approach, the idea of an equilibrium might be too strong a notion.

Although an institution may be originally based on pre-existing design, when it takes material form it can take on particular forms unique to the context, a phenomenon Granovetter referred to as embedding (Granovetter, 1985). This process of institutional design has been described as a model of adaptation (Lejano & Shankar, 2013) where as a universal template takes on particular form, policy actors necessarily specify design details that are but described in general terms in the universal template (a process of specification).

Adaptation requires the action of lower-level policy actors who interpret a broad policy goal into reality. For example, commenting on a new policy directive from central leadership, Xi Jinping said: "When studying the document, we should not stop at the surface, quote it out of context, copy it mechanically or apply it blindly. We should straighten out the relationship between the general policy arrangement and a particular policy, between a policy chain and a link, between top-level policy design and policy interfaces at different levels, between policy consistency and diversity, and between long- and short-term policies."[4] The search for a relationship (even a balance, as long as we do not insist it is a static one) between a policy's consistency and its diversity is something that Figure 2.3 can help describe. We will use Figure 2.3 throughout this book as a mnemonic device to guide the analysis of the different case studies.

26 New Modes of Institutional Description

Undoing rigid categories also means we be more liberal concerning what the idea of a policy "text" is. Conventionally, these texts are the formal policy-setting or rulemaking language of a legislature or chief executive. But, letting go of the assumption about what constitutes such a policy text, we become open to the possibility that institutional life is molded by multiple, interweaving texts, what Kristeva (1980) referred to as intertextuality. In subsequent chapters, we will examine how even informal speech contributes to policymaking. Indeed, one can imagine Figure 2.3 reinterpreted in completely textual fashion, where context is understood as text, as well. Ricoeur pointed out the possibilities for considering action, itself, as text to be interpreted (Ricoeur, 1971). In an intertextual frame, a policy text gains meaning through its entry into and encounter with a field of other texts.

2.5 Relationality

There are many examples of programs and administrative structures that are poorly captured by classic, Weberian models of governance, the latter pertaining to the way services are carried out through formal, bureaucratic rule systems and lines of authority. Departures from the conventional model include decentralized systems of resource management, such as found in some developing country contexts. In this book, we will make the case that some of the nondescript modes of governance in China similarly represent deviations from the norm. The reason conventional models do not describe these novel institutions well is because the latter operate in ways that constantly depart from the canonical bounds of the formal institution. Using conventional descriptives to describe the nondescript institutional designs leads to superficial analysis, at best.

Scholars of public administration have used the language of networks to describe modes of governance that seem to depart from the formal boundaries between government, the governed, and other bodies (e.g., see O'Toole, 1997; Kickert, Klijn, & Koppenjan, 1997; Mandell, 2001). The network model portrays a system as a pattern of relationships between different actors that span and cross over formal organizational boundaries. Rather than formal organizational lines of authority, the relational links that connect an actor to the rest of the network are thought to be what governs responsibilities and roles in the system. However, the network literature has always been wanting in fully describing how these links or relationships work. In this section, we describe some ways to better understand and analyze the notion of a relationship (drawing, in part, from Lejano, 2008). We will then employ these descriptives in examining hybrid or nondescript modes of governance found in China.

In some nations, modes of governance, as practiced, differ markedly from their formal description. As we will expound in later chapters, China's emerging model of governance has begun to confound classic models. Superficially, one can describe its economy as a mixed market-socialist system, an oxymoron that does not even begin to describe how the market is designed and how it operates (simply stating the obvious fact that the model departs from the classic stylized market of perfect competition). Such innovations are difficult to design and evaluate because the public policy and public administration literature has paid insufficient attention to relationship-based modes of governance, which brings us to the main point of the chapter.

In this book, we employ a phenomenological approach to describing institutions, which involves bracketing (or setting aside) conventional descriptives and, instead, being open to observing or experiencing the institution in its everyday workings and attempting to describe that anew. Phenomenologists (namely Husserl, Heidegger, and Brentano) characterized humans as relational beings – i.e., less described by formal rules or intentions and more by everyday relating – and this is a sentiment we can bring to our analysis. That is, instead of beginning with concepts and assuming real institutions fit into them, we observe how persons and objects relate to each other in a program and describe what we witness. Let us refer to this as a model of care, the latter term representing a partly phenomenological descriptive for the way humans are not simply beings who exist but relational agents who are always seeking out others, making connections and, in a word, relating (Gilligan, 1982). In a sense, we care, therefore we are. When complex inter-actor relationships govern who does what in a network, then formalized roles and rules often tend to look blurred. We will refer to these blurry, dynamic modes of action that depart from formal structures of governance with something of an oxymoron of a term – structures of care (Lejano, 2008), suggestive of the way these modes of governance do follow patterns but that these cannot be codified into formal rules and roles because they are based on relationship. Relationships confound the formal in different ways. Consider, for example, the complex relationship between a mother and child, which cannot be captured by any codified set of rules and roles and really speaks to a multitude of everyday actions, reactions, and intentions which we refer to as caring. In this case, it is the complexity of a relationship and its manifestation in an uncountable suite of everyday actions that cannot be captured by formal codes. Or, consider the complex ritual of gift exchange, which Bourdieu describes as being, in essence, something that should not ostensibly follow a formulaic pattern lest it be considered perfunctory (Bourdieu, 1977). In the latter case, caring for a relationship leads to a dynamic, ever-shifting pattern of actions and responses.

We begin by examining the roots of the idea of structures of care and explain our additional contribution. Comparisons are made with other widely used models of governance, including hierarchies, rational choice, and network theories. We illustrate the model of care through application to the evolving systems of governance in China.

In a Weberian system of governance, institutions are characterized by the hierarchical, bureaucratic organization of authority and responsibilities (Weber, 1864). Such formalized arrangements can be captured by codified rules and constitutions. These texts, then, can be exported to the field and implemented just as written. This is a strongly formal model, the "form" emanating from the code and dictating how the institution is played out in the field. In contrast to this, the idea of structures of care are relationships that drive a system in a certain place. Unlike the classic Weberian system, which specifies a universal template (to be followed everywhere), structures of care are specific to their context. Formal rules and roles are epiphenomenal to the working and reworking of relationships in that context.

The notion of structures of care is our attempt to go beyond the strictures of the idea of a network. Networks, as described in the literature, are patterns of relationships that create a structure. Notwithstanding the capacity of such structures to depart from formal organizational boundaries, these are structures nonetheless, most exemplified in the field of social network analysis (e.g., Cook & Whitmeyer, 1992), where these patterns are quantified and diagrammed. Aside from structural pattern, network analysis sometimes focuses on interactions, as in the exchange of material or information (e.g., Jones, Hesterly, & Borgatti, 1997). In this chapter, we focus not on structure and on patterns of exchange (which can blur in hybrid systems) but on relationship. Relationships are ever evolving, dynamic, and multiplex.

Relationships have to do with how one person perceives or conducts herself or himself in relation to another. In previous work (Lejano, 2008), relationships are characterized as a set of "mappings" carried out along three dimensions. These mappings refer to how a person's identity is constructed in reference to others (capturing the relational nature of identity). Rules, roles, and other effects of these relationships emerge, but relationships exist prior to these. We depict the relations established by a policy actor in three interrelated operations:

- Constitution of Self: Establishing one's own identity or position, in a particular context.
- Constitution of Self-to-Other: Establishing one's identity or position vis-à-vis another.
- Constitution of Self-and-Other: Establishing the identity or position of self-and-other, i.e., the union formed by the two policy actors taken as one group.

It is easy to see how this complex constitution of identity affects governance. One can say that governance is different under Xi Jinping because he is different from the presidents and party leaders who preceded him. But a better way of understanding this, in our opinion, is not to simply attribute it to Weber's idea of charisma but to see how relationships around this particular leader have changed – i.e., how other party leaders see their roles and positions vis-à-vis Xi, how officials at lower levels of government see themselves in relation to central leadership, etc.

But these relationships are ever on the move, so to speak. For this reason, attempts to work out the formal patterns of authorities and institutionalized actions will see ever-evolving ones. Rules and roles are more blurred than in a more static, formalized system. And this makes the challenge of institutional description even greater. The approach we present herein is, in a way, our attempt to bracket the strong notions of system structure and form.

We will use the term "relationality" to describe the complex logic and teleology of governance that emerges with structures of care. It stands in contrast to the formal rationality found in classic Weberian systems. It is an attempt to describe systems that, because they are not well captured by conventional, formal modes of description, are often simply dismissed as imperfect, blurred, hybrid systems. Rather than focus on departures from convention, we seek to find modes of description that respond to the thing itself.

Rationalization, as proposed by Weber, is about designing or subjecting a system upon a strong logic. Markets are governed by the logic of efficiency (a strong form of which is that of individual rationality à la von Neumann-Morgenstern). Bureaucracies are governed by the logic of power or discipline. Much of the design and workings of the system can be traced to the logics of its particular form of rationality. However, relational systems are not built around strong logics but, rather, patterns of interaction and the identities that actors have forged with respect to each other. Should one attempt to model the logic between a parent and the child, it would find rationality to provide unsatisfactory explanations of behavior (e. g., could one possibly attribute all of a parent's actions to pursuing the parent's self-interest). Strong divisions between domains of social and political life help maintain autopoietic systems which, as a result, can be molded upon definitive logics. But what characterizes the logic of relational systems? For the latter, we might find complex, multiple, or shifting logics to prevail. In sociopoietic systems, there are no separate functional domains and, so, action is not as easily traced to simple defining logics. There are no hegemonic texts, no single overarching logics. Or, to put it another way, what we might find is the logic of enactment, where rigid top-down design gives way to the impromptu and phenomenal (Lejano & Del Bianco, 2018).

Autopoietic systems can display legible, overarching rational logics that guide system design and function. In contrast, sociopoietic systems are acted upon from within and without, subjected to the multiple logics of interacting policy actors. Perhaps more accurately, sociopoietic systems function in accordance with the working and reworking of relationships that constitute and act upon the system, blurring any semblance of an overriding rationality (Lejano, 2008). Other scholars have noted this – e.g., Shin (2017), who pointed out how decentralized governance in China blurs boundaries between central and local authority.

2.6 Looking Ahead

Thus far, we have sketched a number of novel approaches to describing innovative institutional forms, namely:

30 New Modes of Institutional Description

- sociopoiesis versus autopoiesis
- plenary institutions and plenary goods
- textualist and contextualist systems
- specification/adaptation and institutional polymorphism
- relationality and structures of care

In succeeding chapters, we proceed to apply these descriptives to a number of areas of institutional reform ongoing in China.

Notes

1 The term "autopoiesis" was used by Luhmann (2003) to describe self-maintaining social systems, though the term itself originated in the field of biology to describe self-reproducing organisms (Maturana & Varela, 1980).
2 http://urbanland.uli.org/Articles/2012/April/ul/RheeChinaBubble
3 Article 3 of the General Principle of the Constitution of China states: "The State organs of the People's Republic of China apply the principle of *democratic centralism*" (italics ours), which ostensibly intertwines the people and the State, accessed at www.npc.gov. cn/englishnpc/Constitution/2007-11/15/content_1372963.htm
4 Xi Jinping, Improve Governance Capacity through the Socialist System with Chinese Characteristics, Speech at a provincial-level officials' seminar, February 17, 2014.

References

Agranoff, R., & McGuire, M. (1999). Managing in network settings. *Policy Studies Review*, 16, 18–41.
Alter, C., & Hage, J. (1993). *Organizations working together*. Newbury Park: Sage Publications.
Barthes, R. (1974). *S/z* (p. 76), trans. R. Miller. New York: Hill and Wang.
Basso, K.H. (1996). *Wisdom sits in places: Landscape and language among the Western Apache*. Albuquerque: University of New Mexico Press.
Bourdieu, P. (1977 [1972]). *Outline of a Theory of Practice*. R. Nice, transl. Volume 16. Cambridge: Cambridge University Press.
Bourdieu, P. (1984). *Distinction: A social critique of the judgement of taste*. London: Routledge.
Brentano, F. (1874). *Psychology from an empirical standpoint* (Psychologie vom empirischen standpunkt, English translation by A.C. Rancurello et al.). London: Routledge.
Cohen, J., & Sabel, C. (1997). Directly-deliberative polyarchy. *European Law Journal*, 3(4), 313–342.
Cook, K.S., & Whitmeyer, J.M. (1992). Two approaches to social structure: Exchange theory and network analysis. *Annual Review of Sociology*, 18, 109–127.
Crittenden, C. (2001). The principles of care. *Women & Politics*, 22(2), 81–105.
Daly, M., & Lewis, J. (2000). The concept of social care and the analysis of contemporary welfare states. *British Journal of Sociology*, 51(2), 281–298.
DiMaggio, P., & Powell, W.W. (1983). The iron cage revisited: Collective rationality and institutional isomorphism in organizational fields. *American Sociological Review*, 48(2), 147–160.
Douglas, M. (1966). *Purity and Danger. An Analysis of Concepts of Pollution and Taboo*. London: Routledge and Keegan Paul.

Dubini, P., & Aldrich, J. (1991). Personal and extended networks are central to the entrepreneurial process. *Journal of Business Venturing*, 6, 305–313.

Friedman, M. (1968). *Why Economists Disagree. Dollars and Deficits: Living with America's Economic Problems*. New York: Prentice-Hall.

Gadamer, T. (1975). *Truth and method*, trans, ed. G. Barden & J. Cumming.

Gilligan, C. (1982). *In a different voice: Psychological theory and women's development*. Cambridge: Harvard University Press.

Granovetter, M. (1985). Economic action and social structure: The problem of embeddedness. *American journal of sociology*, 91(3), 481–510.

Hannan, M., & Freeman, J. (1977). The Population Ecology of organizations. *American Journal of Sociology*, 82, 929–964.

Hassan, M.K., & Reneteria-Guerrero, L. (1997). The experience of the Grameen Bank of Bangladesh in community development. *International Journal of Social Economics*, 24(12), 1488–1523.

Heidegger, M. (1927). *Being and time* (Seid und zeit, English translation, 1962). Albany: SUNY.

Helmke, G., & Levitsky, S. (2004). Informal institutions and comparative politics: A research agenda. *Perspective on Politics*, 2(4), 725–740.

Howlett, M., & Rayner, J. (2008). Third generation policy diffusion studies and the analysis of policy mixes: Two steps forward and one step back? *Journal of Comparative Policy Analysis*, 10(4), 385–402.

Husserl, E. (1900). *Logical investigations*, vol. 1 (Logische Untersuchungen, English translation by J.N. Findlay, 1970). New York: Routledge.

Husserl, E. (1913). *Ideas*, trans. B. Gibson. New York: Macmillan.

Jones, C., Hesterly, W., & Borgatti, S. (1997). A general theory of network governance: Exchange conditions and social mechanisms. *Academy of Management Review*, 22(4), 911–945.

Kickert, W., Klijn, E.H., & Koppenjan, J. (1997). Introduction: A management perspective on policy networks. In W. Kickert, E.-H. Klijn, & J. Koppenjan (Eds.), *Managing complex network* (pp. 1–13). London: Sage Publications.

Kristeva, J. (1980). *Desire in language: A semiotic approach to literature and art*. New York: Columbia University Press.

Kvale, S. (1996). *InterViews: An introduction to qualitative research interviewing*. Thousand Oaks: Sage Publications.

Larance, L.Y. (2001). Fostering social capital through NGO design: Grameen Bank membership in Bangladesh. *International Social Work*, 44(1), 7–18.

Lejano, R.P. (2006). *Frameworks for policy analysis: Merging text and context*. New York: Routledge.

Lejano, R. (2008). The phenomenon of collective action: Modeling institutions as structures of care. *Public Administration Review*, 68(3), 491–504.

Lejano, R., & Del Bianco, C. (2018). The logic of informality: Pattern and process in a São Paulo favela. *Geoforum*, 91, 195–205.

Lejano, R., & Park, S.J. (2015). The autopoietic text. In Fischer et al. (eds.), *Handbook of Critical Policy Studies* (pp. 274–296). Cheltenham, UK: Elgar Press.

Lejano, R.P., & Shankar, S. (2013). The contextualist turn and schematics of institutional fit: Theory and a case study from Southern India. *Policy Sciences*, 46(1), 83–102.

Lindblom, C.E. (1965). *The intelligence of democracy: Decision making through mutual adjustment*. New York: Free Press.

32 New Modes of Institutional Description

Lipsky, M. (1971). Street-level bureaucracy and the analysis of urban reform. *Urban Affairs Quarterly*, 6(4), 391–409.

Luhmann, N. (2003). "Organization." In T. Bakken & T. Hernes (Eds.), *Autopoietic organization theory. Drawing on Niklas Luhmann's social systems perspective* (pp. 31–52). Copenhagen: Copenhagen Business School Press.

Mandell, M. (Ed.). (2001). *Getting results through collaboration: Networks and network structures for public policy and management.* Westport, CT: Quorum Books.

March, J.G., & Olsen, J.P. (1989). *Rediscovering institutions.* New York: Simon and Schuster.

Matland, R.E. (1995). Synthesizing the implementation literature: The ambiguity-conflict model of policy implementation. *Journal of Public Administration Research and Theory*, 5(2), 145–174.

Maturana, H., & Varela, F. (1980). *Autopoiesis and cognition: The realization of the living.* Dordrecht: Reidel.

McGann, J. (1986). *The textual condition* (p. 15). Princeton, NJ: Princeton University Press.

Mossberger, K., & Hale, K. (1999). *Information diffusion in intergovernmental networks: The implementation of school-to-work programs.* Paper presented at the annual meeting of the American Political Science Association, Sept. 2–5.

Neuendorf, K.A. (2001). *The content analysis guidebook.* Thousand Oaks: Sage Publications.

Organisation for Economic Co-operation and Development (OECD) (2012). *The governance of mixed-ownership enterprises in Latin America.* Discussion Paper, OECD/CAF Latin American SOE Network Meeting, October 2012, Lima.

Ostrom, E. (1990). *Governing the commons.* Cambridge: Cambridge University Press.

O'Toole, L. (1997). Treating networks seriously: Practical and research-based agendas in public administration. *Public Administration Review*, 57(1), 45–52.

O'Toole, L., & Meier, K. (2005). Desperately seeking Selznick: Cooptation and the dark side of public management in networks. *Public Administration Review*, 64(6), 681–693.

Piore, M., & Sabel, C. (1984). *The second industrial divide.* New York: Basic Books.

Powell, W. (1990). Neither market nor hierarchy: Network forms of organization. In G. Staw & L.L. Cummings (Eds.), *Research in organizational behavior* (pp. 295–336). Greenwich, CT: JAI Press.

Ricoeur, P. (1971). The model of the text: Meaningful action considered as a text. *Social research*, 529–562.

Ring, P.S., & Van de Ven, A.H. (1992). Structuring cooperative relationships between organizations. *Strategic Management Journal*, 13, 483–498.

Rose, R. (1991). What is lesson-drawing? *Journal of Public Policy*, 11(1), 3–30.

Sabatier, P.A. (1986). Top-down and bottom-up approaches to implementation research: A critical analysis and suggested synthesis. *Journal of Public Policy*, 6(1), 21–48.

Schneider, A., & Ingram, H. (1997). *Policy design for democracy.* Lawrence: University Press of Kansas.

Scott, W.R., & Meyer, J.W. (1983). *Organizational Environments: The Organization of Societal Sectors.* Beverly Hills, California: Sage.

Sevenhuijsen, S. (2000). Caring in the third way: The relation between obligation, responsibility and care in third way discourse. *Critical Social Policy*, 20(1), 5–37.

Shin, K. (2017). Neither centre nor local: Community-driven experimentalist governance in China. *The China Quarterly*, 231, 607–633.

Snow, C.C., Miles, R.E., & Coleman, H.I. (1992). Managing 21st century network organizations. *Organizational Dynamics*, 29(3), 5–20.

Sokile, C.S., Mwaruvanda, W., & van Kopeen, B. (2005). *Integrated water resource management in Tanzania: Interface between formal and informal institutions.* International Workshop on Plural Legislative Frameworks, Jan. 26–28, Johannesburg.

Stone, D. (2000). Caring by the book: How work rules thwart good care. In M. Harrington-Meyer (Ed.), *Care work: Gender, labor, and welfare states.* New York: Routledge.

Strang, D., & Soule, S.A. (1998). Diffusion in organizations and social movements: From hybrid corn to poison pills. *Annual Review of Sociology*, 24(1), 265–290.

Strauss, A.L. (1993). *Continual permutations of action.* Hawthorne, NY: Aldine de Gruyter.

Taylor, R. (1998). The ethic of care versus the ethic of justice: An economic analysis. *The Journal of Socioeconomics*, 27(4), 479–493.

Weber, M. (1864). 1978 translation. *Economy and Society*, ed. B. Roth & C. Wittich. Berkeley: UC Berkeley.

3

GOVERNING BY METAPHOR
The Intertextuality of Institutional Life in China

3.1 Introduction

In the previous chapter, we introduced some concepts that will prove useful in studying innovative aspects of governance in China. One concept was that of textuality – namely, the functions of policy texts in governance, and contextuality – the presence of exogenous factors outside of the policy text. We made the point that these texts are often used in a sociopoietic system, wherein the text alone does not sufficiently prescribe policy but is part of a larger context in which policy is interpreted and enacted. One colorful example of this is found in the role of figures of speech in policymaking in China. As we will discuss, the degree to which these literary expressions play a role in policy is, while not unique, particularly distinctive in the Chinese context. Such use can, in fact, play a role in the evolution of institutions. Things brings us to a deviation from strongly textual policy regimes, where texts exhibit autopoiesis, to one marked by intertextuality.

In this chapter, we examine a variation of this hermeneutic process, where policy texts enter into a context populated by other texts. In such an environment, we should be open to the possibility that even those that are not ostensibly rulemaking or policy-setting texts might play a role in crafting rules and policy. In this manner, we bracket the neat separation between formal-juridical and informal-everyday domains (or, in Goffman's terms, bracketing the distinction between front and back stage).

The role of extra-juridical texts in policymaking is an illustration of a system we referred to, in the previous chapter, as Frame-c. In a strongly textualist system, policy texts prescribe institutional life to a high degree, and implementers need only follow these juridical texts. But in a contextualist system, policy texts gain meaning through intertextuality. In this chapter, we study how texts which should have no formal role in policy formulation, actually exert an influence through inter-textuality. Ceremonial speeches are an example of this. Even more intriguing is the use of figures of speech which, conventionally, are presumed to be simply for rhetoric's sake.

Studying policymaking as a phenomenon means paying attention to how policy is crafted and furthered in everyday settings. The role of language, uttered by leaders in non-juridical (even ceremonial) settings is one such instance. Most institutional scholarship would not consider this an element of policymaking, since this is not part of the formal legislative/administrative process, but a phenomenological stance appreciates the actual functions that such language plays.

China's central leadership makes frequent use of figures of speech (namely metaphor, euphemisms, and aphorisms) when referring to important issues of policy. Such speech should be understood as having more strategic use in policy-making than simply rhetoric. By relaxing the strong assumption of what constitutes a policy text, we open up our analysis to the possibility of non-formal policy discourse having strategic policy uses. First of all, such speech can characterize a particular ideological system. But it can also act upon the polity through different mechanisms. These expressions can be, in Austin's terms, speech-acts (Austin, 1962). For example, consider how ostensibly ceremonial speech can frame certain policy directions and create a meta-narrative for these initiatives. Such meta-narratives can chart a basic course without spelling out the details, leaving agents in the field to work out the latter. This preserves the central leadership's authority, while leaving room for innovation and improvisation. This can allow some balance between centralization and decentralization. Other uses include the ability to use euphemistic speech to dance otherwise delicate policy discourse, allowing a fine balance between engagement and diplomacy. As we will demonstrate, these strategic uses are enabled by the linguistic properties of different types of figures of speech.[1]

In January 2017, leaders of the world assembled in Davos, Switzerland, for the annual World Economic Forum meeting. In a much anticipated speech, China's president, Xi Jinping, gave a keystone address that had as one of its main themes globalization. In doing so, he used a number of colorful aphorisms and figures of speech to embellish his address.

One of the expressions he used was a classic aphorism, saying: "Honey melons hang on bitter vines; sweet dates grow on thistles and thorns," presumably pointing out the possibilities of positive progress from even conflictual situations. He then likened globalization to a tide, and commented that to "channel the waters in the ocean back into isolated lakes and creeks is simply not possible," ostensibly calling for an open global economy: "Pursuing protectionism is like locking oneself in a dark room. While wind and rain may be kept outside, that dark room will also block light and air."

While some have remarked on Xi's penchant for using such figures of speech, we recognize that this type of speech has been a common feature of China's

36 Governing by Metaphor

political leadership, often employed by Mao Zhedong and Deng Xiaoping (Heisey, 2000). As we will develop in this chapter, such speech has strategic uses beyond the rhetorical. It allows leaders to chart policy directions while maintaining a balance between diplomacy and engagement, centralization and decentralization, and vision and pragmatics. It takes on a practical role during a period of economic and political uncertainty for China, perhaps helping foster a degree of institutional experimentation.

Figures of speech such as metaphors and hyperbole are common devices in political rhetoric, used to foster patriotism, capture imagination, and project the charisma of the speaker. They make memorable what otherwise are perfunctory political speeches. No country's leadership has employed these figures of speech as widely and consistently as China's. Perhaps some of the origins of such rhetoric trace back to Confucian thought, which employed metaphorical models to describe essential truths. Figures of speech have been deliberately employed by political leaders in China throughout its history. Mao Zhedong, in justifying the Communist Revolution and the break from colonialist powers, employed the post-Newtonian metaphor of Einsteinean physics of infinite divisibility of energy and matter and opposition of elementary particles. In describing the inexorable force of the Cultural Revolution, Mao said "Wind will not cease even if trees want to rest." Decades later, Deng Xiaoping would urge the nation to take a more open, pragmatic approach to restructuring its economy and society, arguing, "it does not matter whether the cat is white or black if it catches a mouse," the mouse referring to economic development, a way of redirecting Chinese society away from rigid ideology and onto progressive reform (Jing, 2017).

There are conventional reasons for making use of these figures of speech in official discourse. Metaphors, allusions, and others provide simpler frames by which to apprehend complex ideas. They can provide color or dramatic effect to otherwise dry, official language. Aphorisms or old sayings can make a speech seem timeless and memorable. These are what we will refer to as the rhetorical reasons for employing figures of speech in official talk. In this chapter, we explore other, non-rhetorical, strategic reasons for use of such figures of speech in policymaking. We work out its deliberate use for the strategic – i.e., crafting or maintaining institutions, charting policy directions, or signaling relationships with political foes or allies.

In our analysis, we employ a linguistic approach to working out the strategic use of figures of speech in policymaking. These strategic uses are enabled by the linguistic properties of these figures of speech, as we take up in the next section.

3.2 Conceptual Background

In the previous chapter, we introduced a hermeneutic model of institution-making and used Figure 2.3 to illustrate the process by which policy texts come into meaning as they encounter particular contexts. We alluded to a version of the model where, in line with Kristeva's (1980) idea of intertextuality, even context can be understood as text to be interpreted. This opens up the analysis to consider the action of non-formal texts, including off-the-record comments, verbal agreements, tweets, and other speech that is not considered to be part of the formal policymaking process. We re-introduce Figure 2.3 in this alternative form, as Figure 3.1.

In this chapter, we consider how non-formal text can turn into policy as such text enters into a field of other texts and meaningful action. Specifically, we look at ostensibly informal, non-policy talk, as found in leaders' ceremonial speeches. To be sure, speeches can be used for formal policymaking. But in this chapter, we consider elements of such speeches that are ostensibly not meant as formal policy talk, which are figures of speech that are sprinkled into ceremonial speech presumably for primarily rhetorical purposes. But, as we will see, they can also serve the non-rhetorical function of crafting policy.

But how do figures of speech act on institutional life? George Lakoff, in his study of metaphor, observed that it was not simply a literary device, but one that figured in sense-making in ordinary speech. Metaphors are used to construct and order reality and to give meaning to otherwise unintelligible circumstances. They allow us to manage the unknown by imposing familiar worlds of meaning upon it (Lakoff, 1993; Lakoff & Johnson, 1980).

Similarly, metaphor (and other figures of speech) lend meaning to political life. In a time of change, when political uncertainty prevails, such literary devices convey familiar meanings to the unfamiliar circumstances and, in so doing, translate complex initiatives and political decisions into readily understood concepts, allowing the construction of political reality. These literary devices can facilitate governance, especially in situations that are complex, new, or uncertain.

We focus on three types of figures of speech: Metaphor, aphorism, and euphemism.

Metaphors are mappings between domains (in this case, conceptual ones), wherein the properties found in one domain map onto the second (Lakoff & Johnson, 1980). By this device, properties in the second domain, which may be more familiar or appealing, are associated with the first. For example, when Ronald and Nancy Reagan used the term "war on drugs" to introduce a new initiative against drug use, they purposefully used language alluding to the Second World War: "Well, now we're in another war for our freedom, and it's time for all of us to pull together again."[2] Metaphor can be used to lend positive valence to an otherwise controversial initiative, such as the use of metaphor to "sell" the Gulf war (Lakoff, 1991).

Aphorisms are sayings that express some age-old or universal truth. They are most often short witticisms or pithy quotations that can be used away from their original context (Morson, 2004). In this category we combine proverbs and wise sayings that, even if ancient (e.g., Confucius' Analects), can still be used today.

Euphemisms are substitutions in terms, in which a more innocuous term is put in place of that which can carry negative connotations or which can be overly confrontational. Euphemisms are often employed both to present the self in a more positive way and reduce the disconcerting effect on the other (McGlone & Batchelor, 2003). Examples of this are Orwellian terms such as "protective custody," which can mean imprisonment without habeas corpus. Euphemisms change the valence of the passage from negative to positive. Strategically, this literary device allows the introduction of more ambiguous, nonaggressive speech that does not require an overt response from the other party.

Conventionally, figures of speech are used for rhetorical flourish or more effective explanation. We refer to these as the rhetorical/literary uses of figures of speech, which include the following:

- A clarifying concept that, by allusion or simplification, describes a complex situation in a more effective or understandable way.
- A type of rhetorical flourish, providing memorable aspects to speech.

In the rest of the chapter, we examine the non-rhetorical uses of figures of speech and study their strategic uses. Strategic usage refers to use of figures of speech for reasons beyond simple exposition of ideas and rhetorical effect, and strategically pursuing certain political aims.

In our analysis, we consider three types of figures of speech and illustrate their use in a policy arena.

3.2.1 Brokering Relationships

There are some political positions that are difficult or awkward to state directly. When trying to convey the politically unspeakable, euphemism and metaphor can work where plain language does not. As an example of this, we will examine

FIGURE 3.1 Intertextual Model of Institutions

rhetoric around the South China Sea conflict. In this case, figures of speech can convey a government's policy not to compromise its assertion of territorial rights, but in ways that do not directly mention outright conflict with neighbors or the US.

3.2.2 Framing Policy

In other cases, figures of speech can frame a policy issue, setting a basic direction for policy without spelling out the complexity of its detail. Another way of saying this is that rhetoric can constitute a meta-narrative that can provide broad guidance to the interpreters and implementers of policy (Schon & Rein, 1995). Many policy situations are characterized by inherent, sometimes intended, ambiguities (Brugnach & Ingram, 2012). Such speech can set the general tone, rallying people around a common idea, while leaving the specifics unspecified. This process is known as framing, which is the process by which a basic scheme is used to organize participants in a movement and create shared meanings (see Goffman, 1978; Snow & Benford, 1988).

Figures of speech are often used to create a frame or meta-narrative that guides subsequent policy formulation and interpretation. It is consistent with an adaptive type of governance, as well (Lejano & Shankar, 2013). It allows leadership to claim (if only formally) authority over policy reforms, transmitting ethical (and other) norms that guide rulemaking, while allowing experimentation at lower levels of government.

In this chapter, we will use the evolving Chinese economic model to illustrate its use as meta-narrative.

3.2.3 Establishing Convention

Aphorisms are wise sayings, expressed in pithy ways, that convey age-old wisdom ("a chain is as strong as its weakest link"). Metaphors can be used to the same effect and, as in the last example, are implied in many aphorisms. Thus, text like "a strong hand is needed to strike the iron," referring to the metaphor of the blacksmith in forging new metal, can signal, to others, the need to further consolidate the power base and conveys the sense that such need is a natural order of things. As to the question of whether or not the speaker (Xi) actually had this meaning in mind when he spoke it, our response is that of Barthes (1974), who wrote about writerly texts, where the reader or listener decides what the text means, and Ricoeur (1981), who saw meaning as emerging from the fusion of horizons (in this case, speaker/author and reader/listener). In the discussion below, we speculate about what the text is doing, without assuming what the speaker meant to do with it.

In the ensuing discussion, we take three policy areas, each pertaining to a different function of figures of speech. The method of interpretation is based on a hermeneutic (Ricoeur, 1981; also Lejano & Leong, 2012), where the meaning of a text emerges from alternatively reading the text and examining the context

40 Governing by Metaphor

around it, a type of mixed scanning (Etzioni, 1986). Context, in this case, can mean other texts that influence the reading of the central text, or the social-physical setting in which it is uttered or read. The meaning of the text is influenced by a logic of fit between it and its context. While we can never directly infer what a speaker intends by an utterance, we can interpret the text and infer meanings from the hermeneutic analysis.

3.3 Case Studies

3.3.1 Brokering Relationships

The site of a fermenting territorial conflict, the South China Sea is an area of roughly 3.7 square kilometers and contains three groups of islands and one submerged bank, which are: Nansha Qundao (the Spratly Islands), Xisha Qundao (the Paracel Islands), Dongsha Qundao (the Pratas Islands), and Zhongsha Qundao (the Macclesfield Bank) (Wu, 2013; Wu, 1996). Most of the disputes revolve around claims over the Spratly Islands, or Nansha Qundao, which contains more than 230 features including islands, shoals, reefs and banks (Li, 2003). Claimant states include Brunei, the People's Republic of China, the Philippines, and Vietnam.

China claims most of the South China Sea on the basis of the so-called nine-dash line, which first appeared in an official map published by the Chinese government in 1948 (Zhao, 1996). Of the original 11 dashes, two were removed in 1953, due to Mao Zhedong's decision to hand over the Gulf of Tonkin to Vietnam (Beech, 2016).

Xi's trip to Seattle in September 2015, was his first state visit to the US. Just prior to his trip, an international tribunal began proceedings to decide on the merits of the Philippines' claims to the South China Sea. In May that year, a US surveillance plane flew a reconnaissance mission over the Spratly Islands, and the Chinese Navy dispatched a plane to warn it about encroaching on the contested area. It is at this juncture that Xi Jinping began his official visit to the US with a speech to a group of business interests. The choice of the audience was perhaps symbolic, perhaps suggesting that practical, commercial concerns should outweigh the political.

But he also came with a warning. How does a statesman warn a powerful combatant without engaging in directly hostile language? In this case, part of it can be done through euphemism and metaphor. Xi goes on to use an allusion to a Greek epic: "There is no such thing as the so-called Thucydides trap in the world. But should major countries time and again make the mistakes of strategic miscalculation, they might create such traps for themselves." What does it mean to invoke Thucydides? First, it can be a warning against fomenting conflict through a war of words. Second, it is (whether he meant it or not) an allusion to the possibility of war itself. But any such allusion necessarily avoids overt mention of conflict. There is no need for overt language when euphemism will serve the purpose. Interpreted in the light of the South China Sea dispute, it is a dire warning, as we are reminded that Thucydides wrote of a war that came about when a nation that began amassing power, Greece, began to threaten the established hegemon, Sparta.

But Xi also uses metaphor to conjure up a vision of a more harmonious future. How did he put this? By using the adage, "Peaches and plums do not talk, yet a path is formed beneath them." Conventionally, the adage refers to trees that silently bear fruit, speaking with actions, not words. But we can also interpret it as the idea of two different species, peaches and plums, that do not speak to each other and, yet, form a path between them. We can intuit that the path might mean harmonious relationships, such as through trade or cultural exchange, as he immediately follows up the passage with mention of international cooperation. The statement is ambiguous, but perhaps that is reflective of the relationship between the two nations, as well.

Later, he discusses how differences can be turned around into areas of mutual cooperation. What is notable about this speech is that he did not once mention the South China Sea conflict and, yet, we can all glean its import for this issue. Such is the power of metaphor.

3.3.2 Framing Policy

During the Cultural Revolution, it became mandatory for Party members to carry a copy of Mao's book of quotations (known outside China as the "Little Red Book"). The book, which was used as a reference for governing the nation, did not contain any detailed prescriptions for institution-building, nor did it contain rules and regulations. Instead, it consisted of 267 aphorisms from the chairman, which served as an ethical compass that guided the nation, not by specification, but by the spirit of Mao's ethical thought.

A similar phenomenon may be occurring around Xi Jinping, whose quotes have recently been published by the Party's political machinery. Analogous to Mao's red book, the *Excerpts of Xi Jinping's Remarks on Overall Deepening Reforms* consists of 274 quotes from Xi, many of which are aphorisms drawn from traditional Chinese sayings. How do these texts guide institutional life in China? Clearly, they do not specify actual practices or institutions but, rather, provide broad guidelines that people can interpret and translate into working principles on the ground. In short, they work as meta-narratives.

One particularly interesting area of institutional life that seems to make use of meta-narrative is the idea of constructing a "socialist market" system. What exactly the Party means by a socialist market is unknown – perhaps no one has a clear idea of what institutional design corresponds to this notion. What this institutional design would be is something being worked out in incremental fashion, crossing the river by feeling the stones, as Deng alluded to. An example of this is the evolving system of rules governing the Shanghai Stock Exchange, where the Party tried different strategies to curb market volatility.

42 Governing by Metaphor

China's transition to a socialist market economy started in the late 1970s when Deng Xiaoping, chief architect of the country's reform and opening up, was convinced that the traditional planned economy alone would be unable to revitalize China's economy. In his efforts to incorporate the market into the planned economy, also known as "building Socialism with Chinese characteristics," Deng argued: "It is wrong to say a market economy only exists in capitalism. Why can socialism not use a market economy?" Initial reforms included agriculture decollectivization and allowing private businesses and foreign investment. The 12th Communist Party of China (CPC) National Congress in 1982 made "the planned economy primary and market economy supplementary" as the direction for economic reform. In 1984, the CPC for the first time decided to develop "a planned commodity economy by public ownership."

Three years later, the 13th CPC National Congress further raised the significance of a market economy, saying the government should regulate the market and also enable the market to guide enterprises. In June 1989, Deng said, "We must combine command and market regulation to develop the economy." In his famous south China tour in 1992, Deng said, "It does not matter whether we have more planned or market economy. That is not the fundamental difference between socialism and capitalism because they are both economic tools." The 14th CPC National Congress, for the first time, officially confirmed that China was to develop a socialist market economy. In the 1990s, major reforms included partial privatization of the state sector, trade and price liberalization, and dismantling of the so-called "iron rice bowl" system of job security to boost efficiency. Since 2000, China has continued to carry forward the market-oriented reform and meanwhile enhanced macro-economic control. For example, the Chinese government is trying to create globally competitive industries by consolidating state-owned enterprises into large national champions.

In crafting the socialist market system, policy actors are guided by broad principles that set the general direction but do not provide policy specificity. Many of these guiding ideas are given as aphorisms, metaphors, and traditional sayings, meant to evoke the spirit of institutional reform without spelling it out in detail. One can look at Xi Jinping's comments on this theme, to date, and see in them just such a pattern of broad guidance affirming, but not specifying, the socialist market idea. To create a master frame, such text uses aphorisms and metaphors that are familiar to many. In some cases, Xi crafts his own, personal aphorisms, such as the following:

"learn to correctly use both the 'invisible hand' and the 'visible hand,' and become experts in balancing the relationship between the government and the market."[3] "[W]e must adhere to the 'two unswervinglys' in order to continue and improve our basic economic system."[4]

In this, Xi creates an image of a dialectic system, perhaps invoking Taoist yin and yang, that seemingly goes hand in hand coherently. The phrase "two unswervinglys" simply refers to developing both the public sector and the non-public sector of the economy. A similar dialectic is evoked in combining both the invisible hand of the market and the visible hand of the state (or Party). As institutional prescriptions, these aphorisms are inexplicit. But prescription is not their purpose. Rather, they serve as master frames that allow other policy actors to experiment with different institutional designs under the purview of Xi and the Party.

As discussed above, we can never ascertain what is in the speaker's (e.g., Xi's) mind, but we can interpret. In the above instance, we can intuit possibly strategic use of these expressions by their place in the larger context. They obviously do not hold any substantive prescriptions for specific policy actions, since they are mostly vague. Upon inspection, one sees that the rest of the speech is in a similar vein – general exhortations and advice without specific instruction. But these messages may be meant to signal a policy stance. What stance is being communicated? We can interpret this vis-à-vis the larger political context, which is an uncertainty over the direction of China's development model at a time of declining growth rates and a seeming exhaustion of Deng's doctrine of economic openness. The image of coherent, complementary systems signals a willingness to continue Deng's economic experiment. It signals that, with the present regime, it is allowable to experiment with market instruments without threatening the primacy of the state. Furthermore, the use of figures of speech and aphorisms can serve as master frames that help affix these ideas in the public psyche and discourse.

At times, these expressions can serve as general guiding principles. In other instances, they can be used to craft the idea that a coherent ideology exists, that steady hands and clear ideas guide the ship of state. It does not matter as much that the expressions may have no literal meaning, other than to create the illusion of governance.

3.3.3 Establishing Convention

Soon after taking office as president, Xi Jinping proceeded to lead a purge of corrupt Party members from within their own ranks. It was a widespread reform, but it was not a completely transparent plan. Perhaps part of the detail of the plan was kept out of public knowledge in an effort to keep the purge an "inside" matter for the Party. Or perhaps the plan was something worked out in evolving fashion over time, gaining specificity with implementation. It needed a master frame to organize the effort and have multiple policy actors, throughout the ladder of power, act in collective fashion.

But this effort also illustrates the idea that figures of speech can help establish convention in situations that otherwise are extraordinary. After all, a purge of one's own party is a radical task, fraught with struggle. It can easily be seen as a simple power play. In this case, the use of euphemism and aphorism can help ameliorate the negative connotations of the purge and, perhaps, help portray it as not an overtly political move but one that people might view as a natural course of events.

44 Governing by Metaphor

The attempt to "naturalize" the extraordinary is not uncommon – for example, some of this same dynamic was in evidence in ex post analysis of the recession of 2008 where the volatile changes in property and equity markets were explained as natural corrections of artificially inflated conditions (Horwitz, 2012). In an important speech at a meeting of the Commission for Discipline Inspection, Xi used the following expressions to set the tone for the anti-corruption campaign:[5]

> He who is good at governing through restriction should first restrict himself then others.
> Step onto the stone and you should leave your footprint on it; clutch a piece of iron and you should leave your handprint on it. This means one should take forceful steps and deliver tangible results in our anti-corruption campaign.
> We should continue to catch "tigers" as well as "flies."

In using nature metaphors, these texts reinforce the idea that such purging is a natural course of events. In the same speech, he provides the underlying reason behind such purging, which is "preserving and developing the Party's advanced nature and purity ..." In so doing, he associates the Party with a state of nature, reinforcing the idea of the Party as an ineluctable outcome of historical evolution. But, in order to maintain this symbolic status, it must be presented as something pure and advanced.

Xi uses the image of self-purification of the Party, elsewhere likening the anti-corruption reform to strong medicine needed to cure the illness. This coheres with the larger backdrop of power in China, where the Party strives to maintain its singular rule over the state into the foreseeable future. But, in order for the Party to do so, it must maintain the notion of purity and rectitude, never forsaking its mythical ties to the people. This occurs as polls indicate some drop in public satisfaction with quality of life.[6] In this case, the use of figures of speech seems to produce another naturalizing effect, which is to evoke the traditional state of affairs, that which has been the order of things since Confucian times. It is a return to the mythical past when China was a fortress unto itself and all was in harmony on the earth and in the heavens. It is this evocation of mythology that typifies text connecting the cleansing of the party as part of tradition, a hearkening back to the wisdom of the ages.

We also discern how multiple strategic uses can be associated with particular language. In the passages above, the phrase "tigers and flies" also works as a euphemism that connotes, but does not explicitly call out, corrupt Party comrades.

3.4 Discussion and Conclusion

In this chapter, we examined the role of language, uttered in non-juridical settings, in influencing policymaking. It is not unique to China, but is particularly distinctive how formal and non-formal speech by its leaders can play a role in the crafting of institutions and governance. No formal process would admit of such a role but, indeed, it undoubtedly does exist. Within the ambit of such speech, even more particularly interesting is the use of figures of speech (metaphors, aphorisms, euphemisms) for such functions. The usual notion is that these expressions simply function in a rhetorical way, but closer inspection of the policy process suggests that these quotations have a life of their own beyond the ceremonial occasion in which they are uttered. We speculate on the possible effects of such speech without assuming any intention on the part of the speaker. A text can exert an effect on its own completely apart from what the speaker or writer meant to say.

Using a hermeneutic approach, we examine possibilities for non-rhetorical use of such language. Studying their relationship to the larger context of real situations and other texts, we find a number of strategic uses (and, as discussed above, the question of intention is not a concern for the hermeneutic). In general, these expressions signal different intended meanings. In the case of the South China Sea conflict, they help convey a fine balance in the relationship between China and other nations, a kind of détente achieved through literary means instead of explicit diplomatic language. When we examined another case, that of crafting a development trajectory for China, we found such language to help convey a meta-narrative that frames the general agenda without specifying the details of such. The language helps convey the "big picture" of what a socialist market economy might prove to be. And, looking at the case of anti-corruption campaigns, literary language is part of how extraordinary actions are portrayed as canonical, a natural event in the evolution of the life of the nation.

We end with a note that these reflections are not just about China. In fact, while we take China as an exemplar of the use of literary expressions for strategic purposes, we maintain that this is in fact operative for other contexts, as well. It is just that exemplars and limiting cases delineate the phenomena so much more clearly that we examined the Chinese context. It is hoped that this research leads to more concerted analyses of the role of non-juridical speech acts in the institutional life of a nation.

Notes

1 Portions of this chapter are taken from a working paper (Lejano, Wei, & Li, 2018).
2 Speech by Ronald Reagan, September 14, 1986, as cited in Lejano, Ingram, & Ingram (2018).
3 Xi Jinping, The "Invisible Hand" and the "Visible Hand," Speech at the 15th Group Study Session of the Political Bureau of the 18th CPC Central Committee, May 26, 2014.
4 Xi Jinping, Explanatory Notes to the "Decision of the Central Committee of the Communist Party of China on Some Major Issues Concerning Comprehensively Continuing the Reform," Nov. 9, 2013.
5 Xi Jinping, Power Must be "Caged" by the System, Speech at the Second Plenary Session of the 18th CPC Central Commission for Discipline Inspection, January 22, 2013.

46 Governing by Metaphor

6 Lyon and Liu (2016). For example, between 2014 and 2015, satisfaction with the level of household income dropped from 66% to 58%, and optimism over the standard of living dropped from 76% to 71%.

References

Austin, J.L. (1962). *How to do things with words*. Oxford: Clarendon Press.

Barthes, R. (1974). *S/z* (p. 76), trans. R. Miller. New York: Hill and Wang.

Beech, H. (2016). Just where exactly did China get the South China Sea nine-dash line from? *Time*, July 19, http://time.com/4412191/nine-dash-line-9-south-china-sea/.

Brugnach, M., & Ingram, H. (2012). Ambiguity: The challenge of knowing and deciding together. *Environmental Science & Policy*, 15(1), 60–71.

Cheng, X. (2009). *Chinese metaphors in official discourse: How the government of the People's Republic of China criticizes the independence of Taiwan*. PhD dissertation, Ball State University, Muncie, IN.

Etzioni, A. (1986). Mixed scanning revisited. *Public administration review*, 8–14.

Goffman, E. (1978). *The presentation of self in everyday life* (p. 56). London: Harmondsworth.

Heisey, D.R. (Ed.). (2000). *Chinese perspectives in rhetoric and communication* (No. 1). Greenwood Publishing Group.

Horwitz, S. (2012). Causes and cures of the Great Recession. *Economic Affairs*, 32(3), 65–69.

Jing, Y. (2017). The transformation of Chinese governance: Pragmatism and incremental adaption. *Governance*, 30, 37–43.

Lakoff, G. (1991). Metaphor and war: The metaphor system used to justify war in the Gulf. *Peace Research*, 25–32.

Lakoff, G. (1993). The contemporary theory of metaphor. In A. Ortony (Ed.), *Metaphor and thought* (2nd Ed.), Cambridge: Cambridge University Press.

Lakoff, G., & Johnson, M. (1980). *Metaphors we live by*. Chicago: Chicago University Press.

Lejano, R., Ingram, M., & Ingram, H. (2018). Narrative in the policy process. In R. Hoppe & H. Colebatch, *Handbook of the policy process*. London: Edward Elgar.

Lejano, R.P., & Leong, C. (2012). A hermeneutic approach to explaining and understanding public controversies. *Journal of public administration research and theory*, 22(4), 793–814.

Lejano, R.P., & Shankar, S. (2013). The contextualist turn and schematics of institutional fit: Theory and a case study from Southern India. *Policy Sciences*, 46(1), 83–102.

Lejano, R., Wei, D., & Li, L. (2018). *Governing by metaphor: Rhetoric and institutions in China*. Working Paper, Institute for Water Policy, Singapore.

Li, J. (2003). *Nanhai Zhengduan yu Guoji Haiyangfa (South China Sea disputes and the international law of the sea)*. Beijing: Ocean Press.

Lyon, L., & Liu, D. (2016). Chinese satisfaction drops amid economic slowdown. Gallup Poll, January 18, 2016, accessed June 30, 2017 at: www.gallup.com/poll/188474/chinese-satisfaction-drops-amid-economic-slowdown.aspx?g_source=confidence+in+government+China&g_medium=search&g_campaign=tiles

McGlone, M.S., & Batchelor, J.A. (2003). Looking out for number one: Euphemism and face. *Journal of Communication*, 53(2), 251–264.

Morson, G.S. (2004). Aphoristic style: The rhetoric of the aphorism. In W. Jost & W. Olmsted (Eds.), *Rhetoric and rhetorical criticism* (pp. 248–265). New York: Blackwell.

Ricoeur, P. (1981). *Hermeneutics and the human sciences: Essays on language, action and interpretation*. Cambridge: Cambridge University Press.

Schon, D.A., & Rein, M. (1995). *Frame reflection: Toward the resolution of intractable policy controversies*. New York: Basic Books.

Snow, D.A., & Benford, R.D. (1988). Ideology, frame resonance, and participant mobilization. *International social movement research*, 1(1), 197–217.

Wu, S. (2013). *Solving disputes for regional cooperation and development in the South China Sea: A Chinese perspective*. Oxford: Chandos Publishing.

Zhao, L. (1996). *Haiyangfa Wenti Yanjiu (Study on questions concerning the law of the sea)*. Beijing: Peking University Press.

4

RELATIONALITY IN RURAL PROPERTY REGIMES

In this chapter, we examine China's institutional experiment in the area of rural land reform and use this case to develop the idea of relationality in property rights (产权 chan quan). Responding to lagging rural incomes and the scarcity of developable urban land, the central government sanctioned the pilot implementation of a new type of tradeable development right. In the municipality of Chengdu, one of the pilot sites, the new instrument is called the construction land quota and is used to trade development rights between rural and urban sites. Using a comparative analysis, we describe the essential features of the quota, comparing it to a similar program in Chongqing and to more conventional instruments like tradeable development rights. We argue that extant institutional models come up short in describing distinctive features of Chengdu's quota program and develop the idea of the plenary good as a mode of description. Examining and characterizing the Chengdu program provides a lens with which to view the larger, national project of constituting a socialist market system. We end the chapter with a note on the distinctive nature of China's institutional environment, evoking the idea of a Confucian ethos in describing what we refer to as a relational system.

4.1 Introduction and Background

China's ongoing experiments in governance are an important laboratory from which to learn about institutional design. This is no more evident than in the area of land use and urbanization, where the scale and pace of such change in China is unprecedented. Moreover, the government's practice of adaptive incrementalism allows us a chance to see a kind of institutional innovation at work. For example, China's leadership routinely evoke the idea of a "socialist market economy," but what institutional forms this will translate to is an open question. Leaders will often use metaphor and aphorism in their speeches when describing China's future. Perhaps part of the motivation behind this practice (other than, of course, rhetorical effect) is the open-endedness of the details behind its institutional model, which are being worked out in incremental fashion as we speak (Lejano, Wei, & Li, 2017). As Deng Xiaoping once said, China is "crossing the river by feeling the stones."

Over the last decade, China has embarked on significant reforms in its system of rural land ownership and management. While the natural inclination of scholars is to characterize this as a step along a path to a full-fledged private property market, a more careful examination suggests that it may not be as simple as this.[1] Scholars have pointed out that the outcomes of privatization are never predetermined (e.g., Araral, 2009). This chapter argues that what we are seeing is the evolution of institutional designs that are unique in some respects, taking on some elements of a private property market while retaining elements of collectivization. The aim of this chapter is to better characterize these changes and to describe how the new institutional model may be something altogether innovative. To do this, we will focus most closely on the pilot program that Chengdu has embarked on around a new form of transferable development rights (TDR) that links rural farmland to urban development.

Our research focuses on a case study of institutional experimentation in the municipality of Chengdu, the capital of the southwest region of Sichuan. The municipality has 11 districts, five county-level cities, and four counties under its jurisdiction. As of 2016, its population stood at nearly 16 million, of which around 6 million live in the rural, outermost (third-circle) periphery of the area. Chengdu has been the site of a vigorous process of urbanization, its urban area estimated to have grown from 75 square kilometers (km^2) to 807.9 km^2 between 1976 and 2010, with an annual urban growth rate of 7.7% (Qu, Zhao, & Sun, 2014). Under these conditions, the pressure to convert rural land to urban land use is great.

In 2007, the central government selected Chengdu as a pilot area for comprehensive reform under the Commission for Balanced Urban-Rural Growth (CBRUG). Along with the municipality of Chongqing, Chengdu would be a site for experimental use of a new tradeable development permit (the "quota"), which could be used to transfer land use rights from more remote rural areas to urbanizing areas of the city (PRC NDRC, 2007). As discussed below, the new institutional mechanism is a response to a push for reform from both national and local levels.

The chapter introduces the background of the institutional experiment – its origins in development agendas at central state and local levels and the evolution of the new quota system. We then compare it against conventional regulatory instruments, as well as Chongqing's closely related program. The chapter will attempt to more richly describe the new program, proposing a unique institutional model that better characterizes what is new and innovative about it. Towards the end of the chapter, we sketch out where this evolution of institutional configuration might be headed and why its endpoint is not necessarily a conventional private property market, as implied in some literature. In our analysis, we will apply concepts from earlier chapters – such as autopoiesis, multi-corporality, and relationality – that help us better describe the unique properties of these evolving institutions as a relational institutional design.

4.1.1 Initiatives for Land Reform

One important rationale for reform has been the so-called urban–rural divide. Development has concentrated in cities and stagnated in the countryside. As of 2010, it was estimated that average incomes in urban areas were more than three times that in the rural.[2] This owes, in part, to decades of government-sponsored industrial development in cities, focusing infrastructure investment in urban places (Park, 2008; Ye, LeGates, & Qin, 2013), along with a higher level of subsidies/transfers (Yang & Cai, 2003) and higher levels of education (Sicular et al., 2007) in urban areas. Compounding this is the considerable income inequality between rural areas, both between and within provinces (Yu, Luo, & Zhang, 2007). The urban–rural divide is exacerbated by constraints to free labor mobility between rural and urban areas – i.e., China maintains a residential registration (hukou) program, where people's residential status is classified as urban or rural. The Household Responsibility System, which began in 1978 and grants each rural household usufruct rights to individual plots of land, is additional incentive for rural residents to stay in place. Notwithstanding the effect of hukou residential registration and household responsibility systems in fixing rural populations to the countryside (Chan & Zhang, 1999), rural-to-urban migration has been unprecedented (e.g., see Chan, 2013 for estimates).

Proponents for land reform initiatives, such as the pilot program in Chengdu, draw general guidance from directives from the central government, especially those set forth in the Third Plenary Session of the 18th Central Committee of the Communist Party of China. Some relevant passages are excerpted below:[3]

> We will allow rural collectively owned profit-oriented construction land to be sold, leased and appraised as shares, on the premise that it conforms to planning and its use is under control, and ensure that it can enter the market with the same rights and at the same prices as state-owned land. We will narrow the scope of land expropriation, regulate the procedures for land appropriation, and improve the rational, regular and multiple security mechanism for farmers whose land is requisitioned. We will broaden the scope of compensated use of state-owned land, and reduce land appropriation for non-public welfare projects. We will establish a mechanism for the distribution of incremental benefits from land that takes into account the interests of the state, the collective and the individual, and appropriately raise individual income from such benefits. We will improve the secondary market for land leasing, transfer and mortgage.

It is clear that a key concern of the central government is the gap in incomes and quality of life between urban and rural areas. State policy also promotes fair treatment of rural farmers whose homestead lands have been expropriated with little compensation. Later in the document are relevant passages that directly support TDR:

> We will select several pilot areas to steadily and prudently push forward the mortgage, guarantee and transfer of farmers' residential property rights, and expand the channels for farmers to increase their property income. We will set up a rural property rights transfer market, and promote the open, fair and procedure-based operation of rural property rights transfer.

At the same time as the central government sets policy goals toward unified rural and urban construction markets, it stresses the desire to maintain the nation's store of arable land. The Second Land Survey in 2015 shows an average of 0.1 hectares of arable land per capita, which is low compared to other nations. As a result, the government has set a minimum total arable area of 1.8 billion mu (1.2 million km^2 or 120 million hectares) as a national policy (CCCCP, 2014).

On the part of municipal and local governments, there is a constant struggle to find new developable land in the expanding, densifying city. The supply, which is the amount of rural land that the state allows to be converted for urban development, constantly falls short of demand in the fastest growing cities. Along with local government's dependence on urban expansion for revenue (Hsing, 2010), the result is a perceived need for new ways to carve out new areas for urban development.

4.1.2 Conventional Procedure for Converting Rural to Urban Construction Land

The current process for converting rural agricultural land to urban construction land might be well described, at least formally, as a system of nested institutions (Ostrom, 1995, p. 41; March & Olsen, 1998, p. 995). That is, land allocation proceeds in stepwise fashion from state to provincial to municipal to local levels and, ultimately, to private parties.

The central government sets the overall framework within which land use planning occurs. A central concern of national leadership has been the steady loss of rural farmland across the country, leading to the "red line" of 1.8 billion mu, as specified in the National Land Use Master Plan. Some scholars suggest that another reason for setting this limitation stems from government's concern over growing rural unrest over land expropriation by local governments and low levels of compensation to the dispossessed farmers (Cai, 2011).

First, the central government sets goals for preserving arable agricultural land across the entire country. To do this, it allocates arable land requirements on a provincial level as part of the National Land Use Master Plan. Similarly, quotas for allowing conversion of rural agricultural land to urban construction land are allocated on a provincial level. Each province then allocates its quota to municipal governments, and the latter proceed to allocate their quotas to districts and counties below them, which translate these into zoning plans. In turn, townships in each county carry out the allocations on a parcel-level basis.[4]

Property rights differ between urban land, where all land is the property of the state, and rural land, where land is collectively owned by the village. In order to convert land from rural to urban construction land, it has to be first converted from collective ownership to state ownership. This is done by the municipality, acting formally on behalf of the state, which expropriates land from farmers, paying them according to predetermined rates of compensation. The land is held in reserve in the municipal or provincial land bank, and then leased to private parties through auctions or bid invitations. The funds from the auction are then deposited in the municipal or provincial financial center. Private parties purchase the right to use and benefit from the land for fixed terms.[5]

Expropriation has allowed local governments to obtain a large source of revenue, equivalent to the difference between the amounts paid by the buyers and that paid out to the farmers. The terms of compensation are set according to the Land Administration Law (LAL), passed in 1986 and amended in 1998 and 2004. The LAL sets compensation according to the opportunity cost of the agricultural land. Specifically, it sets compensation for the expropriated land at six to ten times the average annual agricultural output value of such land in the preceding three-year period. This is essentially equivalent to the present value of the future stream of income from farming the land. Contrast this to the amounts received from auctioning off the land to urban developers, amounting to the present value of the stream of benefits from urban use.

In previous work (Lian & Lejano, 2014), we discussed the large discrepancy in these two streams of revenue. In many cases, the amount received by local government can be more than a hundred times the compensation rate received by the farmers. Moreover, life in the newly urbanizing area proved difficult for the displaced farmers (or 失地农民, shidi nongmin). Amounts received from the land would prove inadequate, given rising costs of living in the city. The inability of farmers to change their hukou from rural to urban meant they could not access many services in these urbanizing areas. Having lost their opportunity to farm, many former farmers also find themselves without needed skills to find work in the city (Lian & Lejano, 2014, p. 5). Attendant to this is the loss of self-subsistence associated with farming (i.e., food, water, and livestock that the farmer's family can live on). Conceptually, one can say that this is a result of the quick transition from collective, rural life to an individualized, urban one. This is signified most of all by the provision, in the LAL, for substituting cash payments for the erstwhile practice of working out re-employment of the farmers (LAL, 1998 revision).

Relationality in Rural Property Regimes   53

A related issue is whether or not the individual farmers really have a say over the decision to sell rights to their collectively owned farmland. Ambiguity over which collective institution (e.g., village council, township, etc.) oversees these decisions leaves it an open question as to whether or not farmers have a voice in these forums (Ho, 2001).

4.1.3 Transition to and Design of the Quota System

This process of stepwise allocation can have inherent inefficiencies, since allocations tend to reflect other considerations, such as inter-jurisdictional parity and bureaucratic formalism. For example, central government allocations cannot reflect, in detail, differing levels of productivity of agriculture (or urban development) across the country. Allocations within the municipality can themselves have inefficiencies. In the case of Chengdu, the municipal government distributes the total quota (for rural land conversion) among its approximately 20 cities and counties equally in an effort to maintain a sense of even-handedness, regardless of the level of demand for urban construction land in these different areas (interview with author).

In order to meet some of the pent-up demand for urban construction land in rapidly growing areas, the Ministry of Land and Resources allowed 20 cities to initiate a linking program beginning in 2004. The policy was known as Linking Increase in Urban Construction Land with Decrease in Rural Construction Land, or Link (挂钩, gua gou) for short. The Link program was the forerunner for the present quota program in Chengdu. The detailed evolution process will be provided later.

Comprehensive land consolidation (土地综合整治 tu di zong he zheng zhi) coincided with the acceleration of land registration in Chengdu. To be clear, the land is still owned by the collective, but land certificates acknowledge the individual household's claim to sole use of the particular parcel. The quota system requires strict accounting of parcels, determining which collective rural land would be subject to the quota program and who would receive compensation. By the end of 2010, about 1.66 million households received titles for rural land for housing or other construction use (Li, 2012).

A parallel development was the unification of urban and rural hukou in Chengdu (Ye & LeGates, 2013). Rural residents of Chengdu may now use public and social services in the city after an initial period (one year), when they pay into the urban social security system. Essentially, this does away with much of the distinction between urban and rural hukou.

This represents a significant increase in income to rural households. One source estimates that about RMB 120,000/mu was received by farmers in 2012 (Xiao, 2014, p. 186). Compare this to another study, which found a range of RMB 16,000–54,000/mu for compensation received by farmers for expropriated land (Li, 2012, p. 61). The municipal government receives a fee of 0.5% of the transaction amount but, more significantly, gains revenue from new development in the urban area.

4.2 Methodological and Conceptual Approach

The primary goal of the research is to characterize the new institutional design of the quota program. In other words, we attempt a thick description of it that delineates in what ways the new institution is unique and even innovative. To do this, we make use of several analytical strategies.

First, we more finely describe the new institution by analyzing differences between it and other models. A number of comparative analyses will be done. We begin by departing from the assumption that the reforms might be tending to a fully privatized property market. This entails comparing the quota program with a conventional marketable instrument with private property rights. The second comparison will differentiate the quota program from the closely related TDR. Another comparative assessment can be done by differentiating the Chengdu and Chongqing programs. The idea behind the comparative approach employed in this analysis is to emphasize not isomorphism, but polymorphism – i.e., differentiation of programs to fit context (Lejano, 2006; Lejano & Shankar, 2013; Lejano, 2016).

The second conceptual framework is to view the new institutional design as a set of relationships. Institutions are more conventionally designed as sets of rules or practices. However, they are also new configurations of relationships between different policy actors. The transition from state-owned property to private property regimes is characterized by a transfer of property rights and authorities. However, the new quota system in Chengdu does not attempt such a clear displacement of rights and authorities. To understand the networked design of the quota system, we describe it in relational terms (see Qiao & Upham, 2015).

The empirical evidence consists of archival material (scholarly articles, program material) and interviews. A total of 14 interviews were conducted with: Four exchange center staff, one village officer, one academic involved in design of the program, and nine village residents. A portion of the fieldwork was conducted at the Chengdu Agricultural Exchange Center, where collective construction land use rights are traded. Owing to personal relationships with staff in Sichuan Provincial Government, the author gained access to the Center by way of official introduction, and the research team was able to interview a person who played a key role in drafting the quota program, who was one of the staff in Chengdu Bureau of Land and Resources and is now the assistant manager at Chengdu Agricultural Exchange Center. This person was one of our main informants. He also introduced the team to another interviewee, a university professor who was his colleague in the Chengdu Bureau of Land and Resources and also involved in the design of the quota program.

In order to understand how the quota program is processed, the research team also interviewed several other staff in the exchange center. The research team then visited several villages they mentioned and interviewed several villagers, randomly selected, to see the outcome of the quota program. Interviews were digitally recorded, transcribed, and translated into English. The research team also visited the agriculture exchange center and observed proceedings and collected archival information (trading data, trading rules, etc.).

4.3 Institutional Evolution and Design of Chengdu's Quota System

4.3.1 Institutional Evolution of the Chengdu System

Before characterizing the unique and innovative institutional features of the quota program, we first briefly review the process by which institutional design occurred in incremental fashion (akin to "crossing the river by feeling the stones"). The Chengdu quota system, initiated in 2008, is now quite different from the initial design, which underwent three design phases, as discussed below.

4.3.1.1 Policy Relaxation Phase of Post-Quake Reconstruction

In 2004, the state council proposed, in the Decision on Deepening Reform and Strengthening Land Management, to encourage rural construction land consolidation and to link the increase in urban construction land with the decrease in rural construction land. Thereafter, the Ministry of Land and Resources started to set up pilot areas of link programs, and Chengdu was among the first pilot areas.

In order to create new urban construction land, an equivalent area of rural residential land must be freed up and converted back to agricultural use. To do this, the residents have to agree to relocate to higher-density housing elsewhere in the village. This then frees up the former residential area, which is then reconverted to farmland.

As one informant shared with us: "Chengdu is in fact, doing best in terms of the Link policy. The first pilot project was conducted in Changxing Village in Bi County, Chengdu. At that time, the project was very effective so as to be attached high importance by the Ministry."

But the process was slow – because the urban and rural properties were "linked," the reconversion process had to be carried out before the development rights could be transferred to the urban land, a process that took years. Official documentation about linking the increase and decrease of urban and rural construction land (建设用地 jian she yong di) in some provinces and municipalities throughout the country was formally issued in 2006. Linking was confined to within-county transfers and, so, matching up urban demand with rural supply from different counties was not possible. But all this changed in 2008.

On May 12, 2008, the great Wenchuan earthquake devastated rural parts of Chengdu. Millions of homes were destroyed. In the ensuing recovery, the government struggled to rebuild homes at a pace needed by those displaced by the earthquake. In response, the government sought to enlist private capital for reconstruction, but the incentives for building in remote rural areas were limited.

56 Relationality in Rural Property Regimes

As a result, the Ministry of Land and Resources relaxed the within-county requirement for linking of rural and urban land.

This allowed the demand in more rapidly growing areas of Chengdu to spur investment, across county lines, in consolidation and resettlement in the stricken rural areas (Xiao, 2014). Upon a recommendation by Zhou Qiren, a noted economist, Chengdu began piloting the quota system that spanned the entire municipality – i.e., the City of Chengdu and the ten counties around it (interview with author). For example, a Qionglai index could be used at Shuangliu, Wuhou, Jingjiang areas, etc. Essentially, a developer could purchase a quota, generated by consolidation in rural Chengdu, and use it for development of parcels in the central city (中心城区 zhong xin cheng qu) and so-called second-circle (二圈层 er quan ceng) areas.

But Document no. 10 issued by the state council in 2010 clearly stated that the Link policy cannot be carried out across different counties, the only exception to this rule being the reconstruction for disaster-stricken sites. The policy relaxation phase of post-quake reconstruction was followed by the regular period.

4.3.1.2 Trial Operation Phase of "Permit for Access" (持证准入 chi zheng zhun ru)

The Chengdu Agricultural Exchange Center (农交所 nong jiao suo) began quota trading on December 4, 2008. Initial implementation of the quota system was problematic. At that time, the quota was a prerequisite for being qualified to bid for urban land, and developers did not want to be shut out of the bidding. Demand for the quotas was great, and bids were inordinately higher than officials thought acceptable, reaching RMB 920,000/mu at one point. Within 11 days of its first trade, the center was shut down by the Ministry of Land and Resources, fearing it would lead to a sudden increase in costs to urban residents.

4.3.1.3 Optimizing Phase of "Permit for Use" (持证准用 chi zheng zhun yong)

Ministry officials visited Chengdu to study issues with design of the quota program. The ministry subsequently allowed the exchange to begin operating again in April 2011 only after the Chengdu municipal government revised its rules to require quota acquisition only after a developer has already acquired a piece of property. In a sense, this lowers demand for the quota since developers need only to match the number of properties acquired and not the properties they might potentially bid for. In addition, Chengdu fixed a default guiding price (指导价 zhi dao jia) for the quota of RMB 300,000/mu, which is the level that policymakers felt would suffice to compensate for the work of resettlement and conversion to agricultural land. Evidently, recent demand for quotas has not pushed the price above this baseline, as recent trading data we obtained showed no movement away from the current guiding price.

4.3.2 The Design of Chengdu's Quota System

We now describe, in more detail, the design features of the quota program, before proceeding to the comparative institutional analysis.

Chengdu, located in the western edge of Sichuan Basin, is the provincial capital of Sichuan Province. Chengdu served as the economic, cultural, logistical and technological center in southwest China, and built a competitive and broad industrial base which now helps the city maintain its leading position in the region. In the rural parts of Chengdu, 60% of the land area comprised sparsely populated hills and mountains, the remaining 40% of land is found in the plains, where population density is high and the conflict between people and land is intense. How to maintain the arable "red line" and ensure food safety, to provide a powerful guarantee for the rapid development of urbanization and industrialization, and to solve agriculture issues and balance the urban and rural development at the same time, has become a primary area of tension in Chengdu's economic and social development process.

As mentioned earlier, the policy of Link was put forward by the state council in 2004 to deepen the reform and facilitate land transfers. In 2007, the state council designated Chengdu and the neighboring municipality of Chongqing as "National Comprehensive Reform Pilot Regions for Coordinated Urban-Rural Development." In October 2008, Chengdu established the first rural property rights exchange center in the country. After finishing the conferment of ownership certification, the reform of rural property rights in Chengdu initiated the practice of quota transaction. The specific operational procedures of the construction land quota transaction system in Chengdu are as follows:

Quota Generation

There are three steps to generate quotas. First, developers consolidate the rural collective construction land (including homestead and subsidiary facilities, land for township enterprises, rural public facilities and public welfare construction land) and reclaim it as arable land. Second, the reclaimed construction land would be assessed and checked, deducting the land reserved for the farmers' concentrated residential units. Third, the Chengdu Municipal Land Resources Bureau would register detailed information about the construction land quota and issue a Construction Land Quota Certificate for developers. The certificate indicates the technical information about the generated site, including acreage, acceptance projects and so on. If developers use the saved collective construction land directly, they would not receive a Construction Land Quota Certificate.

Quota Acquisition

The construction land quota can be obtained in either of two ways: Through consolidation projects or market transaction. Natural persons, legal persons and other organizations can purchase construction land quotas from agricultural exchange center.

Quota Transaction

The construction land quota, which is obtained by developers through comprehensive land consolidation projects, can be used directly by the developer or sold via public transactions at the agricultural exchange center. The construction land quota is valid for two years from the original generation or last transaction. During the period of validity, the quota cannot be transferred again. If the quota holder fails to use the quota within the prescribed time limit, the Chengdu Municipal Government buys the quota back at the minimum protective price published that same year. The minimum protective price of the construction land quota is based on the cost of implementation of a rural land consolidation project, including the construction of rural infrastructure, public service facilities, and rural housing construction.

Quota Usage

Holding a construction land quota is the precondition for the purchase of state-owned construction land. The bidder shall possess the corresponding area of construction land quota, and only then will the bidder sign the State-Owned Construction Land Use Right Transfer Contract upon successful bidding for state-owned construction land (excluding industrial land) that falls within the so-called second-circle (or peri-urban area) of Chengdu City. If bidders bid for state-owned construction land (excluding industrial land) sold for the first time in the third-circle counties, they pay an amount equal to the price of the corresponding area of construction land quota (according to the minimum protective price announced by the municipal government that same year). Only then can the State-Owned Construction Land Use Right Transfer Contract be let.

Quota Revenue Distribution

If the rural collective implements the comprehensive land consolidation project, then the collective receives the net revenue from the generated quota. If investors or the official land consolidation department (which are entrusted by the collective) implement the land consolidation project, then a portion of the benefit will accrue to them. After the construction land quota transaction, the supplier pays the infrastructure supporting fee at 10% of the transaction price. If the quota is used directly rather than transferred in the agricultural exchange center, it is also necessary to pay the infrastructure supporting fee at 10% of the negotiated price or the minimum protective price. The municipal government of Chengdu collects the infrastructure supporting fee, and then returns it to district government where the consolidation project is located to improve infrastructure construction in rural areas. The cost of planning, surveying, designing, reclamation, checking and other necessary fees, like the cost of infrastructure support and public service facilities in the concentrated residence, are shared by the peasant collective, farmers and investors. If the rural collective raises funds and finishes the project itself, the cost can be distributed between the collective and the individual participating farmers, according to agreed-upon local arrangements. A resident who gives up their homestead and foregoes living in the concentrated residence, may be paid the price of a corresponding homestead reclamation area, after deducting the cost of homestead reclamation and other necessary expenses.

4.4 Distinguishing Chengdu's Quota Program from Conventional Market Approaches

One way of delineating how a new program is unique or innovative is by comparing it against an established or conventional institutional template (as in Lejano & Shankar, 2013).

4.4.1 The Market Platform for the System

Having held more than 20 special meetings and modified relevant policy documents more than 60 times, experts from economic, financial, legal and other fields worked with various departments in order to design the construction land quota transaction system. During "two sessions" in 2007, provincial and municipal leaders, including the provincial governor, Jufeng Jiang, and the Party secretary, Chuncheng Li, paid a special visit to the Ministry of Land and Resources to request support for land reform efforts, including the quota transaction system. Through this arduous planning process, Chengdu, together with Chongqing, were officially approved to become the country's only two pilot cities to explore quota transaction by the Ministry of Land and Resources in 2007.

In October 2008, Chengdu established the first rural property rights exchange center in the country. This center has become the market platform of the system. Though the quota system aims at a market mechanism, it still includes limiting conditions and special stipulations to protect local interests – e.g., investigating whether the land consolidation project is consistent with land use plans, verifying whether the farmers are aware of the project and participate in it, preserving local environmental amenities such as hills or pools, etc.

Comprehensive land consolidation in Chengdu has become a central piece in the national government's rural reform effort, which has been endorsed by the

60 Relationality in Rural Property Regimes

Ministry of Land and Resources. In 2010, after years of discussion, Chengdu Municipal Government put forward a new idea, which includes promoting innovation in the rural land comprehensive consolidation mechanism, serving peasant collectives and farmers as the dominant power rather than the government, encouraging social investors to participate in rural land reclamation, putting the saved construction land quota to tangible land market to trade publicly, with all proceeds returning to the rural area.

After eight years' development, Chengdu's rural property rights exchange center adheres to a market-oriented concept, and actively pursues system innovation. It initiated the development model of "one trading platform and three-level service system," which includes the three levels of "municipality, county and township." A "six unified" management model has been established including unified trading rules, unified transaction verification, a unified information system, unified service standards, unified supervision, and unified transaction settlement. Such an institutional system generates many benefits, such as encouraging various types of rural property rights to join the transaction, activating the rural market, liberating the values of rural property rights, increasing the income of rural collective economic organizations and farmers, and others.

Up to June 30, 2016, Chengdu's rural property rights exchange center had conducted 12,997 cases of various kinds of rural property rights transactions, with a total turnover of RMB 5.32 billion. The scale and variety of transactions topped similar exchange centers nationwide. At present, under Chengdu Municipal Government's support, the rural property rights exchange center continues to make vigorous efforts to build a provincially comprehensive rural property trading platform, to cover the whole province, and strives to build a rural property rights trading market with complete functions and orderly circulation.

4.4.2 What is Different about Chengdu's Market Instrument?

Much of the commentary on China's ongoing institutional reforms paints it as an inexorable march toward full marketization of property rights and other aspects of the economy. Part of this is undoubtedly true and, in fact, explicitly stated in the central government's platform – e.g., the Third Plenum's directive to "promote market-oriented reform … promote resources allocation according to market rules, market prices and market competition, so as to maximize the benefits and optimize the efficiency."[6] On the other hand, the Party still points to the need to "strike a balance between the role of the government and of the market" and, specifically referring to land use rights, establish a mechanism that "takes into account the interests of the state, the collective and the individual …"[7] It is our thesis that, in part, the joint and multiple nature of the goals surrounding land reform reflects on the design of the quota system, and what has evolved in Chengdu is something unique.

The conventional market-based design is one that maximizes efficiency within external constraints like zoning, building height and density requirements, and others. It is through these constraints that the state protects public interests. But, within these bounds, the trade of goods is itself geared around maximizing individual (and, through the "invisible hand," aggregate) utility. In China, however, we may find institutions designed upon the simultaneous pursuit of multiple values – i.e. not just efficiency, but equity, stability, coherence with the network of relations. For this reason, we might find something like a quota program to be designed and implemented to pursue these multiple goals. To do this, decision-making cannot be simply left to individual buyers and sellers but, instead, shared in a network of interested parties. It is a form of networked decision-making, wherein individual and collective units negotiate jointly with the local government and private interests.

The Chengdu quota program might be understood as a form of TDR, which has now become a conventional development tool in the US and other countries. While the term "TDR" encompasses a broad range of configurations, we can describe some of the most commonly found features. Like Chengdu, it is an exchange of rights to develop and use land for desired purposes between two areas: A sending area, where land is to be conserved or a certain non-urban land use maintained, to a receiving area, where development is allowed (Pruetz & Standridge, 2008). The owner of the parcel in the sending area and the developer negotiate a purchase price, after which the developer can use the TDR to build additional development in the city. These have been used for various purposes, such as preserving farm or forest land in the countryside (Nickerson & Lynch, 2001), to saving historic landmarks in the city (NYC DCP, 2015).

TDRs are based on a conceptual/legal framework that treats property rights as a bundle of goods. In this bundle are elements which include rights to own, use, lease or rent land, and possibly others. The conventional form of right is that of fee simple private property, where the owner, by virtue of purchasing the property, possesses all the rights of ownership, usufruct, and use (Kaplowitz, 2004). When viewed as a bundle of rights, some elements such as the right to use may be severed from the rest of the bundle and transferred. With a TDR, this would be the right to a restricted category of use such as urban development. The seller still retains the ownership of the property and use that excludes the specific right that was traded away (e.g., commercial development). Sometimes, the location of the sending and receiving areas are contiguous (i.e., part of a continuous special development zone), but more generally, they can be in completely separate areas. The theory is that transaction costs will be kept as low as possible, meaning that negotiations are conducted directly between two private parties through an efficient mechanism that allows these parties to locate each other (e.g., through an exchange). Having conducted the transfer of the right, the developer then proceeds to carry out the project without much additional transaction. Our analysis will use this conventional model of the TDR against which to compare Chengdu's quota program.

It is evident that Chengdu's program shares much of the design of the conventional TDR and, in fact, it can be classified as a type of TDR itself. But there

62 Relationality in Rural Property Regimes

are important elements that make Chengdu's program unique or, at least, distinct from the conventional description of the TDR.

In Chengdu, the right to develop a parcel to commercial or residential use is severable from the property itself, as with the conventional TDR. However, it is not divisible (or individualized), in several respects. First, while individual farmers and their households are consulted, the transfers require the entire collectively owned area in order to be converted into a quota.[8] Individual, non-contiguous parcels cannot enter into a quota agreement on the supply/sending side. At a minimum, decisions have to be reached by the group of affected farmers collectively. In practice, a host of other players are involved. The village collective formally transacts on behalf of the farmers. The local government (municipality or township) manages the consolidation process, which involves selecting the parcels, reclaiming them for agricultural use, and moving the families to higher-density housing. In Chengdu, the consolidation process can be managed by companies that specialize in it. Beyond indivisibility of rights and responsibilities, the quota program also inherently involves the joint action of multiple groups (i.e., not just the collective but the municipality, local developer, and other village units described below). This is what distinguishes the quota program from conventional market instruments like the TDR. Throughout the remainder of the chapter, we will refer to the ability of an individual actor to negotiate as an individual as autonomy. The converse (non-autonomy) is, as with Chengdu, when the actor (which can be an individual or a group) must collaborate with other actors/organizations in order to decide on and conduct the transfer.

The joint nature of decision-making around the quota program means that multiple actors, in multiple levels of governance, are involved in the transaction. There is much that is unique about the arrangement found in Chengdu and, later, we will use this example to construct an alternative institutional model that, while applicable to every context, is well delineated by the Chengdu case. Joint decision-making allows, formally, consideration of multiple societal goals. Note that we do not assume the motivations behind it to necessarily be benign. Perhaps, some local actors pursue these reforms not out of concern for the welfare of rural households but simply to maximize the potential revenues from urban development. Perhaps, as some authors claim (but not something we discovered in our own interviews), new opportunities for rent-seeking allow some individuals to earn extra income. But, as we will discuss later, the mere construction of an institutional mechanism that gives a role to multiple parties opens up the process for multiple rationalities. To compare it to something more familiar, in the US, the design of the real estate market is such that concerned individuals have no say over creeping gentrification or the loss of open space, since the market is designed as purely private transactions. And, of course, these problems are found in Chinese cities, as well, but there is a possibility for an alternative logic with a differently designed institutional mechanism.

What are the other societal goals that might be achieved by this type of net-worked decision-making? There are, as in a private property regime, the benefits to the sellers and buyers. But there is also the benefit of equity when the village collective is involved, as individual rural homeowners do not have to negotiate individually because, were they to do so, they might end up with poorer terms or compensation rates that vary from person to person. Were the negotiations indi-vidualized, the natural monopsony (a few large buyers, many individual sellers) might lower the levels of compensation. There are benefits vis-à-vis the process of relocating, as well, since households do not move on their own but, instead, are part of a group transition. The local government, to the extent it participates, oversees the process and maintains standards for the consolidation projects. There are benefits to the state, such as preservation of arable land, avoidance of rural unrest, and control over the growth of its cities. The state participates indirectly, when it sanctions the new institution or corrects it (such as when initial prices for quotas were too high).

As a matter of fact, the construction land quota transaction system is not yet complete, and essentially uses a qualified certificate. It is not a completely unified market. At present, there are two markets: That for rural land consolidation (the supply side) and the market for city estates (the demand side). The current supply side is fully marketized while the demand side is not, which takes pricing listings rather than open bidding. In other words, Chengdu's construction land quota system is an institutional innovation based on the Link policy rather than a completely marketized property exchange regime. Why not have open bidding on the demand side? In the discussion that follows, we introduce the notion of autopoiesis and will argue that the design of the quota market corresponds to a sociopoietic, rather than autopoietic, system.

4.5 Distinguishing the Chengdu and Chongqing Programs

Our interviews and archival material suggest a deliberate effort, on the part of policymakers in Chengdu, to differentiate their quota program from Chongq-ing's. This is reflected in terminology, first of all. Chongqing's program preceded Chengdu's, and the former instituted what it termed the Construction Land Ticket (建设用地票 jian she yong di piao, or di piao, for short). Chengdu, which had initially used the same term, subsequently called their transferable permit the Construction Land Quota or Index Certificate (建设用地指标 jian she yong di zhi biao). (Document no. 27). Sale of the certificate is referred to as a Quota Transaction (指标交易 zhi biao jiao yi).

One of the first areas of differentiation begins with the process of conversion of rural construction land to agricultural. In Chongqing, this is all done by the municipal government with the townships and village committees acting as developers. Chengdu, however, has tried to cultivate local entrepreneurs around this process and encourages local developers to plan and implement the

64 Relationality in Rural Property Regimes

conversion process. This allows Chengdu to take advantage of private capital and private entrepreneurs to conduct this time-consuming and expensive work (Xiao, 2014).

In Chongqing, the total number of land tickets (地票 di piao) sold each year is capped at no more than 10% of the total construction land allowance received from the central government. Despite the crimp on supply, prices for Chongqing's land tickets were not as high or as volatile as those of Chengdu's quotas, though they did rise to RMB 250,000/mu one year (Xiao, 2014, p. 95). Early trades revolved around RMB 80,000/mu (Cai, 2014) and, to this day, prices hover around two-thirds of those in Chengdu. This may reflect differences between the two municipalities: Chongqing, being larger than Chengdu, may have a larger potential supply of consolidated land and a "thicker" market than Chengdu, despite the cap on di piao. Property values (i.e., lease prices) are significantly higher in Chengdu than Chongqing.[9] Doubtless, it should also reflect the particular history of each institution and the details of the design of their tradeable instruments.

The logical sequence of purchase of the quota and development rights over a parcel differ, as well. In Chongqing, a developer (or other buyer) who wants to bid for a parcel of land in the urbanizing area needs to have purchased a quota, first. In contrast, in Chengdu, purchase of the quota is required only after the buyer has already acquired the urban development right. As previously discussed, Chengdu decided on this practice in order to lower the demand, level of speculation, and price for the quota.

In our interviews, some informants suggested that this may result in more rent-seeking behavior on the part of developers in Chongqing and more administrative effort on the part of the municipality, compared to Chengdu. The comments, from one staff member from Chengdu, are shown below.

> Chongqing designed their auction this way. After you buy the land ticket, you choose a (parcel of) land. But if you weren't able to obtain the land, then whoever bought the land will return the money to you, equivalent to giving you the money for the land ticket. It was designed like that, but in reality, this doesn't happen. That is, if I have chosen a (piece of) land, I will do everything I can to get the state-owned construction land in my hands. Honestly, there is too much room for negotiation. I'll give an inappropriate example. Say there is a piece of land near the People's Liberation Monument, can I also use the land ticket to get it? If, in the end, I can do it, then I will be super-rich. This kind of theoretical situation may, in fact, exist. There are many strategies, to exclude others.

In principle, if a developer in Chongqing purchases a quota and, then, is not able to successfully bid for a parcel, then the quota goes to waste (ultimately to be purchased by the successful bidder). In practice, however, this usually does not happen, since the municipal government works with the developer to secure a parcel (Cai, 2014, p. 75), in some cases maybe even getting special privileges in selecting which parcel to take (Xiao, 2014, p. 10). At any rate, the local government in Chongqing assists the quota holders secure urban land use rights. In Chengdu, on the other hand, developers have less discretion over which parcel they end up with – i.e., after winning a bid, they are simply assigned a parcel by the municipal government or choose from a pre-prepared list (interview with author). Formally, the rules found in Chongqing and Chengdu are not dissimilar, so one surmises that part of the story lies in differing relationships between actors in both places.

4.6 Characterizing Local Decision-Making around Land Consolidation

One stated goal of the reform was to strengthen the degree of participation of community residents. In fact, this may have been the point most greatly emphasized by the interviewees. In this section, we describe the process by which the village reaches a decision around land consolidation and quota generation.

There are multiple groups involved, and the exact nature of the process undoubtedly varies from community to community. In general, decision-making revolves around the village council (村民议事会 cun min yi shi hui), which is made up of representatives from each village group, and each representative serves a three-year term. The council takes up issues and votes on them, with a two-thirds vote required to pass a motion. For an issue such as land consolidation, there is a prior discussion where village groups meet with each household. Village groups recommend consolidation to the council if all its households agree to it. In principle, each household should have equal say in the matter. This process, by which each individual household can choose to participate in land consolidation or not, is a type of right that can strengthen the bargaining power of the individual farmer. It is further strengthened by the municipal government's initiative toward land titling.

The details of the process are then worked out in council meetings. The villagers' general assembly authorizes the council's recommendation and enters into an agreement with the Bureau of Land and Resources. Proceeds from the quota transaction are distributed among resident households according to arrangements decided within each village group.

In addition to the village council, there are other bodies that are involved in the process. These include the village committee (村民委员会 cun min wei yuan hui), a supervisory committee (监督委员会 jian du wei yuan hui), and a deliberation panel (评审小组 ping shen xiao zu), all of which share in the overall process of deciding on and implementing the consolidation project.

The process of consolidation, itself, can be planned and carried out by the local government or specialty contractors working for the village. These are often

66 Relationality in Rural Property Regimes

referred to as social investors (社会投资人 she hui tou zi ren), which seems to allude to sources of capital outside the government. In some cases, village residents can set up a group asset management company and mortgage their land use titles to obtain loans to implement the project themselves (interview with author). The policymakers we interviewed all saw the local process of deliberation as an important reform. We quote one of them below (whose positive impressions about deliberation were echoed by other interviewees).

> First of all, the reform of rural property rights system, is issuing the certification of land rights. We want to clarify property boundaries. The second is to renew the grass-roots governance mechanism. This is very important. What do we rely on? The village council will promote all the major affairs and decision-making. It's no longer the sole decision of the so-called village head, village director, and village secretary. Not them, but the people elected, similar to how it is with Western parliaments. The village council can be referred to as grass-roots democracy, yes, this is very important. Every major event has to go through this deliberative mechanism 议事机制 (yi shi ji zhi) …
>
> Rural land consolidation is basically a combination of the previous things. First, you need to have the right of the land before you can consolidate the land. You need to know who has a large family, which households are smaller, so that when you participate in the project, there is a basis for you to distribute the money. Second, how you would implement the plan will also rely on the new deliberative mechanism. You need to have the spirit of ownership in order to actively promote the project.

The somewhat bureaucratized, formalistic structure of local deliberation can be interpreted as increased transaction costs. But this formalization may be a necessary step in democratizing land use planning. While state policy has hailed the rights of the village collective, there has always been ambiguity over what the collective is, exactly, and who represents it. Some scholars suggest that this has opened up the process to manipulation by local elites (e.g., Ho, 2001). As we can see, there is more structure to local participatory processes now.

Our interviews suggest a general accepting attitude toward the village council process, with most of the informants thinking the process was fair. One resident shared her thoughts.

The research team spoke with a 71-year-old resident from Nan Xin village, which recently went through the land consolidation process. She received RMB 11,900 (US$1,785) from the transaction of cultivated land in the village collective. In addition, for every homestead that was demolished, the government paid about RMB 1,100 per square meter per head, based on the cost of materials. This supplements her monthly social security income of RMB 330. The consolidation was agreed to by all voluntarily, she said, partly because there was less reason to stay in their homestead properties anymore.

Young people don't want to stay at home anymore. They all left, and it is
hard for old people to do farm work, and the old houses are too big for
those who are left behind ... You don't get much from a mu of land. Corn
is sold at 1 RMB a catty, and a mu of land can only produce a few hundred
catty. If you work outside, you might earn RMB 2,000-3,000 a month [so]
nobody wants to farm lands anymore. Young people all left, only the elderly
still stay at home, with some small children (still studying).

And she had a positive opinion about the new village council:

We elected the members ourselves. We hold general meetings, and members
openly discuss and decide on matters together. The farmers are very much
respected ... At the general meeting, you can voice your opinions and
voting is done anonymously. We discuss matters like road building, and if
you consent, you sign, and if not, then don't sign. But most people sign.

About 80% of those interviewed echoed similar, positive impressions. The above
comments suggest some positive development in local participation, but they also
speak to the larger issue of the decline of rural agricultural livelihoods.

4.7 Characterizing the Institutional Model

It seems to us that institutional scholars over-emphasize the disjuncture between
public and private property regimes (as political scholars have over-emphasized
the divide between socialist and capitalist). Part of it is a failure to imagine what a
market-centered socialist system would look like. The response, on the part of
scholars, is to suppose that China's land management system is progressing into a
fully westernized private property market. The central government is undoubtedly not absolutely clear, itself, what a socialist market economy would look like,
hence its unique form of incrementalism, where it relies on localized institutional
experiments (such as Chengdu and Chongqing) and its unique form of "governance by metaphor."[10]

Another difficulty is the relatively narrow classification schema used in the
institutional literature to define property rights. The public-private distinction,
mentioned above, is paralleled by a conceptual framework around types of goods.
The classic schema is to categorize private goods as those that are rival and
excludable, and public goods as those that are non-rival and non-excludable. In
between these two are club goods (non-rival, excludable) and common-pool
resources (rival, non-excludable).

But where would we locate collective property, such as rural collective land
in China? Is it a club good or more like a private good? Or is it something
altogether unique?

In this section, we proceed to refine the typology of goods, in order to better
characterize the complex nature of property rights in China. The main idea is that

68 Relationality in Rural Property Regimes

there is something unique in the property regime evolving in China that extant classification systems do not fully capture.

Let us proceed methodically through the argument. First, we recognize that rural collective land is excludable (i.e., it is assigned to one collective and not others) and, so, cannot be considered a public good.

Might it be considered a club good, where a group (not an individual) has ownership over the resource? We think otherwise – unlike a classic club good (which is non-rival), use of the land by one farmer eschews use of the same plot by another – i.e., it is rival. But, it clearly is not a private good, since the individual farmer, whose use of a parcel precludes use by another farmer, does not own that parcel.

This suggests a third descriptive which is divisibility of the right. In the case of a private good, the right over the land (which includes ownership, but also authority over its use or disposition) is divisible among individuals using the resource. But this is not the case with rural collective land where, even when the municipality assigns titles to individual parcels or individual households, ownership is still collectively shared and indivisible. The collective, in this case, is ambiguous, but for simplicity's sake, we can take it to mean the group of individual farmers/households with a claim to the land. In this case, the entity is not the individuals who make up the group but the group itself.

This allows us to define a distinct category, which is the collective good, which can be characterized by excludability, rivalry, and indivisibility.

The question is, can rural collective land in China be considered a pure collective good? We propose that if we did, it would be a special class of collective good. The reason for this is the complexity of what collective, and the overlapping nature of multiple collectives, are involved in determining the disposition and use of the land. The ambiguity over what constitutes the collective, which can be represented by different associations (village council, village assembly, etc.), is underlain by a fundamental institutional complexity. First, authority over disposition of the land (i.e., use of it, selling of limited rights to it, and others) is distributed among a number of different and overlapping entities.

An additional level of complexity stems from the fact that the sale of the quota is not simply a transaction between a buyer and seller. Rather, a network of entities are involved in the transaction. The village organizations work with the municipal government and, sometimes, private developers, to plan and implement consolidation and prepare the quota for sale in the exchange. Decisions around when, where, and how to consolidate (and create a quota) involves joint actions by these different entities, and not just the collective owners of the land. This is not simply a nested process of decision-making but a conjoint one. Whereas a private or club good need only require decisions on the part of the individual or club regarding disposition of the property, the system found in Chengdu's quota program requires joint decision-making and action by a set of entities located at different scales or levels of governance. Decisions are a matter

Relationality in Rural Property Regimes **69**

for collaboration between farmers, village association, municipal government, and possibly private parties. Indirectly, the central government is also involved by sanctioning and monitoring the process (occasionally intervening in the process as they did when shutting down the exchange in 2010).

We believe that this is not accidental. The shared form of governance around rural collective land and, by extension, the quotas, corresponds to the desire of the state to pursue multiple goals (individual, collective, state) at the same time or, at least, to reconcile them somehow. It is perhaps for this reason that there is no thought given, as yet, to creating a conventional rural private property market.

In a club good, the "club" has decision-making authority over the resource. Reading into the practice of the quotas, the state (through its delegate, the municipal government) sponsors the consolidation and quota creation process. It can have veto power over such proceedings and, more so, needs to guide it and, often, will be the lead proponent of it. This is a kind of shared governance, where authority and responsibility are collocated in multiple bodies at different levels in the network. As presented in Chapter 2, because of the joint, all-inclusive nature of authority around quotas, it falls exactly as a kind of plenary good, which is a new category with the properties of excludability, rivalry, indivisibility, and multicorporality.

It is the last property which distinguishes the plenary good from the pure collective good. Multicorporality is the property of shared authority over a good, especially the right to decide on the disposition of the good. This is distinct from Ostrom's notion of nested institutions, which describes hierarchical domains where an actor has purview over a resource within its limited scope of authority. With plenary goods, decision-making is not subdivided, necessarily, but more generally, shared.

Rather, the concept of plenary goods is most closely related to the notion of network governance (which will be referred to later), where authority over some good or service is shared among multiple actors often located at multiple (sometimes overlapping) locations in a constellation of policy actors. To further delineate the plenary nature of some institutions, we might contrast this with the model of common-pool resources. As Ostrom described it, one solution to the common-pool resources issue is to have local community enact a workable system of use rights over a resource through social capital (mutual monitoring and enforcement of rules). Authority, in this case, is seen to inhere in the local community. In contrast, a plenary good might be jointly managed by local community, regional authorities, the national government, and even private actors. Here we can reproduce Table 2.1 from Chapter 2.

The idea of a plenary good may be relevant to related systems in other parts of the world, such as mixed-ownership enterprises (OECD, 2012). But the multicorporal nature of these goods, as we understand them, pertains not just to ownership but decision-making, implementation, and other aspects of stewardship.

The shared nature of governance around the quotas is an important way of protecting different interests. Individual farmers are not subject to the difficulties of individual negotiation to the extent that the village council and municipality intercede for them. The village, itself, may not be equipped, in terms of technical expertise and staffing, to negotiate and carry out consolidation and quota generation. So being, the process can be managed by the local government or private parties. Rather than being nested institutions, where different actors at different levels act separately, these are conjunctive institutions. Rights and roles are not formally separated from one actor to the other – instead, they are embedded in each other. The actual decisions correspond to mixed rationalities (e.g., not just maximizing return on investment, but other objectives as well).

As presented in Chapter 2, a classic private market is what we might call an autopoietic system. It is meant to function independently of the state, and decision-making occurs only between private actors. The market transaction is a self-encapsulated thing, where it functions outside the intervention of actors (the State, the Church, society). In contrast, we can think of an alternative mode of governance as sociopoietic (Lejano & Park, 2015). Going back to the market transaction, in a sociopoietic system, the transaction involves the actions and interests of actors other than the two private parties. The transaction does not occur completely independently of these other institutions, such as local government, the party, etc., and prices are not simply endogenous to the private transaction but something influenced by the interaction of all these actors.

Commentators on China's evolving model of governance will sometimes point to the need for greater primacy of "the rule of law." What they mean by this term is that the law, as a text or encoded set of rules, act like an autopoietic system, where decisions and actions stem directly and only from the encoded text. In contrast, in a sociopoietic system, the text is not all of the institution, and other social forces weigh in, in the implementation of the law. Often, the central government will issue directives that are broad guidelines (sometimes using metaphor to describe the policy direction), and it is up to regional or local actors to bring specificity to these through everyday practice. This, of course, assumes that there are sufficient incentives for local actors to spend effort and resources, as well as take the risks, needed for developing new institutional rules and practices.

Sociopoietic systems are relational systems, because the actual institution is determined by the working out of social relationships among policy actors. Describing the relational system goes deeper into this phenomenon by uncovering the nature of the relationships and relating this to how the different policy actors act – this is the micro-dimension of relational analysis. There is a macroscopic perspective to characterizing something as a relational system, which is describing the network arrangement that is the web of relationships that make up the system. Conventional ways of describing systems for collective action separate solutions into state-centered, individual-centered or privatized, or communitarian. Similarly, strategies for development are said to vary depending on whether the strategy revolves around the state (e.g., expert bureaucracies), the individual (e.g. markets), or the community (e.g. nongovernmental and

Relationality in Rural Property Regimes 71

TABLE 4.1 Types of Goods: Expanded Classification System

	private	public	common-pool	club	collective	plenary
excludability	1	0	0	1	1	1
rivalry	1	0	1	0	1	1
divisibility	1	0	0	0	0	0
multicorporality	0	0	0	0	0	1

community-based organizations). But what if the actual system involves all these actors working and negotiating jointly? This has been referred to as network governance, but this literature does not really work out what the relationships are between policy actors (simply, that they all act as one group). A relational analysis should be able to delineate how each policy actor acts in the network, and to distinguish one kind of network from another.

This pertains directly to property rights. Qiao and Upham (2015) use the term "relational property rights" to describe the system where the actual meaning of property rights depends on the set of social relationships (between village, individual, business, and state) in a place. When the actual institution is determined by the working out of social relationships, then formal rules and roles will be blurred (Lejano, 2008). Formally, the rules behind both Chongqing's land ticket and Chengdu's quota are similar, but networked forms of governance rely on relationships and interactions among a heterogeneous group of actors that cannot be codified as rules. If there is any accuracy to the claim by informants in Chengdu that a very different political dynamic occurs between developers and municipal government in Chongqing, it reflects the contextual nature of relational systems, where processes and outcomes depend on the working out of complex relationships in particular places.

On the other hand, networked decision-making represents significant transaction costs. This goes against the conventional thinking behind tradeable instruments which are designed to increase the ease of transaction. There is also the possibility of excessive rent-seeking. While interviewees from Chengdu point to Chongqing's system as having the greater potential for influence peddling, the fact is that these possibilities can exist in both systems. And there is the possibility that farmers are not allowed to act as independent agents but, rather, are manipulated by local governments and developers seeking to profit from their need for supplementary income.

What is the difference between the relational system just described and the idea of *guanxi*, which describes the central role of interpersonal relationships in fostering and facilitating transactions both in the private and public sectors? These are closely related, of course. In our view, while guanxi is all about the importance of interpersonal relationships in improving or facilitating the functioning of institutions, relationality is all about the under-determinedness of institutional design, such that formal features of the program are left unspecified (and filled in by relational processes). Guanxi may act like the grease that helps the institutional design to function, but such design can be complete and pre-exists the functioning of relationships. With relationality, relationships form part of the basic essence of the institutional design. For example, a completely designed (or determined) market system will have in place all the rules that determine how prices are set. In contrast, a relational system may allow negotiations within a network of policy actors to influence market prices.

But what is to be gained by the relational system? The answer is corollary to what is lost, which is the independence of the market and autonomy of market transactions. Other considerations can be pursued outside of the private interests of seller and buyer. There are protection mechanisms, at least potentially, for checking the market when it runs off course. The central government's intrusion into the quota exchange market, shutting it down when prices rose too much, is a check against speculation. Likewise, the municipality's fixing of the quota price at RMB 300,000/mu is a way to dampen the volatility, increase the predictability of the quota market, and assure villages and "consolidation entrepreneurs" of a reliable return for their project.[11] It is undoubtedly true that there will be allocative inefficiencies with interfering with the market, but there are other goals that are pursued. One is the greater equity of a system where farmers, who might not be able to stay in the market for so long, do not have to settle for a temporarily depressed quota price.

Setting quota prices will be interpreted as an artificial intervention in the smooth functioning of the new market. But perhaps it is just one way to divide up the surpluses accruing from the exchange of property in the urban area with the exchange of development rights in the rural. It is uncertain what the real opportunity costs are to the farmers, whether it is the foregone benefits from farming or potential benefits from future commercial development of their land. And even a smoothly functioning market cannot guarantee that what is received by the farmers will suffice to support them in their new residences.

Collective institutions (such as the village council) protect the individual from the burden of working out complex transactions. Contrast this to the weakened purchasing power of dispossessed rural residents whose land has been expropriated. In previous work, we found much dissatisfaction among rural residents of differing levels of compensation received between one family and another (Lian & Lejano, 2014).

4.8 Looking Ahead

The question to ponder is: Where is the institutional experiment, now underway in Chengdu and Chongqing, headed? The ultimate motivation for local-scale pilot tests is presumably the idea that the new institution might diffuse outward to other municipalities. Pushing the idea even further, one might even conceive of a quota system that extends beyond a single municipality, creating a regional or national trading regime. The idea of opening up its land tickets to a national market, even derivatives trading, has been discussed in Chongqing (Cai, 2014). The logic of it stems from the nature of the goal of maintaining 1.8 billion mu of arable land, which can, in principle, be anywhere in the country.[12]

But there are potential problems from creating a nationwide quota program. There is a possibility of a loss of balance between productive land uses within each municipality. There are problems to this kind of spatial unevenness – higher transportation requirements for goods and services, greater vulnerability of communities to ups and downs of the economy, and others. Most of all, perhaps, is the loss of cultural resources in the form of rural community life that ever recedes from view.

Where might the institutional experiment be headed? With extensive land titling underway, it will look more and more like a private property regime. If there is a common presumption that the end product is inexorably the creation of a fully privatized rural property market, we suggest it can be otherwise. The question, then, moving forward, is whether evolving institutional rules can maintain some forms of collective decision-making and involvement by bodies located at different levels of the governance structure. Rather than an inevitable evolution of a common set of rules for land transfers, what we may find in China, years from now, might be a rich diversity of contextually designed institutions. The differences in design between Chongqing's land ticket and Chengdu's quota system may foreshadow a more decentralized and richly varied spectrum of designs across the country. Running counter to this, however, is the still present overarching authority of the central government, which sets policies that are often simply adopted in toto at lower levels of government.

Most deeply, there is an inherent reduction involved in creating a tradeable good, whether it is the right to commercial development or maintaining the stock of arable land. It is the assumption that the good can be completely captured by the right that is traded. But what is transferred from place to place is not simply a development right or a quantity of arable land – it is, in fact, culture, social ties, and rural communal life. What might ultimately be traded away is a kind of lifestyle and heritage of rural communities, as people move to more urban residential communities and farms are taken over by large corporations. Years from now, the sweep of modernization may transform the country into high-rises and mechanized fields, at a loss of authentic community life.[13]

The process of consolidating rural residential land to free up quotas has its limits, though scholars have differing opinions on how great this potential supply of new urban construction land might be (Xiao, 2014). Ultimately, discussions will move on to further expanding the process of unifying urban and rural markets, though it is not entirely clear what scholars and policymakers mean by this. It is clear that part of it pertains to unifying or eliminating the hukou system. It is less clear if they mean removing the system of collective ownership in rural areas and converting all land to state (or, perhaps, even private) ownership. Most scholars, political scientists and economists alike, tend to assume that land use is best determined by a fully privatized market, but this seems to be a mostly ideological straitjacket. The most important question may be how to foster collaboration between the national leadership, local government, and private capital to carve out development agendas for the countryside, whatever the legal definition of property rights.

The looming problem is how to envision productive livelihoods in rural China, where agricultural households are moving to higher-density towns and away from farming as a lifestyle (Chan, 2013). The irony of freeing up hundreds of millions of hectares of arable land that increasingly few are willing to till is not lost on policymakers. At the same time, unemployment is growing in many of China's cities (Cao et al., 2012). If the future of rural China is mechanized agriculture operated by large corporations, will there be sufficient and adequately paid employment for rural residents? If not, what alternative livelihoods are available to them, short of joining the mass exodus to the city? And, without overly romanticizing it, will rural villages and community life disappear?

In conclusion, we might extrapolate from the special case of Chengdu and reflect on what it might mean for China. Though this is pure speculation on our part, we suggest that it is possible that the complex kind of institutional design we saw in the case of Chengdu's quota may be an indicator of a larger institutional logic that may characterize the national institutional experiment. We have already seen how decision-making can be relational, drawing together multiple entities that normally operate in different domains. Contrast this to the classic bureaucracy with its circumscribed authority or the market which reduces transactions to that between two individual actors.

Without exaggerating the point, it may help to see this as a contrast between Weberian and Confucian systems. The classic Weberian ethic is one of utilitarian rationalization and a formal delineation of boundaries (between state and community, public and private). It displays the logic of formal rationality, where authorities and jurisdictions are divided up among policy actors. Rationalization is an optimizing logic, such as when markets are completely privatized in the effort to maximize the utility gains by two private parties, or when an area of regulation is delegated to a specialized agency to maximize pursuit of a public end.

In contrast, the Confucian system is not modeled after optimality but similitude. The ideal government is patterned upon an ideal form, whether, as in Taoist terms, it is to be found in the heavens, or in Confucian terms, located in the family and congruent relationships. While we can think about division of labor within a family, the latter is a collective of members bound by relationship. It is not the division of labor but its integration that characterizes the Confucian system. The contrast is between the utilitarian ethic (maximizing efficiency) of the Weberian ideal versus the virtue ethic (working like a family) of the Confucian. Whereas government in one system emphasizes formal rules and delineations of authority, in the other we find the system to be governed by less-than-formal or underspecified relationships between policy actors. Whereas one exhibits an exclusionary logic that delimits purview over a resource to an agency or to the exchange between two individuals, the other system is characterized by an inclusive logic, where all interact in joint fashion. There are no absolute boundaries between public and private because in a relational system, the goal is to have interaction between private and public policy actors.

In other words, the Chengdu case may be a harbinger for where China's grand institutional experiment is headed. Scholars might assume that all of it ultimately evolves into a classic Weberian system of governance, where the public domain is carved up into domains exclusive to different bodies of government and the private is consigned to the arena where private individuals meet to the exclusion of the state. On the other hand, we may see the evolution of more complex systems, where heterogeneous groups of public and private actors interact in ways not completely determined by formal rules but, rather, the relationships between them.

Notes

1 Not all scholars assume that a classic system of private property rights is the necessary end of land reform in China – e.g., see Cheng and Xiaoqin (2017).
2 NBSC: Urban Household Survey Guideline, www.stats.gov.cn/tjzd/gjtjzd/t20090601_402562259.htm; NBSC: Rural Household Survey Guideline, www.stats.gov.cn/tjzd/gjtjzd/t20090601_402562258.htm. Note that some, dated, sources suggest a lesser gap in cost of living – e.g., Brandt & Holz (2006) estimate that the cost of living in urban areas is 39.7% higher than in rural areas.
3 Decision of the Central Committee of the Communist Party of China on Some Major Issues Concerning Comprehensively Deepening the Reform, January 16, 2014, at www.china.org.cn/china/third_plenary_session/2014-01/16/content_31212602.htm, accessed February 9, 2017.
4 The township is the lowest level of the administrative state, and the village, which exists under it, is a unit for self-administration by village residents (Alpermann, 2003).
5 Article 12, Provisional Regulations on Grant and Assignment of Urban State-owned Land Use Right.
6 Decision of the Central Committee of the Communist Party of China on Some Major Issues Concerning Comprehensively Deepening the Reform, January 16, 2014 at www.china.org.cn/china/third_plenary_session/2014-01/16/content_31212602.htm, accessed February 9, 2017.
7 Ibid.
8 This could involve increased transaction costs over the conventional individual transaction. With the quota, part of these transactions costs would involve the time and effort spent mobilizing community and engaging it in joint decision-making.
9 www.numbeo.com/property-investment/compare_cities.jsp?country1=China&country2=China&city1=Chongqing&city2=Chengdu&tracking=getDispatchComparison, accessed February 8, 2017.
10 Lejano, Wei, and Li (2017).
11 This logic holds true even when we consider the fact that local government may have faulty information and can get the prices "wrong," as Xiao (2014, p. 167) suggests. Officials will never possess perfectly quantified information since some of these values (e.g., political stability) are never monetized.

76 Relationality in Rural Property Regimes

12 We should note, however, that availability of agricultural land does not necessarily translate into agricultural production, since there are no provisions on maintaining quality of land, productivity of local agricultural communities, etc.
13 Take the example of the 71-year-old resident we interviewed. Though she expressed satisfaction with the community decision-making process, one cannot but detect the hint of nostalgia she expressed for the old way of life in the community.

References

Alpermann, B. (2003). *An assessment of research on village governance in China and suggestions for future applied research*. Beijing: EU-China Training Programme on Village Governance.

Araral, E. (2009). Privatization and regulation of public services: A framework for institutional analysis. *Policy and Society*, 27(3), 175–180.

Brandt, L., & Holz, C.A. (2006). Spatial price differences in China: Estimates and implications. *Economic development and cultural change*, 55(1), 43–86.

Cai, M. (2011, November). *Local determinants of economic structure: Evidence from land quota allocation in China*. Conference paper, 16th Annual Conference of the International Society for New Institutional Economics. Available at: http://extranet.sioe.org/uploads/isnie2012/cai.pdf.

Cai, M. (2014). Flying land. In J. Teets & W. Hurst, *Local governance innovation in China: Experimentation, diffusion, and defiance* (pp. 60–83). New York: Routledge.

Cao, G.Y., Chen, G., Pang, L.H., Zheng, X.Y., & Nilsson, S. (2012). Urban growth in China: Past, prospect, and its impacts. *Population and Environment*, 33(2–3), 137–160.

Central Committee of Chinese Communist Party (CCCCP) (2014). *A decision on rural development 2014*. www.xinhuanet.com. Accessed February 4, 2017.

Chan, K.W. (2013). *China: Internal migration. The encyclopedia of global human migration*. Blackwell.

Chan, K.W., & Zhang, L. (1999). The hukou system and rural-urban migration in China: Processes and changes. *The China Quarterly*, 160, 818–855.

Cheng, E., & Xiaoqin, D. (2017). A theory of China's "miracle": Eight principles of contemporary Chinese political economy. *Monthly Review – An Independent Socialist Magazine*, 68(8), 46–57.

Ho, P. (2001). Who owns China's land? Policies, property rights and deliberate institutional ambiguity. *The China Quarterly*, 166, 408–409.

Hsing, Y.T. (2010). *The great urban transformation: Politics of land and property in China*. New York: Oxford University Press.

Kaplowitz, M.D. (Ed.). (2004). *Property rights, economics and the environment*. New York: Routledge.

Lejano, R.P. (2006). *Frameworks for policy analysis: Merging text and context*. New York: Routledge.

Lejano, R. (2008). The phenomenon of collective action: Modeling institutions as structures of care. *Public Administration Review*, 68(3), 491–504.

Lejano, R. (2016). 政策分析框架 融合文本与语境,. Beijing: Tsinghua University Press.

Lejano, R.P. (forthcoming). *A phenomenology of institutions: Comparative perspectives on China and beyond*. New York: Routledge.

Lejano, R., & Park, S.J. (2015). The autopoietic text. In Fischer et al. (eds.), *Handbook of Critical Policy Studies* (pp. 274–296). Cheltenham, UK: Elgar Press.

Lejano, R.P., & Shankar, S. (2013). The contextualist turn and schematics of institutional fit: Theory and a case study from Southern India. *Policy Sciences*, 46(1), 83–102.

Lejano, R., Wei, D., & Li, L. (2017). *Governing by metaphor*. LKY School of Public Policy, working paper.

Li, L. (2012). Land titling in China: Chengdu experiment and its consequences. *China Economic Journal*, 5(1), 47–64.

Lian, H., & Lejano, R. (2014). Interpreting institutional fit: Urbanization, development, and China's "land-lost." *World Development*, 61, 1–10.

March, J.G., & Olsen, J.P. (1989). *Rediscovering institutions*. New York: Free Press.

March, J.G., & Olsen, J.P. (1998). The institutional dynamics of international political orders. *International organization*, 52(04), 943–969.

New York City Department of City Planning (NYC DCP) (2015). *A survey of transferable development rights mechanisms in New York City*. New York City, Department of City Planning, February 2015.

Nickerson, C.J., & Lynch, L. (2001). The effect of farmland preservation programs on farmland prices. *Am J Agric Econ*, 83(2), 341–351.

Organisation for Economic Co-operation and Development (OECD) (2012). *The governance of mixed-ownership enterprises in Latin America*. Discussion Paper, OECD/CAF Latin American SOE Network Meeting, October 2012, Lima.

Ostrom, E. (1995). Designing complexity to govern complexity. *Property rights and the environment: Social and ecological issues*, 33–45.

Park, A. (2008). Rural-urban inequality in China. In S. Yusuf (Ed.), *China urbanizes: Consequences, strategies and policies* (pp. 41–63).

People's Republic of China, National Development and Reform Commission (PRC NDRC) (2007). *A notice approving Chongqing and Chengdu to establish national trial and experimental pikot programs of coordinated urban-rural development comprehensive reform*. (June 7, 2007), Beijing (Chinese).

Pruetz, R., & Standridge, N. (2008). What makes transfer of development rights work?: Success factors from research and practice. *Journal of the American Planning Association*, 75(1), 78–87.

Qiao, S., & Upham, F. (2015). The evolution of relational property rights: A case of Chinese rural land reform. *Iowa Law Review*, 100(6), 2479.

Qu, W., Zhao, S., & Sun, Y. (2014). Spatiotemporal patterns of urbanization over the past three decades: A comparison between two large cities in southwest China. *Urban ecosystems*, 17(3), 723–739.

Sicular, T., Ximing, Y., Gustafsson, B., & Shi, L. (2007). The urban–rural income gap and inequality in China. *Review of Income and Wealth*, 53(1), 93–126.

Xiao, Y. (2014). *Making land fly: The institutionalization of China's land quota markets and its implications for urbanization, property rights, and intergovernmental politics*. Doctoral dissertation, Massachusetts Institute of Technology.

Yang, D.T., & Cai, F. (2003). The political economy of China's rural-urban divide. *How far across the River*, 389–416.

Ye, Y., & LeGates, R.T. (2013). *Coordinating urban and rural development in China: Learning from Chengdu*. Cheltenham, UK: Elgar.

Ye, Y., LeGates, R., & Qin, B. (2013). Coordinated urban-rural development planning in China: The Chengdu model . *Journal of the American Planning Association*, 79(2), 125–137.

Yu, L., Luo, R., & Zhang, L. (2007). Decomposing income inequality and policy implications in rural China. *China & World Economy*, 15(2), 44–58.

5

RELATIONAL INSTITUTIONS AND ENGOS IN CHINA

From Nu River to Changzhou

In earlier chapters, we discussed the phenomenal nature of institutions, which departs from the strict sectoral (or organizational) boundaries drawn in formal models of governance. Rather than see the blurring of boundaries as departures from the norm, we should instead see the thing as it is in itself. We need to bracket strong delineations between the spheres of institutional life. In this chapter, we blur the neat separations between state, civil society, and other actors. We find taken-for-granted terms, such as NGO (nongovernmental organization) to presume too much. For example, what would one make of an NGO that included government actors? Or environmental nonprofits that included members of industry? And why does the blurring occur, and what is its effect on the organization and its advocacy? How does it change the conventional notion of pluralism? As we will discuss, extant descriptives, including the notions of clientelism or corporatism, do not adequately capture the nature of the phenomenon.

In this chapter, we examine the rise of environmental NGOs (specifically, ENGOs) in China. The problem we face is that conventional ideas of what NGOs are and civil society's role in a nation's governance, are strongly influenced by the literature on pluralist political systems where there is a separation (formally as well as on the level of practice) between government and nongovernmental actors. Much of this literature focuses on the nonprofit sector, as well. This is a problem because when we apply these conceptual a priori to NGOs in China, all we end up saying is, well, they do not seem to be sufficiently "NGO-like." But that is missing the point, which is to understand what NGOs really are like in China and how they function.

To develop a richer description of this evolving institution, we contrast it against the template of what the conventional NGO is supposed to be. We find that these new NGOs constitute something altogether distinct from the nonstate actor as conventionally defined. The conventional template for civil society is that the groups are formally/legally separate from the state. This also holds for membership, in that, usually, civil servants and elected officials are not members of these NGOs. Their mode of action is often protest, sometimes collaborative inquiry, but it is always as a fiscalizer and critic of government action. Often, too, there is a distinction made between the knowledge base possessed by the NGO and the government agency. While there are technically expert NGOs, often one finds a distinction made between the community-based knowledge of the NGOs and expert knowledge found in the government agency. Lastly, in many polities, the NGO is assumed to play a role as one of many competing stakeholders in a pluralist political system. This chapter compares environmental ENGOs in China to these conventional templates.

5.1 Introduction

The rapid development of NGOs in China, especially given the more complex institutional hurdles these NGOs face compared to their western counterparts, has already attracted increasing scholarly attention, particularly focusing on their interaction with the Chinese government. The conventional understanding of NGOs refers to private actors completely independent from government, what is referred to in the literature as civil society. This is a problem because when we apply these conceptual a priori to NGOs in China, all we end up saying is that they do not seem to be sufficiently "NGO-like." What we find in China is something less than independent of government, both in terms of composition and policy stance. One can understand this through the concepts of sociopoiesis and relationality. In other words, the NGO-government interaction deviates from conventional explanations which highlight clear lines between the state, the market, and the NGOs as their western counterparts.

Indeed, NGOs in China adopt smart strategies to fit into institutional contexts which are sometimes antagonistic to them. Hence, understanding NGOs and their interaction with government and institutions in China may enrich the literature on NGOs and civil society as well as institutional theory in general.

Hence, some scholars are searching for a conceptual framework, beyond both the conventional models of civil society and corporatism, to fully understand NGOs in China (Saich, 2000). A number of studies illustrate various strategies adopted by Chinese NGOs under this sociopoietic scenario to cooperate with government by pointing out the importance of key factors affecting relations among different actors, including leadership of social organizations, personal connections, organizational resources, and political opportunities from resource-mobilization and institutional theory perspectives (Zhang & Guo, 2017). Some studies also describe the nature of NGO-government interaction in China as adaptive cooperation (Yu & Shen, 2017). However, much of this work focuses on service delivery-oriented groups and has not examined dynamics over time.

In this chapter, we examine the advocacy activities by ENGOs in China and explore the way they adapt and fit to institutions governing them, through a comparative case study approach. Two cases are examined, including the much-publicized dam-building case in Nu River, Yunnan Province, and the polluted land public litigation case in Changzhou, Jiangsu Province. The main research question is how ENGOs adapt and fit to institutional contexts under an authoritarian regime using the notion of sociopoiesis.

Most interestingly, the second case in this chapter provides a new way to think thoroughly and deeply about this issue. Friends of Nature (FON, the most influential grassroots ENGO) is the major actor in the second case regarding land pollution in Changzhou, Jiangsu Province in 2016, more than a decade after the Nu River case. The formal institutions regarding NGOs and civic participation regarding environmental issues have changed a lot during this span of time. The top leaders have already realized the importance of NGOs working with government and urged the transformation from social management to social' governance in 2012. The revised Environmental Protection Law endorses the legitimacy of NGOs enrolling in environmental disputes in 2014. The newly released Philanthropy Law relaxes the control over NGOs by dismissing the dual-management system in 2016. All signals seem to be in favor of ENGOs in China. Theoretically, ENGOs should have more power to affect government policies if formal institutions are settled as in their western counterparts. But the Changzhou case tells a different story.

5.2 Governing NGOs in China

NGOs in China have already become influential actors given their growing size and important roles in the policy process. There are more than 700,000 registered NGOs in China, which are divided into three types according to the government regulation, including social organizations (shehui tuanti), social service organizations (sehui fuwu jigou), and foundations (jijin hui). In addition to formal registered NGOs, there are also numerous NGOs not yet registered.

In contrast with a civil society approach, some scholars adopt a so-called clientelist/corporatist approach to explain development of NGOs in China (Unger & Chan, 1996), which assumes that NGOs in China are still under the tight control of the government (and/or the Party). In this situation, NGOs are not the same as how NGOs are defined classically – i.e., private, independent, and autonomous. The typical type of NGO is a government-controlled nongovernmental organization (GONGO). They are components of formal institutional arrangements of the state aiming to facilitate control over society.

In order to maintain tight control over NGOs, the dual-management registration system was introduced in the late 1980s which means NGOs should be managed by two government agencies, namely an operational agency (yewu zhuguan danwei) and a registration agency (dengji zhuguan danwei). Otherwise, they were not allowed to be enrolled into the registration system. The dual-management registration system was changed a bit when the Charity Law was released in 2016. However, only charitable organizations are allowed to be set up without an operational agency. Others, such as environmental protection and labor rights organizations, are still under tight control. In 2017, the Law of Activities of Overseas Nongovernmental Organizations in the Mainland of China was promulgated to regulate overseas NGOs in China.

However, the reality of NGO/state relationships in China has evolved beyond the clientelism/corporatism model. A number of grassroots NGOs have already become more and more popular and influential regarding public issues than GONGOs. And, yet, as we will discuss, their action is not entirely separate from government, and sociopoiesis may be an appropriate concept to describe this. The dam-building case captioned in this chapter is a good example. FON co-worked with other actors to postpone dam-building in Yunnan although formal institutions at that point were not pro-civic participation on environmental protection. In a word, FON found opportunities to achieve their goals by utilizing personal connections of organizational leaders with the government, the press and mass media, as well as, to some extent, international actor involvement, even though formal institutional connections were absent.

5.3 Policy Advocacy in China and Analytical Framework

Policy advocacy is broadly defined as any attempt to influence government decisions through direct or indirect actions, including contact with government, public education and grass-roots mobilization (Reid, 1999). Although many NGOs engage in policy advocacy activities, their advocacy investments and strategies are different from each other (Boris & Mosher-Williams, 1998; Jenkins, 2006; Mosley, 2011). Some scholars have pointed out that marginalized NGOs are more concerned with organizational constraints, political environment, and other variables when doing policy advocacy; their participation in the process of advocacy will use different strategies to balance these concerns (DeSantis, 2010). Gen and Conley Wright (2013) analyzed 35 differing advocacy strategies, and they emphasized the impact of strengthening the democratic environment on increasing public pressure for policy reforms. From the perspective of the organization's resource environment, the literature has pointed out the importance of leadership, personal relations, group cooperation, organizational resources and political opportunities.

Regarding NGO advocacy in China, from the institutional domain, due to the strengthening of civil society forces, there has been an "official – social group" mode of cooperation. The expansion of social groups in China did not lead to the processes of democratization and protest, but toward consultation under authoritarian conditions, and citizens' satisfaction is also increasing in some issue areas (Teets, 2013). Some scholars attempt to explain how the action of advocacy coalitions and resources they brought to bear on the Nu River dam case coerced the government to reduce the scale of the project (Han, Swedlow, & Unger, 2014).

A relatively small proportion of resources and time is devoted to policy advocacy in China. Some scholars have shown that among the current NGOs in China, especially civil organizations, policy advocacy intensity is extremely low, and only 9% of the resources is used for policy advocacy. At the same time, the more volunteer work, the higher the intensity of policy advocacy – in contrast, the more staff work, the less significant the level of policy advocacy, and many NGOs cannot engage in effective public participation (Zhang & Guo, 2012). This again differs from the conventional notion of the ENGO, especially in pluralist systems like the US, where their central mission involves policy advocacy.

A number of studies also illustrate sociopoiesis through various advocacy strategies adopted by Chinese NGOs to work with various levels of government by pointing out the importance of key factors affecting relations among different actors. Under an authoritarian regime, foundations use multi-year grants to develop and support NGOs, and nonprofits can strengthen their degree of participation in advocacy by collaborating with other nonprofits and foundations (Li, Tang, & Wing-Hung Lo, 2016). One interesting aspect of the NGO/state relationship in China is how the previous career paths of its directors and founders influence advocacy. Scholars have shown that the resource strategy of an NGO often depends on the experience of its founders – e.g., if its founder is a former national government official or has related government work experience, then the policy advocacy process tends to ally with Party or government organs (Hsu & Jiang, 2015). Zhan & Tang (2013) highlight the importance of leadership of social organizations, personal connections, organizational resources, and political opportunities from resource-mobilization perspective and institutional theory. They found that strong social capital and personal ties may enhance the capacity of NGOs regarding advocacy activities. This differs from the conventional model of the NGO as separate, formally and substantively, from government (in its culture, allegiance, and membership). At the same time, research has also pointed out that NGOs have led to the development of their organizations by manipulating opportunities and resources, avoiding external risks and mobilizing informal activities (Gåsemyr, 2017). The size of NGOs and their capacity also matters. Due to the dual role of resource dependence and legitimacy pressure, political relations and policy advocacy have an inverted U-type relationship – i.e., too strong or too weak a political association will have a negative impact on the policy advocacy of NGOs – for example by keeping the government at arm's length, NGOs are more likely to be involved in policy advocacy (Li, 2017).

However, much of this work focuses on service delivery-oriented groups and has not examined dynamics over time. This chapter adopts the notion of

Relational Institutions and ENGOs in China **83**

institutional fit to illustrate the complex dynamic of NGOs and their interactions with institutions.

The model of institutional fit, as depicted in Figure 2.3, frames the analysis in this chapter. In this case, we have the conventional model of the nongovernmental organization (the text) transforming itself as it encounters the influence of the institutional milieu (the context) in which is finds itself. In order to be effective, the NGO transforms its activities to incorporate new avenues for advocacy (including litigation). Moreover, it incorporates elements of government into its very identity, as it seeks out modes of action that work in its particular institutional setting. This blurs the separation between distinct fields (public/private, governmental/nongovernmental), and is a product of the web of relationships in which the two cases, to be discussed, are embedded.

As mentioned in previous chapters, the sustainability of a program depends on the constant generation and employment of resources while institutional fit comes out of multiple processes: Material exchange, symbolic and cognitive effects, political strategy, and local cultural dispositions. Hence, the analytical framework focuses on institutional constraints and environment constraints to understand the embedding relationship between formal institutions (text) and context (advocacy activities by ENGOs in China).

5.4 From Nu Dam-Building to Changzhou Poisoned Soil

5.4.1 Nu River Dam-Building

Nu River is an international river in the southwest region of the country. The Nu River flows to the Sino–Myanmar border with a total length of 742 km and a natural drop of 1578 meters. The installed energy generation capacity along the river is 21.32 million kilowatts, making it one of the most important hydropower resources in China. In 2003, the National Development and Reform Commission organized experts through the review of the "Nu River hydropower resources development planning report." In the discussion of the construction of the dam, there were two competing opinions: Approval or denial. The main reason for the opposition was that the construction of the Nu River hydropower station could cause harm to the environment, as well as the question of how much benefit the hydropower project would actually bring to the local residents. Another chief concern was the dislocation of residents, including ethnic minorities, along the river.

This controversy was widely covered in the mass media. Some environmental organizations had to take actions to resist the construction of dams on the River Nu. After many environmental experts and ENGOs took sides in this situation, in 2004, Premier Wen Jiabao issued the following instructions regarding the construction of the dam on the Nu River: "Such large-scale hydropower projects with high social concern and environmental concerns should be [subject to]

84 Relational Institutions and ENGOs in China

careful and scientific decision-making." After Premier Wen's instructions, the Nu River plan and environmental assessment were rejected by the state.

On June 9, 2005, the Chinese Social Transformation Forum ranked the environmental protection organizations' achievement in preventing the River Nu hydropower dam project as the ninth-ranked of 20 major events in China's social transformation, pointing out that NGOs began to have a significant impact on public policy from this time onward, and their efforts have ultimately changed the government's policies. The following statement was issued: "This is a great leap and a milestone in the process of social development in China."

5.4.1.1 Institutional Constraints

As mentioned in the introduction, formal institutions during that period were not conducive to environmental protection and civic participation. In the case of the Nu River dam-building, due to the provisions of the Administrative Procedure Law, the plaintiff must sue for his or her own legitimate rights and interests, and the administrative action against it must have a direct interest. Therefore, it is difficult for NGOs to enter the judicial process for environmental litigation in a classic (autopoietic) pluralist system. However, the environmental organizations utilized the advantages of a sociopoietic milieu and adopted alternative strategies (that is, other than litigation), for discussing the public interest and the question of legitimacy. In this public welfare campaign, the civil society organizations used consultation, lobbying, public opinion and other links to promote the process.

First of all, Green Earth, FON and a number of other environmental organizations successfully attracted attention in the international arena by informing *New York Times* reporters about the conflict. The newspaper reported on the construction of the dam on March 10, 2004, and the article's reprint in the international Chinese media led to an international response. By the end of November, the World River and People's Anti-Dams Conference was held in Thailand, and ultimately drew participants from more than 60 countries, various types of NGOs. In the name of the General Assembly, conference participants sign a statement jointly to protect the River Nu. The statement was submitted to the United Nations Educational, Scientific and Cultural Organization (UNESCO), which replied and said it would be concerned about the development of the River Nu.

In addition, some environmental organizations set up specialized websites and held exhibitions to lobby against the construction of the dams. Through signatures of lecturers and celebrities who joined the lobbying against the Nu River dam, thus, the outcry against the dam and its undemocratic decision-making became more and more intense. In addition, throughout the government's regulatory process, the environmental organizations earned the support of the Yunnan local environmental bureau and also held several expert evaluation meetings. In the ensuing meetings, experts in hydropower, ecology, agriculture, forestry, and geology questioned the rationality and legitimacy of the Nu River project.

Finally, as part of the legal strategy, environmental groups put emphasis on the public interest as well as the mobilization of national sentiment, giving the issue wide-scale legitimacy. The end result was a call for convergence of public opinion around the idea that protecting the ecological environment of the River Nu was the government's primary responsibility.

Therefore, we can say that the maintenance of national authority, legitimization and discussion of public interest issues, could be a most important strategy of NGOs to promote policy advocacy. Drawing attention from the international community is also a very effective way to provide pressure on the Chinese government. It induced the involvement of the central government. By utilizing all these strategies, ENGOs, such as FON, successfully overcame the institutional constraints.

5.4.1.2 Resource Constraints

Strategic Alliance

Strategic alliance is an effective way for NGOs to overcome resources scarcity in this issue. Due to the limitation of government capacity, governments cannot pay equal attention to the demands of each individual or organization. Hence, when several environmental groups join together and become socially influential, the government is most likely to pay attention to their advocacy. In the Nu dam case, environmental organizations such as FON, Yunnan Green Watershed and Green Earth actively contacted national environmental experts, asked experts on the construction of the River Nu dam for environmental hazards assessment, and with the opposition experts formed an alliance, together to carry out policy advocacy to government and other relevant departments. At the same time, the coalition organizations together signed the letter of appeal "Please keep the final ecological Jiang – Nu" and "a civil appeal to publicize the River Nu hydropower EIA report open letter," which collected 99 individual and 61 environmental organization signatures, and was then presented to the state council, the National Development and Reform Commission, the State Environmental Protection Administration and other relevant ministries. This was an important development, as all these different groups agreed upon the goal of "protection of the River Nu, careful development." In addition, these environmental groups used professional knowledge to propose alternative energy solutions, tourism development and other issues. The joint advocacy of these civil society organizations was effective because of its organization level, the huge community groups, members of the social background and cohesion in the momentum of the masses. Therefore, the environmental organizations in the form of strategic alliances policy advocacy to the government, to a certain extent, pressured the government to limit dam construction.

Leaders' Background

The resource constraints within the NGOs were also crucial for policy advocacy. In the authoritarian state, the resource strategy of an NGO is largely influenced by its founder's personal experience, beliefs and expertise to create opportunities and circumstances; the initial strategy of an NGO is strongly influenced by its founder's system experience. It is also a very typical characteristic of sociopoietic society.

In the case of the Nu dam-building, leaders of environmental groups have used their own experience, knowledge and means to call a stop to building the dam. Green Earth's founder, Wang Yongchen, contacted acquaintances of Yunnan University professor and Asia International River Center Director He Daming in the advocacy process; he not only strongly protested the construction of the dam in the symposium of the Nu River hydropower development activities of ecological and environmental protection experts held in Beijing, but was also the only expert holding opposition to the construction during the initial period of the dam at local level. Similarly, Yu Xiaogang, the leader of Yunnan's local private environmental organization, Yunnan Green Watershed, also made use of influence at Oxfam Hong Kong and the Asian Development Bank, that the River Nu should be protected as an ecological river and strengthen the pressure of public opinion.

During the two sessions, the founder of FON, Liang Congjie, through its channels to members of the Chinese People's Political Consultative Conference (CPPCC) members, submitted to the CPPCC National Committee and the National People's Congress "Protecting River Nu, stop hydropower cascade development" and "The classification planning river basin, coordination of ecological protection and economic development proposal" – two proposals, which were written by the Chinese People and Biology of the National Committee members Shen Xiaohui during his tour in Yunnan. It is worth noting that many of the members of the private organizations involved in the media background, in addition to the Green Earth founder Wang Yongchen, had worked as reporters for the Central People's Broadcasting Station, 10% of the members in FON were media practitioners, in order to pour out to the media and manufacture public opinion. These environmental groups used their founders' backgrounds to promote their advocacy strategies and actions.

5.4.2 Changzhou Poisoned Soil

In mid-April 2016, China Central Television (CCTV) news and other media press reported on the Changzhou Foreign Language School environmental pollution incident, causing social concern, with the 500 students suspected of chemical plant pollution plots poisoning to the north of the school area over about 26.2 hectares of flats. Three chemical plants had been thriving there: Jiangsu

Chang Long Chemical Co. Ltd, built in 1958; Chang Yu Chemical Co. Ltd, built in 1983; and Changzhou Huada Chemical Plant, built in 1990.

Around 2010, three factories were relocated, followed by land repairs by the local government. The repair unit, Changzhou Black Peony Construction Investment Co. Ltd, has submitted a "construction project environmental impact report form" to the Jiangsu Environmental Protection Department. The report revealed of the three companies: The use of a large number of toxic and hazardous chemical raw materials, some chemical raw materials and intermediate products with high toxicity or carcinogenicity. However, the Environmental Impact Assessment (EIA) report approval time is March 31, 2012, but the school foundation construction time is August 21, 2011 – that is to say, the school's construction time is in advance by more than seven months of the EIA approval time, which makes it a building constructed without approval first.

But in fact, from the end of 2015, Changzhou Foreign Language School parents began to send reports to the school, a number of government departments, and the press, of the emission of a pungent odor on the north side of the school in the original Changlong block during the soil repair process. They reported adverse reactions among some of the students. Facing the questioning of the parents and the press, Changzhou Municipal Government conducted air quality tests through the city environmental monitoring center and published test results that were in line with national standards. The relevant government departments in turn published the views of experts: The expert group concluded that the air quality monitoring met standards. In late March, they published test results reporting that indoor air, soil, and groundwater were in line with national standards.

On April 29, 2016, FON, the China Biodiversity Conservation and the Green Development Foundation (known as Green Development), as joint plaintiff, initiated litigation proceedings in Changzhou Intermediate People's Court, filing public interest litigation against Jiangsu Chang Long Chemical Co. Ltd, Changzhou Chang Yu Chemical Co. Ltd, and Changzhou Huada Chemical Group Co. Ltd. Civil indictment pointed out that the three defendants seriously polluted the original site of Changlong block in the production and operation process. After moving away, they did not properly restore the polluted site, seriously damaging the public interest. As the firms' behavior was in violation of environmental law, solid waste pollution prevention and control laws and regulations, and other relevant laws and regulations, the plaintiffs demanded that the firms should bear the legal responsibility for environmental infringement. Moreover, the plaintiff asked the court to order the defendant to clean up the original site of the impact of pollutants on the surrounding environment, and bear the cost of ecological restoration. On January 25, 2017, Changzhou Intermediate People's Court made the decision that FON and China Green Development had lost the case

88 Relational Institutions and ENGOs in China

and had to bear the burden of 1.8188 million in legal fees. The plaintiffs are dissatisfied and are preparing for an appeal.

5.4.2.1 Institutional Constraints

In the Changzhou poisoned soil case, the institutional environment is much more friendly than the Nu dam-building case. In this case, FON and China Biodiversity Conservation and Green Development Foundation were allowed to be public plaintiffs in the filing of the lawsuit, due to the revision and approval of relevant laws and regulations. The newly revised Civil Procedure Law in 2012 added a legal provision on environmental public interest litigation, article 55, which clearly states: "on the pollution of the environment, against the legitimate rights and interests of many consumers and other acts of social and public interests, the provisions of the law and the relevant organizations may bring a lawsuit to the people's court." However, the new law does not clearly define the main body of environmental public interest litigation, leading to conservative practices among the courts with regard to the question of environmental public interest. For example, in 2013, the China Environmental Protection Association filed eight environmental public interest litigations which were dismissed due to the main lawsuit lacking clear legal provisions. By 2014, the new Environmental Protection Law was revised, article 58 providing a clear definition of the conditions, with the result that, now, many environmental organizations qualify to file public interest litigation. As a consequence, many environmental organizations have adopted public interest litigation as part of their policy advocacy strategy and are beginning to get initial results.

In the Changzhou case, the staff and volunteers of the two environmental organizations arrived at the site immediately to collect information, contact the relevant interests of the public and prepare for the proceedings to the lawsuit. They also filed a report according to the existing Environmental Law to the plaintiff to the court. After the filing of the case, the environmental organizations arranged for another expert assessment of environmental contamination at the site. However, in the first instance of decision-making, the environmental organizations lost and bore a high trial fee. The case shows how, first, the legal status of NGOs has improved, allowing them to initiate litigation. But, also, it indicates the continuing existence of difficulties in the legal process and obstacles in the pursuit of environmental litigation.

Another observation is that the improvement of the institutional environment for the NGOs also provides avenues and instruments for enterprises and local governments to fight against ENGOs and their partners, including through the mass media and the central government. In the Nu River case, the central government supported ENGOs by issuing a direct order to local government to postpone dam-building. But in the Changzhou case, local enterprises and local government worked together to go against FON by law.

5.4.2.2 Resource Constraints

Leaders' Background

Leaders' personal connections with the government still matter in the Changzhou case, although formal institutions allow grass-roots NGOs to participate. The China Biodiversity Conservation and Green Development Foundation, which was approved by the state council in 1985, is a nationwide foundation, and its leaders include the vice chairman of the CPPCC National Committee, Lv Zhengong, as well as Qian Changzhao and Bao Erhan. The current chairman is the former deputy minister of the United Front Work Department of the Communist Party of China Central Committee, the National Federation of the former Secretary Hu Deping. Moreover, the current Secretary-General Zhou Jinfeng is the member of the CPPCC National Committee and the Standing Committee of the National Federation of Industry and Commerce. After the suit was defeated in the first instance, he repeatedly organized meetings, experts, and lawyers to apply for appeal, proposed to use the Changzhou poisoned soil case to solve the plaintiff's cost problem, but also to solve a series of other issues of environmental public interest litigation.

It can be seen that the two environmental organizations' good relationships with government, registered by the Ministry of Civil Affairs, showing positive records over five years, have become the stepping stones in their motion to qualify for the subject. Those organizations no longer have to advocate outside the legal system, and now interact with the media to discuss the rationality and legitimacy of the problem itself.

Human Capital and Financial Resources behind Litigation

The improvement of institutional arrangements in China not only provides more opportunities to ENGOs regarding their advocacy activities, but also challenges their capacity in terms of human capital and financial support, in particular to support initiating a public litigation.

First of all, only two environmental groups have the wherewithal to engage in policy advocacy in the Changzhou case, making the influence of NGOs slightly "thin" in this case. The secretary-general of the China Biodiversity Conservation and Green Development Foundation Conference stressed that although the law recognizes many environmental organizations' litigation qualifications, for various reasons, many organizations do not want to serve as plaintiffs of environmental public interest litigation and, as a result, the current environment of environmental pollution litigation makes it difficult to form a consortium to negotiate with the government. Secondly, the environmental public interest litigation in this case did not get the assistance of many public lawyers vis-à-vis the preparation of relevant legal knowledge, underscoring the need for environmental public interest litigation lawyers. Thirdly, the media began publicizing the case even before the environmental

90 Relational Institutions and ENGOs in China

organizations were involved in this issue and, therefore, to a large extent, the Changzhou poisoned soil practice was resolved through media exposure, the government's own investigation, and public accountability. When the two environmental groups sued the three factories through environmental public interest litigation, they did not get the media's attention and follow-up. Unlike the Nu dam case, where non-profit organizations captured the media's attention, public participation in the Changzhou case was particularly inadequate, the policy advocacy approach being too simple and lacking flexibility.

In the Changzhou court ruling, the two environmental organizations needed to bear an "astronomical" cost of 1.84 million yuen. NGOs are largely self-financing and do not have a fixed source of funding. Because there are no fixed funds, the main source of income depends on their fundraising, and much of the money may come from government funding and corporate assistance. Even though they have decent financial resources, it is still difficult for them to pay the cost of litigation. Besides, environmental organizations in the process of public interest litigation need to pay a number of costs, including the costs of litigation, expert fees and research fees, etc. In this issue, environmental organizations can only apply to delay payment of fees to the Changzhou court, and on the platform Environmental Public Interest Litigation Fund, asking people to donate for the various costs, with a personal limit of 2 yuan. Nonprofit organizations' financial resources are essential to support the advocacy process. Looking at this issue and many other environmental protection litigation cases, for the vast majority of environmental organizations, compared to the verdict of the outcome of the decision, the biggest pressure may be the failure to afford high costs of litigation, which for many organizations is an unbridgeable gap for them to cross.

In this way, NGOs may be dissuaded from using the legal form of policy advocacy when there are no strong financial resources to support them. The Civil Procedure Law and the new Environmental Protection Law may become mere scraps of paper, and the public interest will be damaged. Therefore, to protect NGOs' ability to engage in public interest litigation, it is necessary to build a more favorable mechanism, in the relevant laws and regulations, to reduce the public interest litigation costs for these organizations.

5.5 Conclusion

After examining these two cases, this section returns to the main research questions raised in introduction. Generally speaking, ENGOs in China utilize their resources to overcome institutional constraints and fit the institutional milieu.

The dam-building case discussed in this chapter is a good example. FON worked with other actors to postpone dam-building in Yunnan, although formal institutions at that point were not pro-civic participation in the area of environmental protection. FON found opportunities and venues to achieve their goals by utilizing personal connections with organizational leaders within the government, the press and mass media, as well as, to some extent, international actor involvement, even though formal institutional connections were absent.

Most interestingly, the second case in this chapter provides a new way to think thoroughly and deeply about this issue. FON is, again, the major actor in the second case regarding land pollution in Changzhou, Jiangsu Province, in 2016, more than a decade after the Nu River case. The formal institutions regarding NGOs and civic participation regarding environmental issues have changed a lot during this span of time. The top leaders of the state have already realized the importance of NGOs working with governments and urged the transformation from social management to social governance in 2012. The revised Environmental Protection Law endorses the legitimacy of NGOs enrolling in environmental disputes in 2014. The newly released Charity Law relaxed the control over NGOs by dismissing the dual-management system in 2016. All signals seem to be in favor of ENGOs in China. Theoretically, ENGOs should have more power to affect government policies if formal institutions are settled as for their western counterparts. But the Changzhou case tells a different story.

In summary, over time, NGOs have contributed to China's current institutional environment diversity through proactive innovation, and the ways of policy advocacy have been gradually shifted from informal means to formalized legal actions. While these developments can open up new opportunities for NGOs, they may also deprive other stakeholders of the flexibility to develop beyond the formal system for many years, and the way they advocate is evolving. The government has also changed the way to deal with advocacy approaches: NGOs still have to rely on the government to manage the system, and this is reflected in the background of leaders, sources of funding and other aspects. Therefore, the relationship between the government and NGOs in policy advocacy interaction still is relationship-based.

However, as we have seen, the lines between civil society, government, industry, and other sectors are blurred. The classic notion of an NGO (which is devoid of government actors, funded by private, charitable donors) blurs when examining the networks of people that participate in and support these NGOs in China. For this reason, policy advocacy and public participation around environmental issues in China is an example of sociopoiesis, where strict divisions between sectors does not well capture the nature of institutional life. Instead, we employ more of a relational approach to understand this complex institutional arrangement.

To sum up, in order to increase its influence over environmental decision-making, ENGOs in China have transformed themselves to take advantage of new legal avenues for advocacy. At the same time, they have transformed their own composition to incorporate actors and resources that traditionally lie outside the bounds of the nongovernmental. For example, membership in the ENGOs includes prominent persons from government, and funding can derive from government and corporate sources. In this chapter, the idea of institutional fit, where the constitutive design of an institution (the text), is modified by the action of the social and legal milieu (the context). To understand ENGOs in China in deeper ways, we open up our analysis to the phenomenon as it appears and is experienced.

References

Boris, E., & Mosher-Williams, R. (1998). Nonprofit advocacy organizations: Assessing the definitions, classifications, and data. *Nonprofit and Voluntary Sector Quarterly*, 27(4), 488–506.

Desantis, G. (2010). Voices from the margins: policy advocacy and marginalized communities. *Canadian Journal of Nonprofit and Social Economy Research*.

Fyall, R. (2016). The power of nonprofits: Mechanisms for nonprofit policy influence. *Public Administration Review*, 76(6), 938–948.

Gåsemyr, H.J. (2017). Navigation, circumvention and brokerage: The tricks of the trade of developing NGOs in China. *The China Quarterly*, 229, March, 86–106.

Gen, S., & Conley Wright, A. (2013). Policy advocacy organizations: A framework linking theory and practice. *Journal of Policy Practice*, July.

Gen, S., & Conley Wright, A. (2016). Strategies of policy advocacy organizations and their theoretical affinities: Evidence from Q-Methodology. *The Policy Studies Journal* (online).

Gronow, A., & Yla-Anttila, T. (2016). Cooptation of ENGOs or treadmill of production? Advocacy coalitions and climate change policy in Finland. *The Policy Studies Journal* (online).

Hana, H., Swedlowb, B., & Ungerb, D. (2015). Policy advocacy coalitions as causes of policy change in China? Analyzing evidence from contemporary environmental politics. *Journal of Comparative Policy Analysis*.

Hsu, C.L., & Jiang, Y. (2015). An institutional approach to Chinese NGOs: State alliance versus state avoidance resource strategies. *The China Quarterly*, 221, March, 100–122.

Jenkins, J.C. (2006). Nonprofit organizations and political advocacy. In W.W. Powell & R. Steinberg (Eds.), *The nonprofit sector: A research handbook* (pp. 307–332). New Haven, CT: Yale University Press.

Li, H., Tang, S.-Y., & Wing-Hung Lo, C. (2016). Nonprofit policy advocacy under authoritarianism. *Public Administration Review*, 77(1), 103–117.

Li, S. (2017). Resource dependency and legitimacy pressure: Does political connection affect environmental grassroots NGOs' policy advocacy? Based on the comparative case studies in the view of organizational theory. *Journal of Public Administration*.

Mosley, J.E. (2011). Institutionalization, privatization, and political opportunity: What tactical choices reveal about the policy advocacy of human service nonprofits. *Nonprofit and Voluntary Sector Quarterly*, 40, 435.

Portney, K., & Berry, J.M. (2015). The impact of local environmental advocacy groups on city sustainability policies and programs. *The Policy Studies Journal* (online).

Reid, E. (1999). Nonprofit advocacy and political participation. In E. Boris, & E. Steuerle (Eds.) *Nonprofits and government: Collaboration and conflict* (pp. 291–325). Washington, D.C.: The Urban Institute Press.

Saich, T. (2000). Negotiating the state: The development of social organizations in China. *The China Quarterly*, 161(1).

Teets, J.C. (2013). Let many civil societies bloom: The rise of consultative authoritarianism in China. *The China Quarterly*, January, 1–20.

Unger, J., & Chan, A. (1996). Corporatism in China: A developmental state in an East Asian context. In P. Bowles, B.L. MacCormick & J. Unger (Eds.), *China after socialism: In the footsteps of Eastern Europe or East Asia?*Armonk: ME Sharpe.

Yu, J., & Shen, Y. (2017). Adaptive cooperation: The strategic reform of the government-social organizations relations since the 18th CPC National Congress. *CASS Journal of Political Science*, 3.

Zhan, X., & Tang, S.-Y. (2013). Political opportunities, resource constraints and policy advocacy of environmental NGOs in China. *Public Administration*, June.

Zhang, C. (2015). Non-governmental organisations' policy advocacy in China: Resources, government intention andnetwork. *China An International Journal*, 181–199.

Zhang, Z., & Guo, C. (2012). Advocacy by Chinese Nonprofit Organisations: Towards a Responsive Government? *Australian Journal of Public Administration*, 71(2), 221–232.

Zhang, Z., & Guo, C. (2017). Chinese Nonprofit in the Shadow of the State: A Literature Review. *Synthesis and Research Agenda*, Arnova Asia Conference.

6

MULTIPLE LEGAL TRADITIONS, LEGAL PLURALISM AND INSTITUTIONAL INNOVATION

The Chinese Criminal Procedure System in Contrast

6.1 Introduction: An Institutional Perspective of the Chinese Criminal Procedure System

China's legal system is an exemplar of system complexity. In terms of law, multiple legal traditions are embedded in the Chinese mentality where legal pluralism and institutional innovation can be widely seen. Lawyers have always treated law as a unique subject with a technical complexity that non-lawyers cannot command, as they argued that it is the only subject regarding positive rules. Positivist theory prevailed in this field even before the recent century witnessed the appearance of socio-legal studies. Black-letter rules require the relevant actors to do something rather than providing what it is. It is seen as the only subject concerning what it ought to be, though it is not a truth. In this field, there is not only a high textuality of institutional life. Later, influenced by scientific theory, normative law seemed to lack practicality in the sense of touching on the world of practice. People's behavior sometimes deviates from what is required by the law.

Then a new theory regarding what is called law in action emerged. Actually, the division between law in theory and law in practice did not work too well. The lawyers, along with the legal scholars, sometimes unintentionally used them interchangeably to suit their particular needs (e.g., in court). These two-dimensional perspectives are coincidental with the need for an institutional perspective for analyzing law. It is understandable because law itself is an important part of an institution. Looking at the law separately may miss the real comprehensiveness and complexity of an institution that operates in a social field.

It is too complicated to discuss the entire legal system. We have chosen the topic of criminal procedure here, as it is regarded as "applied constitutional law" (Lin, 2005) or "seismograph of constitutional law." It is the most sensitive legal area which demonstrates and regulates the most fundamental social relationship, worthy of careful research.

According to *Black's Law Dictionary*, criminal procedure is "the rules governing the mechanisms, under which crimes are investigated, prosecuted, adjudicated, and punished. It includes the protection of accused persons' constitutional rights" (Garner & Black, 2004, p. 403). Chinese criminal procedure is undergoing an era of profound institutional reform, almost going hand-in-hand with other areas of reform, especially socio-economic reform. While the market economy emerged in China, the first formal criminal procedure code was enacted at almost the same time. Whilst a socialist market economy began to take shape, a criminal justice system with Chinese characteristics was also advocated. Similarly, the modernization of criminal procedure does not merely mimic the western system. Rather, the Chinese government is heading toward a unique approach, which claims to be distinct from the Western tradition. In terms of criminal procedure, frequent experiments ensue as a laboratory for justice reform. The traditional positivist theory of law, or even more broadly socio-legal theory of law, cannot well explain these innovations. Explanation is based upon static analysis, a simple and straightforward approach that legal scholars are to use.

Actually, an institutional approach can bring forward a more macroscopic perspective where readership can fundamentally understand how the system evolved together with the ecology. By referring to the concepts of the earlier chapters, we will argue that traditional criminal justice divisions can be well incorporated into an institutional approach if we move out of the narrow-minded "law is law" theory. It is not a simple hybrid of historical, sociological, and legal perspectives. An institutional perspective definitely means a more systematic, dynamic approach for criminal procedure research. To a certain extent, an institutional perspective can assist us in properly understanding the complexity of the criminal procedure system, either present or historical, either in statutes or practice, either the systems or their environment.

6.2 Application of Concepts from Earlier Chapters

When it comes to doing research in criminal procedure, it is impossible to ignore the existing legal literature. Though western institutional categories can still be used to categorize Chinese criminal procedure, such as the divisions between bodies of law (common law, civil law, socialist law, and traditional law), due process/crime control divisions, adversarial/inquisitorial divisions, and coordinate/ hierarchical divisions, the Chinese criminal procedure is found to be a hybrid of the categories mentioned above. Apart from the division between legal families, these categories reflect a superficial stance that falls short of exploring how its function is evolved. We will sketch these categories, applied to Chinese criminal procedure from an institutional perspective. Some of these model divides are really contextual at first glance. For example, legal families divisions are based

96 Chinese Criminal Procedure System in Contrast

upon the dominant features of certain system and legal culture. The form of rules can be seen as partly of this context as well. For example, codification is a common approach to legislate criminal procedure, which is culturally embedded in the continental legal system. Again, due process/crime control seems to be functional and purposeful. In this sense, criminal procedure seems to be a part of public administration. That may be the reason why criminal justice is regarded as a subject of public administration in the US and certain other western jurisdictions. Adversarial/inquisitorial divisions really pertain to the construction of certain organizational phenomena. So are the hierarchical/coordinate model divisions. I would argue that only an institutional perspective can embrace these ideas for dividing models. These divides have already gone beyond the traditional positive theory of law, and are deeply embedded in institutional studies. Some of them are associated with institutional theory, such as coordinate and hierarchical models. As shown in Chapter 1, the institution is a repeatable pattern of actions, allowing us to discuss legal structures, agencies, etc., and bring together the fields of law, public administration, and the legislative, executive, and judicial.

By partially referring to these analytical tools, we will examine the commonalities of criminal procedure as well as the peculiarities of Chinese criminal procedure. We will not ignore the static system as well as the overall principle about how criminal procedure has been developed. In order to know the institutional peculiarities, it is necessary to understand the commonalities, especially when it comes to the legal globalization issue. These commonalities are not distilled from the form of rules but from the institutional function for the procedure. Even though they are not written in criminal procedure code, the relevant working practice must be shown in these summarized functions. The functional development of criminal procedure actually derives from the long-lasting history of civilization in dealing with severe criminal issues. It means that the context predetermines the general structure of text. The institutions must simultaneously fit with environmental changes, even though they might be man-made at the beginning. In contrast, due to the textual change, the context may be adjusted, thus creating feedback to the text. All these processes involve a time lag as the institution has an improvisational certainty if we treat the text as the main body of institutions in a rule-of-law society.

The legal families debate is very much rooted in alternative institutional models: Confucius versus Weber. As many western jurists might anticipate, the Chinese legal system is not a formally regulated and rationalized system but a more traditional, particularly Confucianism-based system. The traditional institution focuses more upon dynamic relations defined by Confucian ethics. But it is not a truth that Chinese law has always been contextualized. Due to external pressure of becoming more efficient in terms of administration against foreign invasion, modern text of codes were called for by the government and intellectuals. We would argue that Chinese law, including criminal procedure, was based on rationale from the Ch'ing Dynasty, but now it is quite similar to many western civil law codes, a rather rational system. Traditional values, especially Confucianism, may appear only in certain potential rules. It may lead to the foundation of a paternalistic culture for practice of current criminal procedure.

From a historical perspective, Chinese criminal procedure is far from a self-referential, autonomous, autopoietic system. It is widely regarded as being politicized rather than being depoliticized. It has its sociopoietic context that should be carefully examined by western scholars who often misunderstand or are prejudiced toward the Chinese system. Just as Karl Marx's theory stated, law is determined by the current political situation; it is shaped and influenced by the social context. Criminal procedure is not a self-contained system and must be understood under the umbrella of social stability and governance, a larger social order. Criminal procedure partly derives ideas from external interlocking systems, such as criminal law, administrative punishment law and their practice.

In defining Chinese criminal procedure, the textuality of criminal procedure code, i.e. Frame-t, will be carefully examined. We can presume that Chinese criminal procedure is logocentric as it has a kind of textuality that is similar to western civilian systems. The textual evolution, especially the revision of the Criminal Procedure Code, has always been regarded as the main issue. However, the contextuality of criminal procedure, Frame-c, also plays a great role in criminal justice. It is necessary to interpret and understand Chinese criminal procedure with reference to its external environment, especially the guidance from the central government, which can be illustrated by those broad policy terms. While the Criminal Procedure Law (CPL) is analyzed from historical and normative perspectives, law in action is also important if we look at Chinese criminal procedure. The text and the context are working together and shaping the institutional reality. However, it does not mean that they complement each other. Sometimes the contextual interpretation means deviation from the text. During the analysis of institutional evolution, Figure 2.3 and the theory of institutional fit will be clearly shown. The CPL fits Chinese social ecology whilst it creates improvement of human rights and civilization in criminal justice. Then it may lag behind the social needs and justice environment calls for a new revision of the text. This ecology is clearly demonstrated in the process of revising the CPL.

With regard to how the Chinese criminal procedure system exhibits its own kind of institutional polymorphism, western scholars may expect continuity between ancient Chinese tradition and the current legal system. However, this relationship may be complicated. The traditional system, especially its legalism, may provide a foundation for establishing a managerial type of criminal procedure, i.e. pre-adaptation. Later, institutional transplants from the Soviet Union and indigenous innovations underpinned by Sino-Marxism were aroused. It may involve the interaction between statute, policy, and practice. Meanwhile, modernity and globalization also influenced the Chinese social environment and thus the criminal procedure system. In such a complicated pluralist milieu, that institutional fit, i.e. as shown in Figure 2.3, is an unavoidable movement. It is necessary to explore how

98 Chinese Criminal Procedure System in Contrast

the statute and policy evolve while social movement must be examined at the same time. Some institutional innovations in China may combine the socialist ideology and civil legal tradition, such as the people's assessor system. People's democracy is demonstrated through assessors; they are not-so-independent triers for the case just like English jurors. The emergence of English jurors is an autopoietic phenomenon which derived from peer review, whereas the Chinese assessor system was a sociopoietic one. These innovations may not only involve specification but also adaptation. Both processes intertwine with each other in terms of text and context. Certain systems are global trends that Chinese criminal procedure follows in its own way. The others are purely embedded in practice and eventually legalized as China's own characteristics.

In order to clarify the system and its real characteristics, we shall contrast it with the English case occasionally where criminal procedure is widely learned by the English-speaking world. Also, compared with the long history of balancing the people and the state in English criminal procedure, Chinese criminal procedure is indeed young, as it was enacted in 1979 and has undergone two revisions. Chinese criminal procedure tends to demonstrate more characteristics of Frame-t, as there is a civilian-style code, whilst English criminal procedure looks more like Frame-c, as all codification must refer to various cases or precedents. English criminal procedure has been always treated as an autopoietic system resulting from long-term battles for the citizens against the regime. However, the Chinese criminal procedure has been seen as a result of top-down reform and a ruling-class-made entity so as to demonstrate greater sociopoiesis. It serves as a tool for maintenance of the larger social order.

In this chapter, we will begin with Weberian ideal types applied in criminal proceedings and extend them to multiple legal traditions. Weber is one of the most influential scholars in defining the Chinese legal system in the western world, including criminal procedure law. In the English-speaking world, he still leaves a strong legacy. By means of Weberian typology, we will first refer to the notion of legal families and then to more widely recognized typologies for comparative criminal procedure, such as the adversarial model and inquisitorial model, coordinate model and hierarchical model. Importantly, we will refer to the prior chapter's concepts to reinterpret these models. The purpose is to properly describe Chinese criminal procedure from an institutional perspective for the readers so that a clear understanding of the general characteristics of criminal procedure in China and its institutional peculiarities can be achieved. We will argue this is not a bureaucratic justification, but to expound not only on the text but also the context. The top-down positivist reform goes hand in hand with low-level adaptive incrementalism.

We will discuss the commonalities of criminal procedure across the world from both textual and contextual perspectives. Then the Chinese characteristics of criminal procedure will be explored gradually before the specific systems and

Chinese Criminal Procedure System in Contrast **99**

practices are discussed. At present, ideologies including paternalism and reform may be Chinese peculiarities. Certain principles including division of powers, coordination and mutual restriction, substantive truth, legal supervision from the procuratorate, justice agencies' independence, and relying on the masses will be examined as Chinese creations. Specific systems including the death penalty procedure will be measured in this part as Chinese institutional innovations. Some of these innovations may be discussed likely in the Frame-t approach, such as the death penalty procedure, whilst certain other innovations unavoidably fall into the Frame-c landscape, such as relying on the masses. All these institutions were designed to fit the surrounding context and then resulted in adaptation for the locale. Some institutions clearly demonstrate a network of relations, such as the division of powers, coordination and mutual restriction. The institutionalized relations really implied a Chinese characteristic. I would argue it is not a means-end logic but a relational logic in a modern sense.

6.3 The Ideal Types and Subsumption of Chinese Criminal Procedure

Weberian ideal types are typological terms for researching the field of social science. Stressing certain elements common to the cases of the given phenomena can help put the seeming tyrannies of details in an orderly way and thus easy for the audience to understand and analyze the existing phenomenon. However, it is rather subjective than objective. Weber never seeks to claim the certainty of ideal types. "Ideal" itself means that every category is mixed rather than pure, whereas pluralist characteristics cannot be ignored. The abstraction-idealization and clear-cut categorization are rather fictional. But in this way, the law's complexity is made more manageable.

Regarding criminal procedure in China, it is embedded in multiple legal traditions. These typological divisions and analysis are not used to complicate the system but are used to clearly interpret the text and context of Chinese criminal procedure. When it comes to these models, they are clearly not only about organizations and rules, but also about governing their practice. In a sense, it is actually based upon institutional categorizations rather than only positive rule division. All these ideal types are based upon analyzing both rules and practice. Textual forms, legal practice and contextual legal culture are altogether counted as the basis for deciding to which group a certain criminal procedure system should belong. Although these ideal types are not our own creation, we will not ignore them in this chapter, as our institutional discourse is descriptive. Those knowledges or analytical tools are an existing mentality that must have influenced the institution itself. What we shall do is to look at these model-divides again by means of our analytical tools for the institutions, making them more profound and reliable for describing criminal procedure in China.

6.3.1 Legal Families Divisions

An easier approach to understanding its peculiarities is to locate it in a wider legal family context where all features of legal systems are idealized and thus more memorable. The widely recognized legal families postulated by David and Brierley comprise: Common law, civil law, socialist law, and "other systems" (most of which are either religious or traditional in nature).[1]

In a previous article, we argued that the Chinese legal system, including criminal procedure, is socialist rather than civil or traditional, though we must recognize that legal pluralism is demonstrated the most in Chinese cases (Yin & Duff, 2010). The 1979 CPL, which is still the main part of the latest 2012 CPL, "was in many ways inspired by earlier drafts prepared during the 1950s and 1963 that had their roots in the civil law inquisitorial system of continental Europe" (Chu, 2001, p. 166). In any event, most articles of the 1979 CPL were based on the text of the 1923 Russian Soviet Federative Socialist Republic Criminal Procedure Code, which was valid in Russia until 1958–60 (Berman, Cohen, & Russell, 1982). For this reason, the Chinese CPL is sometimes seen as a text as being little more than an abridged version of the Russian code (McCabe, 1989). The structure of the Chinese code, resembling its Soviet parent, begins with "general provisions," in which the basic principles and aims are stated, and then there are several chapters concerning pre-trial procedure, trial, appeals, and legal supervision. It has also been pointed out that the CPL shares "certain important features with the rhetoric and technique of the Soviet codes" (Berman, Cohen, & Russell, 1982). These rhetoric and technique actually intertwine with the practice of criminal procedure. Thus, the Soviet or socialist legal legacy cannot be readily ignored in considerations of multiple legal traditions underpinning the current Chinese criminal procedure. Admittedly, in the revisions of CPL, reformers made an effort to throw away the ideological shackles of the Soviet instrumentalist conception of criminal procedure. It is clear that the Soviet criminal procedure was built up upon a civilian background where the codification is used, and so was the Chinese criminal procedure. The Chinese version was regarded as having a strong indigenous tradition including legalism. Arguably, certain legal ideas, especially legalist ones, are by no means inconsistent with the civilian family. It can be regarded as a pre-adaptation for its partial reception in the early part of the 20th century. It reflects the truth mentioned in Chapter 1 that institutions can result from pre-cognitive patterns of behavior. It results in the later sociopoietic transplant which can be readily done.

Certain traditional law family followers may argue that Chinese criminal procedure in practice may be entirely different from the rules. Institutionally, this practice is of real workable rules that provide useful guides to every individual. It is known that traditional Chinese law – comprising both *li* and *fa* – was a flexible instrument used to maintain feudal autocracy and social inequality in a process given substance by personalized punishments. Li is the justified social order of superior versus inferior, relatives versus strangers, old versus young, etc., while fa comprises almost solely the criminal law and other rules with severe criminal sanctions. The distinction between li and fa is now submerged below the surface; it has become less important or less visible than other methods of categorizing law (Head, 2011). For example, public inequality, particularly "ba-yi" (eight deliberations) to mitigate sentences on criminals from the royal families or other types of upper classes, occurring in traditional criminal justice, was repealed under socialist criminal procedure. We could not argue that criminal mediation is from traditional Chinese law, as it is newly created and also referred to western jurisdiction. Certain legal thinking may still permeate Chinese criminal proceedings, such as stratagems (zhi-mou)[2] and supra-planning (mou-lue).[3] This can be reflected by justice agencies and other participants that may manipulate the rules and deviate from the basic legal spirit. For example, in my practicing experience, a presiding judge once made use of a joint accused's definitely unreasonable application to verify his mental disorder in order to extend the time limit for trial.

Nevertheless, we would say that they have not understood the modernity of Chinese criminal procedure and stayed away from Chinese practice. They do not know Chinese legal terminology or even the Chinese language. Their source of understanding of Chinese law comes from prejudicial western reports and old textbooks such as Zweigert and Kötz (1998). It is clear that CPL is a system as rational and formalized as any western criminal procedure code. After several revisions, the magnitude of the CPL and relevant judicial explanations can be very detailed. Precision and clarity have been pursued in the legislation and relevant law-making processes. Insistence on historical continuity may result from perceiving superficial similarities in the function of community pressure as fitting the theoretical mold of li and fa while downplaying the very different modern context (Lubman, 1991).

From the legal family perspective, this modernity partly and indirectly came from the influence of the Anglo-American legal family where adversary and equality of arms are principles. Chinese jurists may regard this change as "reception and recognition of international human rights standards," but those standards regarding fair trial are mostly influenced by common law powers, such as in England and the US. From the dissemination perspective, their values are widespread and accepted due to their influence in politics. Also, the modernization came from fitting ways under the brand of Marxism-Leninism in China. The new criminal procedure law has not deleted the fundamental doctrine regarding socialism. With the rise to power of the Chinese Communist Party (CCP), the government of "new China" first modeled most of its laws heavily on the Soviet model. With the stabilization of the new regime and with the worsening of its relations with the Soviet Union, laws in China were influenced more and more by China's indigenous idea, which can be regarded as China's own variant of Marxism-Leninism (Muhlemann, 2011). Leaders' important speeches and the Party's official documents are often regarded as the outcome of Sino-Marxism,

102 Chinese Criminal Procedure System in Contrast

i.e. Marxism with Chinese characteristics, which must be interpreted, followed and implemented at legislative and practicing levels. For example, the recent dramatic justice reform which resulted in huge revision of criminal procedure law and practice came from a CCP Central Committee Decision concerning Several Major Issues in Comprehensively Advancing Governance According to Law, passed on October 23 at the 4th Plenary Session of the 18th Central Committee of the Chinese Communist Party. In this regard, discussing whether the reform is Anglo-American or socialist in style may distort the readership, who may ignore the real indigenous practical endeavor.

Indeed, Weberian followers in western Chinese law circles may fundamentally misunderstand Chinese law, including criminal procedure. In some aspects, due to Chinese technological advances in terms of the internet, it now allows for online trials for trivial cases, and the western jurisdictions may lag far behind Chinese society, as a member of the English judiciary once said. One might argue that such writers have attached too much importance to the Confucian element in the pre-1949 legal system and have underestimated the effect of modern indigenous legal ideas and influence of globalization in Chinese criminal procedure. This is the context that pushes the repeated and further revision of the text. It actually indicates that criminal procedure is indeed sociopoietic although there are certain autopoietic elements.

Thus, as we argued, in order to know Chinese characteristics and institutional innovations in criminal procedure, it is also necessary to know the similarities and commonalities in global criminal procedure in general without being distracted by legal families and categories which may distract proceduralists from objective observance. Having recognized the basic structure of criminal procedure, reference to certain institutional innovations can be meaningful and objective.

6.3.2 Due Process/Crime Control Divisions

Followed by the legal families division, Weberian illuminations gradually appeared and became a prerequisite study for criminal proceedings. Herbert Packer's dichotomy of crime control and due process designed in his masterpiece, "Two Models of the Criminal Process," contrasts two competing ideal value systems of criminal process (Packer, 1964). This creative dichotomy roughly underpins practical actions in modern criminal procedure, albeit only with reference to American legal practice. It results in the shape and temper of criminal procedure institutions. This model has been widely used for defining the criminal process situation in certain jurisdictions. In the Chinese legal circle, criminal procedure is thought of as being crime control-oriented, while English criminal procedure is due process-oriented. Most Chinese lawyers firmly believed, for various reasons, that English criminal procedure focuses on protection of human rights and maintenance of natural justice. Actually, two fundamental attitudes toward institutions may emerge: The former treats criminal procedure as a tool for governing criminal suspects; the latter regards criminal procedure as a weapon for the accused to defend against the nation.

The models are polarities, and so are the schemes of contextual value that underlie them (Packer, 1964). Under the crime control model, the most important function performed by the criminal process is the repression of criminal conduct so that citizens' security and liberty may be restricted by the necessity of a high rate of apprehension and conviction. It also means a premium on speed and finality (Packer, 1964). It is clear that Chinese criminal proceedings tend to enlarge the possibility of criminalization. For example, the police sometimes intervene in economic disputes and use criminal measures to resolve them. The proceedings tend to be administrative or managerial. The criminal procedure is not used to handcuff the criminal justice agencies but to guide them to convict the accused. Hence, the criminal justice process tends to be an assembly line that moves cases toward disposition. If arrests are made, the related fact-finding, either by the police or prosecutor, will be treated as highly reliable. It means the accused should be presumed guilty from beginning to end. Trial does not play a very crucial role in determining the result of the case. This empirical description indicates that institutions matter and need to be observed from both textual and contextual perspectives.

In contrast, under the due process model, in which English criminal procedure is the representative, fundamental fairness under the law is the most important thing. Section 29 of the Magna Carta has been regarded as the symbol of due process:

No Freeman shall be taken or imprisoned, or be disseized of his Freehold, or Liberties, or free Customs, or be outlawed, or exiled, or any other wise destroyed; nor will We not pass upon him, nor condemn him, but by lawful judgment of his Peers, or by the Law of the Land. We will sell to no man, we will not deny or defer to any man either Justice or Right.

It is clear of the deep context that citizens combat against dictatorship and oppression. Criminal procedure is an autopoietic formation from long-lasting pursuit of liberty for every individual especially those deprived and threatened by the regime. The rights of the accused are the key issue concerned in the criminal procedure so that powers from the criminal justice agencies are limited in order to prevent official oppression of the individual. In other words, criminal procedure should look like an obstacle course, consisting of a series of procedural safeguards that serve as much to protect the factually innocent as to convict the factually guilty. The agencies and officials must be accountable for their irregularities whereas the abuse of process may suffer extreme procedural sanctions.

However, these two models are competing values in most criminal justice systems. Due process is also demonstrated and gradually prevails in modern Chinese criminal procedure as in the English system. The protection of human rights and presumption of innocence before being proved guilty has been confirmed in

104 Chinese Criminal Procedure System in Contrast

Chinese criminal procedure. The rights for the defendant have been drastically improved whereas the defense counsel system has been dramatically enriched. In the 1996 Criminal Procedure Law, a more adversarial trial system was instituted. Nowadays, the Chinese legal system is moving toward a trial-centered system in its reform. All these listed phenomena manifest that crime control and due process are both embedded in Chinese criminal justice. It may be argued, especially from the western liberal regime, that a crime control policy still predominated in Chinese criminal justice. But it shall be considered that due process has been consistently advocated and gradually followed in the Chinese system.

Similar to English criminal procedure, the Chinese CPL claimed to respect and protect human rights (Criminal Procedure Law of the People's Republic of China (CPL) art. 2). Courts, procuratorates, and public security authorities shall protect the defense right and other procedural rights legally enjoyed by criminal suspects, defendants, and other litigation participants (CPL art. 14). The defense lawyer may meet and communicate with his client in custody. The meeting between a defense lawyer and a criminal suspect or accused shall not be monitored (CPL art. 37). A defense lawyer may, from the day when the people's procuratorate examines a case for prosecution, consult, extract, and duplicate case materials (CPL art. 38). Judges, prosecutors, and criminal investigators must, under legal procedures, gather various kinds of evidence that prove the guilt or innocence of a criminal suspect or defendant and the gravity of crime (CPL art. 50). In deciding each case, the court shall focus on evidence, investigation, and research, and credence shall not be readily provided for confessions. All facts found beyond reasonable doubt are based on all evidence of the case (CPL art. 53). A confession of a criminal suspect or defendant extorted by torture or obtained by other illegal means and a witness or victim statement obtained by violence, threat, or other illegal means shall be excluded (CPL art. 54). It is clear that criminal procedure in China is enriched with a due process element. This phenomenon may have resulted from external influence under globalization, indeed a sociopoietic process.

6.3.3 Adversarial/Inquisitorial Divisions

In the article "Evidentiary Barriers to Conviction and Two Models of Criminal Procedure," Mirjan Damaška teased the divided inquisitorial-adversarial models for depicting the features of continental and Anglo-American criminal procedures (Damaška, 1973). These models may be the most common in criminal procedure circles, and it has already seemingly become the self-evident truth in this field. Normally, the Chinese criminal procedure is seen to inherit the continental inquisitorial gene, while the English one is treated as being typically adversarial.

As in most continental jurisdictions, there is an official investigation to establish the truth which builds up to a case file or "dossier" to which the defendant has access in Chinese criminal proceedings. The defendant is expected to assist in finding the truth for the criminal justice agencies. The judge plays a positive part in gathering and selection of evidence. Because of the professional bodies and staff involved in the justice system, evidentiary rules scarcely play any function. The presentation of evidence by the parties is controlled and directed by the trial court. The whole case seems to deal with a cumulative administrative process, which has assembled the dossier of largely written evidence. In some extreme cases, there might be certain inquisitorial action against the accused. Though it has already been eliminated by criminal procedure rules, it may still happen occasionally, especially in duty crimes which rely more on oral confession to convict the accused. The potentially close relationship between the three agencies, i.e. court, procuratorate, and police agency, partly shows the weak position of the accused. The defense counsel may be in rather an awkward position for his role is really limited in assisting the accused. Although this position cannot be clearly seen from the text, it is naturally based on the Chinese political context where all these agencies represent and are guided by a unified party government.

In addition to the adversarial model where the English system is a typical jurisdiction, the parties are partisan and have sole control over the assembly and presentation of their respective cases. They operate at arm's length and neither party is under any obligation to assist the other. The parties are entitled to remain silent about the information they have discovered and the evidence they intend to lead at trial. There are complex and restrictive evidentiary rules which the parties may use to keep evidence unfavorable to their case out of court. The judge is a passive umpire with no prior knowledge of the case when the trial begins. The outcome is determined by a single hearing at which there is a heavy emphasis on the oral presentation of evidence. The debate culture actually is also based upon the context of the relevant equal position between the citizens and the state.

As explained earlier, the Chinese system became more hybridized since 1996. The trial stage became increasingly adversarial and nowadays a trial-centered system is being advocated. Before the 1996 CPL, the court needed to examine the substantive points before the trial and entirely undertook the responsibilities of verifying the facts. Since then, the judiciary has not directly verified cases but is based upon the evidence provided by the parties initially. Nevertheless, the power of ex officio investigating the case has been maintained in the new CPL. This indicated that the Chinese system borrowed certain technical settings of text from the adversarial model. However, the inquisitorial tradition in pursuit of truth is maintained (Long, 1998).

In the adversarial context, it is placed on the adjudication phase where an active advocate manipulates complex rules of evidence to produce substantive results to ensure for the defendant a "fair fight." The judiciary can legally nullify the acts of executive enforcement agency. At present, Chinese trial-centered reform is to ensure the facts and evidence of cases being investigated and examined for prosecution can stand the test of law, and to ensure that the courtroom

106 Chinese Criminal Procedure System in Contrast

hearings play a decisive role in ascertaining the facts, identifying the evidence, protecting procedural rights, and fair trial.[4] It is de facto a new adversarial revolution for the criminal procedure system. It requires the impartiality and independence of justice. In the orientation of trial-centered reform, the role of the defense counsel will be more important than before. The rights of meeting, communication, consultancy, investigation and confrontation will be ensured for the purpose of trial-centralism.

Although Damaška's end is to idealize the type of criminal procedure in two kinds of jurisdictions, his bases are really institutional. He took a phenomenological stance toward institutional description. It is not based upon what is stipulated in the rule. He aspired toward describing criminal trial in an authentic, faithful way, objectively depicting what are the things themselves. It reflects the essence of a comparative institution study.

6.3.4 Coordinate/Hierarchical Divisions

In another influential article, "Structures of Authority and Comparative Criminal Procedure," Damaška created two ideal forms – the "hierarchical" and the "coordinate" models – to illustrate the different features of criminal procedure of the European continent and of the Anglo-US jurisdictions respectively (Damaška, 1975).

The Chinese criminal proceedings are quite similar to the hierarchical model that Damaška categorized. Institutional certainty is much more concerned than individual justice. The authorities tend to be hierarchical, so that the lower echelon of authority likely follows the higher-level authority. In China, three agencies, the courts, the procuratorates, and the police, collaborate with each other. In practice, they are opposite to the accused. Police and prosecutors are really centralized. The saturation of police forces with internal regulation bears a strong resemblance to that of the military. For the court, a comprehensive and widely used system of appeals is used to cope with centrifugal tendencies. Courts and all other justice agencies are treated as units, distinct and separate from their judges. Formalized dossiers are widely used to process the case. Documents and reports are the main form of evidence for the judge to decide on. Even if there are testimonies adduced by the defense counsel, they are written into reports named and distilled by the lawyers.

In terms of the coordinate model, of which the English criminal procedure is a representative, the best solution will be pursued rather than certainty and uniformity of decision-making. The single layer of authority is the ideal system. The ordering of authority is as mild as possible. Police and public prosecutors remain to the present day deeply embedded in local institutions and are in most respects wholly decentralized. Jurors bear the local conceptions of justice upon decision-making. The entire criminal process became identified with the trial. The conclusion of this stage signaled the end of the criminal proceedings. Internal organization arrangements are not clear and rigid. The plea-bargaining can be used by the prosecutor to finalize the case. The adjudicator cherished a flexible attitude toward criminal procedure institutions. The rules are not much more than guidelines susceptible to improvement and reconsideration in light of current cases. The official documentation and bureaucratic techniques are scarcely used while oral presentation and confrontation are the basis for the judge to make decisions.

I would argue that Damaška's paper is in reality an institutional one rather than a comparative law one. It has nothing to do with what is provided by the rules but only describes what it is in practice. The structure of authority is really political and governmental rather than being legal. These model divisions go further to categorize the whole criminal proceedings rather than criminal trial, where the readers can feel how individual institutions work. In some sense, it reveals the clash between what it ought to be and what it is in terms of criminal proceedings. For example, even though there is a jury system in the continental legal system, due to the hierarchical context the system was changed into professional judges together with jurors. Normally, the jurors will yield their decision power to the more professional judge, making a democratic system useless in terms of rulings. It indicates that practicing institutions may change the original meaning of the text which must have an ecological fit between the institution and its milieu.

These model categories are not clear-cut for the Chinese criminal proceedings though. Chinese criminal procedure follows the way of people's assessor to improve mass line and democracy of justice. A restricted approach of negotiated justice nowadays is gradually applied. A guiding cases system is also used in criminal procedure. Oral evidence is increasingly emphasized in Chinese justice reform. In dealing with important cases, social policy and ethical considerations are demonstrated as potential institutions. Although each agency in its own system tends to be hierarchical, three agencies are legally coordinating and may negotiate with each other in dealing with the case. It means that Chinese criminal procedure is quite hierarchical but still retains certain coordinate elements probably due to the mass line and socialist legal ideology which may deviate from the western civilian system. The institutions may not be bureaucratic but they provide an elastic relational mode for governing criminal proceedings.

In the latest criminal justice reform, it is emphasized that adjudication and procuratorial powers shall be exercised independently. It also means that even the higher echelons in the justice system cannot intervene with individual cases. In order to achieve this coordinate purpose, a system for recording, reporting, and pursuing the responsibility of leading cadres' interference in judicial activities or meddling with the handling of certain cases was further established, just as sociopoietic subsystems theory indicates. Internal personnel of judicial organs must not violate provisions to interfere with cases currently being handled by other personnel. Recording and accountability systems for internal personnel looking into cases were established. Meanwhile, case-handling responsibility systems for presiding judges, collegial panels, head procurators and lead investigators were improved so

108 Chinese Criminal Procedure System in Contrast

that the person handling the cases can bear responsibility. Where it causes an unjust, false, and wrongfully decided case, or other serious consequences, a system of lifetime responsibility will be pursued in accordance with the law. Therefore, the centripetal force for creating a hierarchical system was diluted by independence and the system became increasingly coordinated if reform can be practiced. It is clear that the reform of criminal procedure highly relied upon other subsystems, firmly proving China's sociopoietic characteristics of criminal proceedings.

It may be argued that all model categories are polarized so that the objectivity of these models is doubted. Just as Chapter 1 reminded us, these modes of description tend to have strongly dualist frames of reference. Henceforth, legal pluralism is a self-evident argument without any necessity to be proven. However, this is only partial to the story for any legal system. By virtue of the analytical framework alone, readership may not be able to capture the origin and history of the Chinese criminal procedure and, consequently, this could lead to a very superficial understanding. Every legal system may be fundamentally a culture which evolves from the very beginning. In a sense, the text and the context shall be combined and evaluated in terms of criminal procedure. Most of the current scholars often form their perspectives from scratch when they analyze a certain rule, unknowingly falling into an institutional trap. All the lawyers doing the research will become institutional observers gradually without firmly insisting upon what is called "legal ground."

6.4 Commonalities of Criminal Procedure

The multiple legal traditions as well as legal pluralism underpinning Chinese criminal procedure were discussed in the previous section. In the analysis of the subsumption in this particular category, certain peculiarities of the system have been noted. Using this traditional framework may help us understand the general picture of the system. Institutional innovations, however, must be systematically examined before defining the commonalities. The emphasis on the different innovations can often mislead readers. In fact, global criminal procedures tend to be quite similar, with more similarities than differences from an institutional perspective.[5]

By comparison, English law demonstrates a strong tradition of laissez-faire capitalism which is autonomously shaped by market economy, whereas Chinese law is still collectivism-oriented and thus considered socialist which is imposed by Marxism-Leninism. In a sense, English law demonstrates more autopoietic characteristics whilst Chinese law is embedded with more sociopoietic characteristics. English law has a number of common law elements while Chinese law is mainly codified with civilian tradition. China has a long autocratic tradition and this centralized control is deeply rooted in the context of legal culture. In contrast, England has been influenced by classic liberalism and legal institutions demonstrate a very coordinate and decentralized shape. Even when the Chinese system

Chinese Criminal Procedure System in Contrast **109**

has been modernized, many of its institutional elements, including the traditional attitudes, perceptions, ideas, values and much of the traditional mentality, still survive today (Chen, 1999). Noticeably, the ruling CCP in China wants to search for some way to revamp its ideological basis and revive its indigenous Confucianism. The tradition referred to here includes what Mattei defines as the three main sources of social incentives to legal behavior: Politics, law, and philosophical or religious tradition (Mattei, 1997, p. 12). No matter whether the current system is seen as a socialist legal system with Chinese characteristics, it provides a credible, alternative socio-political philosophy to western liberalism. This is regarded as being faithful to China's context of indigenous tradition and current contingent circumstances (guoqing) (Peerenboom, 2003).

It should be firmly realized that every jurisdiction is influenced by and deeply embedded in the context of modernity and globalization. It means that different legal systems will be merged to a large extent due to the common contextual factors. The distinction may become indistinguishable while similar controls are embedded. Robert M. Marsh argues that Max Weber misunderstood Chinese law based on his ideal types being irrational. During the Ch'ing Dynasty (1644–1912), China's legal system represented Weber's substantively rational type more than the substantively irrational type (Marsh, 2000). Most decisions in actual Chinese cases consist of application of general rules to situations which are similar to most western laws, and are unlike Khadi where personal discretion and arbitrariness guides decision-making. In fact, the predictability of decisions can be anticipated. It means due to sociopoietic development, the text of Chinese criminal procedure had been entirely adjusted to meet the need of the certainty of contemporary social order. The text demonstrates a contextual compulsion and influence.

Functionally, criminal procedure in every jurisdiction is charged with giving full effect to penal law itself and, consequently, to the investigation, prosecution, and conviction of the perpetrators of misdemeanors or crimes. Whatever the purposes of the substantive criminal law may be, the tasks of criminal procedure are basically the same. The objectives of criminal procedure include identifying truth, due process and social harmony. All jurisdictions' procedures involve detection, apprehension, prosecution, guilt determination, and punishment of offenders, whereas conciliatory, peace-restoring components are embedded in certain parts of criminal procedure (Ingraham, 1987). Certain common elements must be considered, such as the risks of judicial error, against the violation of human rights and more particularly the rights of defense, against the risk of the dehumanization of a bureaucratic process, the neglect of the interests of victims, the bypassing of the public interest, and so forth (Verin, 1987).

Professor Barton L. Ingraham once established an explicit morphology for criminal procedure, comparable to that of vertebrates. He tried to create an autopoietic theory to justify the self-evident autonomy of criminal procedure and indicate a commonality of criminal proceedings across the world. Using an

110 Chinese Criminal Procedure System in Contrast

analogy with zoology, he describes the skeleton common to all modern procedural systems, at the same time noting the significant differences in their muscles, viscera, and organs (Verin, 1987). He then designed an analytical grid in his cosmopolitan work, "The Structure of Criminal Procedure," distilling a common structure for criminal procedure in France, the Soviet Union, the US, and China. Criminal procedure in all other jurisdictions follows the same structure: Intake, screening, charging and protecting, adjudication, sanctioning, and appeal (Ingraham, 1987). Accordingly, the Chinese criminal procedure follows the same process.

The procedural task of processing persons accused of crime from arrest to disposition is basically the same in Chinese and English criminal procedures. This process can be broken down into six tasks which modern criminal procedure must perform to be complete. First, some methods must be devised whereby reports of criminal activity are brought to the attention of officials and the offender taken into custody for investigation or prosecution. Second, it is necessary to sift and screen these complaints and reports of crime to determine their factual validity, to decide what laws have been violated and whether sufficient evidence exists to support criminal charges, to separate the prosecutable from the unprosecutable complaints, and finally to divert to other social control agencies the unprosecutable cases or cases which do not involve sufficiently public interests. The third task is to formally charge the defendant and to provide him some procedural protections for his defense. The fourth task is to provide a method or procedure whereby the actual guilt or innocence of the accused may be determined. The fifth task of a system of criminal procedure is to prescribe how criminal sanctions are to be imposed and administered. The sixth and last task is to provide means by which decisions as to guilty or innocent and any other pretrial or post-conviction decision regarding the accused may be reviewed by higher authorities to make certain that justice has been done and the laws complied with (Ingraham, 1987).

At first glance, the Chinese CPL is not much different from any western criminal procedure code – demonstrating similar rationality in terms of textuality: The separation between prosecution and adjudication. Especially nowadays, the CPL reduced the deficiencies and ambiguities dramatically. Some important principles including the presumption of innocence, due process, and the right to counsel were established, no matter whether these elements were from foreign origins or through amalgamation. Some western politicians and scholars still argue that Chinese rules are inconsistent with provisions found in the International Covenant on Civil and Political Rights, such as requiring a presumption of innocence, safeguards against self-incrimination, and protections against double jeopardy. It creates the impression that the current reform of Chinese criminal procedure is still mimicking western institutions, where all these values, systems, and practices are firmly espoused. It cannot be denied that China's procedural law has been influenced by international pressure. But this is only one of the influential factors. We will not examine the institution from this prejudicial perspective but examine the real innovations of the institution in an objective approach. Objectively, Chinese criminal procedure and its practice received multiple influences: Modernity, Soviet legacy, traditional Chinese law, and certain other indigenous ideas. Outside influence firmly implies its sociopoietic features.

The procedural system will be examined at each stage of the criminal process from both the perspective of the "ideal" and the "actual": The "ideal" being according to its written law, and the "actual" being according to the way the law is used or manipulated to carry out the functions the analytical model proposes must be performed by every legal procedural system (Ingraham, 1987). We cannot observe criminal procedure only by statute; it is necessary to combine rules and practice together as institutions.

6.5 The Evolution of the Text of Chinese Criminal Procedure

There is limited research about institutional innovations in Chinese criminal procedure in the English language. But it is clear that China has been undergoing an era of profound institutional reform in terms of criminal procedure, or more broadly criminal justice. It is not an isolated issue, as its situation is closely connected with the prosperity of economy and improvement of civilization. China must create an image that the criminal suspect and accused are treated properly and professionally.

In 1988, Yang Chen systematically compared the Chinese criminal procedure with the English one. He summarized the most distinctive features of China's law of criminal procedure as: 1 The social cooperation with the criminal justice organs; 2 the close-knit relationship of coordination and mutual restriction between the various branches of the justice system; 3 the people's assessors' equal rights with the judge in trial and the judicial supervision procedure for the purposes of correct enforcement of the law; 4 the special functions of the independent people's procuracy in criminal proceedings; 5 the active role of the judge in detecting and verifying the facts in criminal proceedings; 6 the application of the doctrines of deterrent and economical justice represented in the speedy trial for serious crimes and the one-appeal system; 7 the somewhat limited role of Chinese defense lawyers compared with English lawyers in criminal proceedings, especially at the stages before trial; and 8 the thorough implementation of the principle of objectivity in criminal proceedings, distinctively represented in the evaluation of the confession, the comprehensive trial of guilty-plea cases, and the rejection of the doctrine of double jeopardy.

Some of the arguments above may still be sound as traditional differences exist in both jurisdictions. However, it shall be noted that after 30 years, a system may change dramatically, especially when it comes to the fact that the Chinese CPL has been revised twice and dozens of judicial interpretations have been made. It is necessary to renew the comparative work. Before understanding the innovations, a historical review is needed for the purpose of knowing its textual evolution. It is

112 Chinese Criminal Procedure System in Contrast

clear that a highly textualized criminal procedure system is established in China and text at least formally is the origin of meaning. Analyzing the Chinese criminal procedure must start from the self-ostensible text of the CPL. Although the text of criminal procedure is highly top-down, made under the modernization of the socialist rule-of-law flag, the influential environment, i.e. the contextual movement, cannot be ignored. A historical approach is a must to assist in evaluating the system. No matter how we categorize Chinese criminal procedure and find certain peculiarities from it, we must try to identify the influential factors during the long sociopoietic development of the system. Here we must go into the historical background to discover the substance of Chinese criminal procedure. Here the textual changes can be the key points as topics, as it is the clear basis for differentiating the stages of criminal procedure institutions. I would not argue that the meaning of Chinese criminal procedure is completely endogenous to the text itself under the Frame-t umbrella. But eventually, the contextualized systems will gradually be transferred into the text. Text is an important symbol in such a codified state.

The 1979 Criminal Procedure Law

After the People's Republic of China (PRC) was established in 1949, there was no criminal procedure code. This is because the entire negation of western capitalist law from the socialist China, Six-Law Overall Regulations (liu-fa-quan-shu) including Criminal Procedure Law left by the nationalist government, was entirely demolished. It meant a break from the civilian tradition accumulated by the nationalist government. Yet some laws and regulations undertook the function of criminal procedure code and provided the basic foundation for later enactment of such code. These include the Interim Organic Regulations of People's Courts of the PRC, the Interim Organic Regulations of the Supreme People's Procuratorate of the Central People's Government, and the General Organic Rules of People's Procuratorates of All Levels, promulgated by the Committee of the Central People's Government in 1951 (Head, 2011). These enactments laid the legal context for establishing uniform judicial authorities and procedures, and became the resources to elaborate institutions of criminal procedure. Furthermore, in 1954, the National People's Congress passed the Organic Law of Courts of the PRC, the Organic Law of Procuratorates of the PRC, as well as the Regulations of the People's Republic of China on Arrest and Detention. These enactments clarified principles such as separate functions, coordination, and mutual checking among public security organs, procuratorates and courts. These rules were partly inherited from the New Democracy Revolution period beginning from 1927, before China's take-over of the Communist Party.[6] It can be seen as a summarization of people's justice practice. It means the context gradually determined and was transferred into the text. Meanwhile, these rules were partly influenced by the Soviet legal model, due to the Sino-Soviet

Alliance in the Cold War. Admittedly, certain elements embedded in ancient Chinese legal tradition have been incorporated into practice. For example, tortured or forced confession, overdue custody, obstacle for the defense counsel, absence of the witness before the court, etc., can be found throughout history (Xiong, 2006).

Partly because of the devastating political chaos during the Cultural Revolution, the agencies and existing legal system were entirely destroyed. The normal administration of justice was entirely substituted by mobilization campaigns of activists and Red Guard youth. Those social customs which were regarded as "feudal" (Confucian thinking), or "bourgeois" (western thinking), were swiftly discarded and discouraged by popular justice. In 1979, the fifth plenary of the China People's Committee's second meeting was held, when seven significant laws were passed, including Criminal Procedure.

The 1979, CPL is the first criminal procedure code after the PRC was founded. It has 164 articles and four chapters. By virtue of this code, the relationship-based principle of separate responsibility, mutual collaboration and control amongst police, procuratorate and court was formally instituted (Xiong, 2006). Criminal proceedings are clearly divided into three separate phases, including investigation, prosecution, and trial. Three agencies resemble three consecutive parts of the factory. A series of measures were introduced for attracting the masses to participate in criminal proceedings. The defense rights were established and the defense counsel can be entrusted at trial. The victim was regarded as a participator rather than the witness. He or she enjoys wider procedural rights, such as the right to complaint and the right to inquiry. An evidence system in accordance with dialectical materialism was adopted. It means that substantive truth prevails in Chinese criminal proceedings. Filing a case became an independent phase of criminal proceedings. The public prosecution by the procuratorate is the dominant form while private prosecution is an exception. For the public prosecution case, the whole dossier must be transferred to the court. The court will review the whole dossier and decide if the trial will be opened up in public. The trial form is mainly inquisitorial. The case will be finalized in at most two instances. The second instance court will comprehensively review the fact and the law, with no limit by the appeal issues. Regarding death penalty cases, a complicated review procedure is provided. As for wrongful convictions, the trial supervision procedure can be used to correct it.

The 1996 Criminal Procedure Law

Though the 1979 CPL is a relatively scientific and systematic code, which fits the context of domestic status quo in China, it was enacted soon after the end of the Cultural Revolution and a historical limit is unavailable. After the 1979 CPL was promulgated, the Standing Committee of the National People's Congress has consecutively promulgated a series of regulations to complement and revise the CPL,

114 Chinese Criminal Procedure System in Contrast

such as the Decision concerning the Implementation of Criminal Procedure Law in 1980, the Decision concerning Death Penalty Cases Review in 1981, the Decision concerning the Revision of the Court's Organic Law and the Decision concerning the Revision of the Procuratorate's Organic Law in 1983, the Decision concerning Promptly Brought Criminals Seriously Endangering Social Security into Trial in 1983, the Supplemental Regulations concerning the Time Limit for Handling Criminal Cases, etc. These improvements actually implied the deficiencies of the 1979 CPL. In this sociopoietic situation, the hermeneutic capacity of the CPL is limited and lags behind the social and political needs for ensuring stability. The 1979 CPL was too general and rough where the criminal justice agencies do not know what to do in dealing with the specific problems due to a lack of institutional guidance. Certain articles in the 1979 CPL do not fit with the constitution and related rules and regulations. For example, the principle of independent exercising authorized by the justice agencies has been established in the 1982 Constitution; however, it was not instituted in the CPL. The intertextuality has not been properly followed. The practice must be met by the CPL as well. The police developed certain practices, such as a reporting system, juvenile justice system, etc., that must be confirmed by revising the CPL. The dramatic change in the political and economic situation in China called for a new code. In other words, contextual change results in the improvement of the text, i.e. the specification. Compared to the 1979 CPL, the 1996 CPL made considerable reform and improvement.

The 1996 CPL is regarded as the landmark of Chinese legal construction (Xiong, 2006). The number of articles increased to 225 with 110 amendments based on the 1979 CPL (Criminal Law of the People's Republic of China, amendment of 1996 (CPL amend. 1996) art. 1). Ideologically, the 1996 CPL tried to dilute the Sino-Marxism, i.e. Marxism-Leninism and Maoism, as well as people's democratic dictatorship. Instead, criminal procedure was targeted at ensuring correct enforcement of the criminal law, punishing crimes, protecting the people, safeguarding state and public security, and maintaining socialist public order. The principle that the courts shall exercise judicial power independently and procuratorates shall exercise procuratorial power independently was provided. Also, in order to protect human rights, the principle that no person shall be found guilty without being judged by the court was established. Specifically, criminal procedure law divided the criminal suspect and the accused. Before the procuratorate prosecutes the case to the court, criminal suspect is used; after that point, he or she is called the accused.

The supervisory function of the procuratorate was also strengthened and clarified. The supervision extended to the phase of filing a case, as well as the execution. Meanwhile, supervision during the trial had been changed to supervision after the trial. Before the revision, the defense counsel could only be appointed seven days before trial. In the 1996 CPL, the criminal suspect was entitled to legal service even in the investigation stage. The rights of the defense counsel were specified, including copying the materials accused in the case, meeting and communicating with the accused, collecting related evidence and applying for the justice agencies to adduce evidence. The rights of the victim had been strengthened. The scope of the private prosecution was enlarged. The victim enjoys similar procedural rights with the accused. He or she can make a statement; enquiry with the accused, witness, expert witness, requires the procuratorate to protest against the verdict if disagreeing with it. Compulsory measures were improved and restricted. For example, the time for interrogation through summons or forced appearance shall not exceed 12 hours. A criminal suspect shall not be detained under the disguise of successive summons or forced appearance (CPL amend. 1996 art. 92).

The most influential reform was borrowed from the Anglo-American adversarial trial system. Before the trial, the court only reviews the procedural formalities for the case. All the substantive issues and whether the facts are clear or the evidence is enough will be resolved before the court. The control of the judge toward the trial had been weakened while the confrontation between parties was strengthened. Certain diversion systems, especially the simplified trial procedure, were introduced to speed up the trial. The appeal trial may be opened up for public hearing. The execution of the death penalty was reformed, and lethal injection could be used to execute criminals.

The 2012 Criminal Procedure Law

Soon after the 1996 CPL was promulgated, many contextual changes called for new revisions of the text. The importance of procedural law had been emphasized and the concept of human rights had been widely accepted in China. Many local courts summarized experiences and made institutional innovations, such as disclosure of evidence, no confessions rules, plea bargaining, simplified trial in the solemn procedure, suspended prosecution, and suspended judgment. For example, in 1995, the Justice Committee of the Changing approved the Several Regulations of Suspended Judgment, the regulatory aspects of which included applied subjects, authority of approval, means of information, resolution for objection against the suspended judgment, supervision during the suspended period, and the confirmation of penalty. These innovated practices lacked legal ground and needed to be justified by the CPL. Most importantly, the United Nations (UN) created, confirmed, and advocated many related justice standards, criteria, and policies, which are the minimum standards commonly enshrined by the international community. China, as one of the founders of the United Nations and a responsible standing committee member of the UN Security Council, must strictly abide by these standards. It was a main force that underpinned the new revision of the CPL. The text must fit the complicated contextual change whilst the text must be advanced in order to ameliorate the environment of Chinese criminal justice.

Based on the 1996 CPL, 100 parts had been revised or added. The number of articles increased by 290, including certain new parts, chapters and sections. It is

116 Chinese Criminal Procedure System in Contrast

truly a major revision. A constitutional principle, i.e. "respect and safeguard human rights," was written into the General Provisions. Specifically, nobody shall be forced to attest his own guilt. The exclusion of illegally obtained evidence was instituted as a system. In the process of investigation, examination for prosecution or trial, if any evidence that should be excluded is founded, such evidence shall be excluded and shall not serve as the basis of prosecution opinions, prosecution decision and judgment.

The conditions of arrest and the procedure for the procuratorate to examine whether to arrest or not had to be improved. The necessity for detainment had to be examined after the approval of arrest. Certain special procedures including conditional non-prosecution for minors, sealing up of the criminal record, etc., had been established. The investigation procedure was improved and regularized. According to the practical needs, technical investigation measures were stipulated in the CPL. To respond to the inconsistencies for the conditions of arrest in legal practice, the dangers to society were articulated in five types: 1 It is probable for him to commit a new crime; 2 there is a real danger of endangering the state security, public security or social order; 3 it is probable for him to destroy or falsify evidence, interfere with the witness in making testimonies, or tally confessions; 4 it is probable for him to retaliate against the victim, reporter and accuser; and 5 attempting to commit suicide or escape.

In order to reduce the extortion of confessions by torture, this CPL stipulates that after a person has been detained or arrested, the criminal suspect shall be immediately sent to the house of detention (Criminal Law of the People's Republic of China, amendment of 2012 (CPL amend. 2012) art. 83). After the criminal suspect is delivered to the house of detention, the investigators shall conduct the interrogation within the house of detention (CPL amend. 2012 art. 116). The investigators may, when interrogating a criminal suspect, record the sound or image of the interrogation (CPL amend. 2012 art. 121).

Criminal defense system have been dramatically improved, while legal aid is enhanced. In the long run, the difficulties for the defense counsels lie in meeting, corresponding with the criminal suspect or accused in custody, as well as adducing related evidence. In this CPL, lawyers can be entrusted as defenders during the period of investigation. If the defense lawyer holding a lawyer's practice certificate, a certificate issued by a law firm or an official letter issued by the legal aid agency requests to meet the criminal suspect or accused, the detention center shall arrange the interview within 48 hours (CPL amend. 2012 art. 37, para. 2). The defense lawyer shall not be monitored when meeting the criminal suspect or the accused (CPL amend. 2012 art. 37, para. 4). The right of the defense counsel to access the file record is ensured. During the phase of examining the case for prosecution and trial, the defense counsel can consult, extract, and duplicate the file record of the current case. The applied subjects of legal aid are extended to those who might be sentenced to life imprisonment but have not entrusted any defenders. Also, the applicable time for legal aid has extended the investigation period. The police, procuratorate, and court have the legal aid center informed to provide defense for the related subjects.

This round of revisions involves the reform of the trial system. Special procedures were added: Procedure for minors, Reconciliation procedure, and Procedure for Confiscation of Illegal Proceeds arising from cases in which the Criminal Suspect or the Accused Escapes or is Deceased, and Procedure for Compulsory Medical Treatment of Mental Patients who are free from criminal responsibility.

With the development of the case load, various approaches were worked out to divert cases. For example, in this CPL, the summary procedure was extended to cases over which the basic court has jurisdiction while the accused admits his own guilt, from those cases of public prosecution where the accused may be lawfully sentenced to fixed-term imprisonment of not more than three years, criminal detention, public surveillance, or punished with fines exclusively.

In order to ensure the fairness of trial, the scope of cases for the second instance trial that will conduct open court sessions were clarified (CPL amend. 2012 art. 223): 1 Appeal cases in which the accused or the private prosecutor and his legal representative dissented from the facts and evidence determined in the first instance, which may affect the conviction and punishment of the crime; 2 appeal cases in which the accused has been sentenced to death; 3 cases against which the people's procuratorate files a protest; and 4 other cases that shall be tried in an open court.

In order to avoid repeated retrial and to finalize the case, the following provision was added: If the facts in the original judgment were unclear or the evidence insufficient, if the court which originally tried the case makes a new judgment with respect to the remanded case, if the accused files an appeal or the procuratorate lodges a protest, if the court of second instance makes a judgment or written order in accordance with law, and shall not remand the case to the court which originally tried the case for retrial (CPL amend. 2012 art. 225, para. 2).

The principle of reformatio in peius has been confirmed. If a case is remanded by the court of second instance to the court which originally tried the case, unless there are new facts of crime or the procuratorate adds supplementary prosecution, the court which originally tried the case may not increase the criminal responsibility of the accused either (CPL amend. 2012 art. 226, para. 2).

The incidental civil procedure has been improved as well. If the victim is deceased or loses his capability of conduct, the legal representative or close relative thereof shall have the right to bring an incidental civil action (CPL amend. 2012 art. 99, para. 1). The plaintiff of an incidental civil action or procuratorate may apply to the court for measures for preservation (CPL amend. 2012 art. 100). In hearing a case of an incidental civil action, the court may conduct an intermediation or render a judgment or ruling according to the material losses (CPL amend. 2012 art. 101).

In order to apply the death penalty seriously and ensure the quality of death penalty review cases, the legal supervision upon the death penalty review

118 Chinese Criminal Procedure System in Contrast

procedure was emphasized (CPL amend. 2012 art. 239). The Supreme Court can remand the case for retrial or change the verdict. Meanwhile, the Supreme Court, in reviewing death penalty cases, must interrogate the accused and hear opinions from the defense counsel if the latter request. In the process of death penalty reviews, the Supreme Procuratorate can address its opinion to the Supreme Court. The Supreme Court shall inform the Supreme Procuratorate of the outcome of death penalty review (CPL amend. 2012 art. 240).

The supervision of the procuratorate was strengthened and improved. Firstly, the content of supervision was broadened. In the 1996 CPL, the supervision was manifested in four aspects: Filing of the case, investigation, trial, and execution. This revision retrieved the original function of socialist procuratorate. The scope of supervision was enlarged. For example, in reviewing death penalty cases, the Supreme People's Procuratorate can address opinions to the Supreme People's Court. And the latter shall inform the former of the result of the death penalty review (CPL amend. 2012 art. 240). For those special procedures, supervision is not absent as well. For example, the procuratorate shall conduct supervision over the decision and implementation of compulsory medical treatment (CPL amend. 2012 art. 289).

In the long run, the measures and effects of supervision conducted by the procuratorate were lacking. In the present revision, additional means were added. For example, in order to implement exclusionary rules and strengthen investigatory supervision, the following articles were added: when the procuratorate receives a case, accusation or report, or finds that any investigator has collected evidence by illegal means, it shall conduct an investigation and check. If the circumstances are true, it shall put forward its opinions on correction; if a crime is constituted, criminal responsibility shall be investigated (CPL amend. 2012 art. 55). It actually enriched the preliminary step to supervision. In other words, the supervision procedure is better articulated. The power to know and investigate facts must be ensured before supervision can be exercised.

Meanwhile, in order to change the retardation of supervision in legal practice and ensure information sharing the legislation clarified that the related agencies must inform the procuratorate of the related conducts and decisions. For example, the prison and the detention house shall send the copy of the temporary service of sentence outside prison to the procuratorate. If the procuratorate considers the temporary service of sentence outside prison improper, it shall within one month from the date of receiving the notification, submit its recommendation in writing to the organ that decided or approved the temporary service of the sentence outside prison, which shall, upon receiving the written recommendation of the people's procuratorate, re-examine its decision immediately (CPL amend. 2012 art. 256).

Certain compulsory provisions were provided. For example, after the criminal suspect or accused has been arrested, the procuratorate shall continue to examine the necessity of the detainment. If there is no need to continue the detainment, it

Chinese Criminal Procedure System in Contrast **119**

shall make a suggestion to release the criminal suspect or change another compulsory measure. Relevant agencies shall notify the procuratorate of the disposal results within ten days (CPL amend. 2012 art. 93).

Statutorily and theoretically, the procuratorate is not only the prosecution agency but also the supervisory agency to safeguard the national statute. Therefore, the procuratorate shall properly deal with the relationship between the prosecution service and supervision service, make efforts to ensure the administration of justice, and protect the legitimate rights and interests of the criminal suspects, accused and defenders. For example, in order to protect the legal rights of the defenders, it is stipulated that when the defender or agent ad litem deems that the public security agency, the procuratorate or the court and their personnel obstruct the performance of his litigation rights, he shall have the right to file an appeal or accusation with the people's procuratorate at the same level or next higher. The procuratorate shall examine the appeal or accusation without delay. If the situation is true, it shall notify the agency concerned to make corrections (CPL amend. 2012 art. 47).

In China, criminal procedure institutions are not confined to the CPL; it includes also the rules enacted by the supreme justice agencies, such as the Supreme People's Court (SPC), the Supreme People's Procuratorate, the Ministry of Public Security, the Ministry of Justice, as well as the Ministry of National Security. Take the judicial explanations enacted by the SPC as an example: the SPC has an unusually broad power of creating judicial explanation. The term "judicial explanation" refers to certain judicial documents issued by the SPC for the purpose of clarifying the vagueness of legislative provisions. Such judicial explanations are different from the replies that are issued by the Supreme People's Court of the PRC. The replies are made to respond to questions posed by lower people's courts. These replies are not generally binding in other cases; however, such replies will occasionally be referred to in cases in similar situations. The judicial explanations issued by the SPC are regarded as binding supplements of the promulgated laws, hence a source of law in and of themselves. In this respect, Chinese judges do enjoy limited legislation power in the Chinese legal system. These judicial explanations are instructions that are not only about concrete issues arising from trials, but also on how to understand and apply laws in general terms even before any trial. Such general interpretations may even rewrite the legislation. In practice, these interpretations have played a very important role to remedy defective or outdated legislation – are indeed an institutional innovation in terms of form. It is actually a specification of institution in order to meet the need of organic context of criminal procedure.

6.6 Criminal Procedure Systems with Chinese Characteristics: Institutional Innovations

Given the history of Chinese Criminal Procedure Law, scholars may claim that every jurisdiction has its own characteristics. But many scholars also think that it is

120 Chinese Criminal Procedure System in Contrast

just a bureaucratic justification. The Chinese system may, in fact, be similar to every transitional regime with the western system as its point of reference. There may be certain contextual innovations but in general it is still based on the western system. Taking Chinese government propaganda into consideration, the Chinese characteristics may not make sense in reality. It is very noticeable that when Chinese officials are proclaiming their main policies in almost all social fields, they would always refer to the maxim "socialism with Chinese characteristics," which was initiated by Chinese reform leader Deng as fundamental guidance to the nation. Government communication is referred to as "a socialist legal system with Chinese characteristics." Chinese Communists have persistently striven to integrate Marxist practice in China and adapt it to Chinese conditions.

What are these Chinese characteristics? There are certain institutional innovations due to the influence of legal traditions, and we will examine these innovations based on ideologies and basic principles. Ideologies reflect not only legislative context but also determine how it is practiced in reality. The Chinese CPL (also true for most codes in China) includes general principles and specific chapters. The specific systems must follow the basic principles. These two parts constitute the institution of criminal procedure in China. However, law in action may deviate from the law in books. The systems will be discussed after the principles are examined. There are certain creative legal practices that have not been clearly denoted in the CPL, and these will be counted as institutional innovations in China. Ideologically, we would argue that paternalism and reform are Chinese characteristics. Division of powers, coordination and mutual restriction, legal supervision from the procuratorate, justice agencies' independence, substantive truth, relying on the masses, and death penalty review are the exemplified principles with Chinese characteristics. Here we demonstrate their unique peculiarities.

6.6.1 Ideologies

Ideology is a comprehensive set of normative beliefs, conscious and unconscious ideas that an individual, a group or a society has. We are not going to take a normative lens to evaluate institutional design in China's criminal procedure. But if principles and rules themselves can be seen from a phenomenal perspective, taking a descriptive lens to summarize them is possible. The principles and rules are neither good nor bad. As institutions with Chinese characteristics, they must be representative for empirical analysis.

We will not use tradition as a metaphor, as well as socialist or capitalist, Confucian or legalist categories, as they are not quite related to the criminal procedure institution itself. These are useful in terms of explaining general law or beyond; however, criminal procedure has a rather technical branch of rules. We would propose more properly guided ideologies for this field. As we explained that Chinese legal platform provided preadaptation for socialist law transplantation where civilian law was the original text and context, traditional Chinese law and

Soviet-styled socialist law shared the same institutional ideology, i.e. paternalism. Again, socialist law is born through revolution. During the past 40 years, Chinese domestic leaders consistently emphasized reform in many different areas. Thus, reform is a fundamental ideology for Chinese criminal procedure. Compared with specific systems, these ideologies demonstrate more contextual sense, not only providing general guidance to the application of legal institutions, but also potentially influencing legal actions regarding criminal procedure.

6.6.1.1 Paternalism

Although institutional paternalism might have been first created in the western legal treatises, it can also be used to describe the peculiar thought for Chinese criminal procedure. We would not say that Chinese criminal procedure is more inquisitorial than European ones, but once the socialist elements are merged into the inquisitorial basis, the characteristics in general turn out to be institutionally paternalistic. This is embedded in a tradition mixed with Confucian-legalist mentality and socialist legality. This can be shown either in text or in context. In England, where liberalism prevails in institutional ideologies, criminal procedure is seen as the basis for the individual to fight against the government, thus a guarantee for the accused against abuse of power by the criminal justice agencies in the process. Compared to the function of weapon against the state for English criminal procedure, Chinese criminal procedure is seen as a guidance for the criminal justice agencies to handle the case. It is clear that article 2 of the CPL stipulates that one of the objectives of the Criminal Procedure Law is to safeguard the socialist legal system, and to ensure smooth socialist construction. It is not strange, as stated in the Marxist doctrine, law is not a self-contained objective system but a coercive "order" or instrument for the ruling class to control the state.

In terms of syntax and style, the Chinese criminal procedure is programmatic and moralistic. In terms of text, active verbs and dynamic sentence structure contrast sharply with the predominant use of nouns, passive verbs of western European texts (Berman, Cohen, & Russell, 1982). The style of sentences used in the CPL cannot be divorced from the Chinese autocratic tradition. Actually, apart from the textuality, China has a long tradition of fu-mu-guan ideology (loosely translated as parent-like government officials), a real legacy of historical civilization. For many centuries, the combination of Confucianism and legalism contributed to criminal proceedings combining leniency with severity, further resulting in a stability unmatched elsewhere in the world (Head, 2011). From Han law to Ch'ing law, criminal proceedings demonstrate a flexibility and tendency for the government to maintain social stability. Certain degrees of tolerance and social harmony were encouraged unless the emperor's jurisdiction was threatened (Hulsewé, 1955). The procedure became as centralized as the government bureaucracy.

Though nowadays the duties toward the socialist state substitute for the duties assigned by the emperor, political control and social harmony must be similarly ensured (Head, 2011). Mao saw law as a suppressive instrument against enemies of the people. Deng saw that the main purpose of law was to maintain social order. In Marxist doctrine, law is seen as being determined exclusively by its political function, since law is created and enacted by the state. Thus, criminal procedure is a coercive "order" or instrument for the ruling class to control the state, "holding down and exploiting the oppressed class," and "safeguarding the interests of the ruling class and the state." It is the process used by agencies working on behalf of the governing class to legitimize and implement punishment in order to maintain order. It is not automatically shaped and articulated, but is enacted and compulsorily enforced by the sovereignty. It has a strong sociopoietic sense. In documents related to criminal justice practice and implementation, socialist jargon such as "implementing criminal procedure law to guarantee the construction of socialist country" is also prominent (Wei, 2000). Such language shows in a straightforward way the programmatic and instrumentalist features of the CPL.

Admittedly, apart from coercive or oppressive elements, there are certain educational and supporting elements embedded in the institution. These elements may come from fu-mu-guan ideology derived from traditional Chinese law. They may also come from socialist ideology. The example is that the function of educating the masses is still upheld in criminal procedure law; one of the stated aims of the CPL is to enhance the citizen's awareness of the need to abide by the law and to fight vigorously against criminal acts. China seems to recognize the importance of this process as an educative tool in commencing the reindoctrination of the offender; the sanctioning phase is supplementary and not the sole instrument of this purpose because there is a heavier emphasis on fighting against crimes and ensuring social stability. It may impair the rights of criminal suspects to a fair trial in practice.

Chinese society is hierarchically organized with power flowing mostly from the top down (Ingraham, 1987). Criminal procedure in China is not only regulatory but, in most cases, an attempt to reconcile the citizen who violates the law with the proper observance of his civic duties (Ingraham, 1987). A great emphasis is placed on rehabilitation, which is conceived of as expiation through labor and reindoctrination of the errant individual to believe in the flaws of his past mode of thinking and behavior, and to seek to conform to the socialist morality, thereby restoring himself to his former position in the community. The relationship between citizen and state, particularly in criminal proceedings, is extremely paternalistic and has deep contextual roots in Chinese history.

This results in a rather managerial version of criminal procedure text. The twofold purpose of the 1979 CPL, according to Jianfu Chen, was "to elaborate the constitutional provisions regarding the division of powers and responsibilities among the people's courts, the people's procuratorates and the public security organs, and to provide working procedures for criminal adjudication" (Chen, 2012, pp. 78–79). It is not an obstacle for the accused to prevent the justice agency from suppressing its rights. From this principle, the CPL is originally not for the accused and the defendant, but for the justice agencies to comprehensively deal with cases.

6.6.1.2 Reform

As David and Brierley claimed, the originality of socialist law lies in its revolutionary nature, in which a socialist order and collectivized economic structure were expected to be formed under the guidance of the Communist Party (David & Brierley, 1985). This revolutionary nature increases the plurality of the legal institutions, as the law is changing always so that many rules are maintained in accordance with early Sino-Marxism. According to Mao's Thought, law is arbitrary in so far as it is treated not as inviolable canon but as a set of codes in constant need of reformation in order to aid the development of socialism. The criminal procedure law was revised frequently and demonstrates more sociopoietic and contextualized features. It reflects the dramatic change in Chinese society, and at the same time demonstrates the revolutionary nature of socialist legal institutions. The revision of law indicates progressivism. This progressivism is not only from international pressure or comparison but also from the reform itself as an ideology. The reform is partly government-led, partly pressured by local experience. This reform is not only sociopoietic in context but also an inherent, self-evident demand, a kind of autopoietic need for all leadership and citizens. In a way, changing is a compulsive institution itself.

Admittedly, English criminal procedure has been changing as well. Over the long period of time when common law was developing, up to the 19th century when dramatic legislative reforms were undertaken, the principal focus of the English lawyer and commentators – including jurists of the sort described more fully below – was on the procedure, not on substance or principle (Head, 2011). In a sense, both laws were modernized. English criminal procedure was modernized because of codification. In that setting, the substance of the law, which is "to adopt the striking phrase of Sir Henry Maine (1822–1888)," appeared to have been "secreted in the interstices of procedure," and indeed the common law did not appear to be a system attempting to bring justice as a conglomeration of designed procedures, in more and more cases, to achieve solutions to dispute (David & Brierley, 1985).

Chinese criminal procedure has been reformed and became more elaborate as shown above. Apart from two major revisions, the Chinese CCP is currently leading a profound and rapid reform of criminal justice under the guidance of "four comprehensives," i.e. trial-centered procedural system reform, which focuses mainly on criminal procedure. China's criminal procedure is changing from investigation-centered to trial-centered, though it is still in experimental and test stages. In order to improve the judicial systems, pilot projects are promoted for separating the adjudication and enforcement powers. Criminal enforcement

124 Chinese Criminal Procedure System in Contrast

systems are reformed to unify. Reform systems for management of judicial bodies' personnel and finances are advocated. A separation between judicial administrative matters and the adjudication or procuratorate powers in the courts and procuratorates is now being explored and implemented. In criminal proceedings, there are many experiments in improving systems for leniency for admitting guilt and accepting punishment. The case-handling responsibility system for presiding judges, collegial panels, head procurators, and lead investigators is improved to implement a system where the person handling the cases bears responsibility. Certain revisions may lack credibility and careful consideration – for example, the supervision committee will take over the power of investigating duty crimes originally owned by the procuratorate.

With regard to the process of criminal justice, it is believed that CPL will face a new revision. It is difficult to anticipate the direction of the new criminal procedure, but it is certain that reforms and changes will continue as reform is a fundamental ideology for the socialist legal institutions, especially for Chinese jurisdiction where reform has always been advocated. During the reform process, inter-transposability and intertextuality will continue as the thickly interwoven layers of text upon text. All rules seems to be improvisational, even though they have been founding texts. It calls for much hermeneutic explanation in order to lend coherence to these myriad rules.

6.6.2 Basic Principles

6.6.2.1 Division of Powers, Coordination and Mutual Restriction

As is provided by the general part of the CPL as well as the constitution,[7] the principle of division, coordination and supervision among police, procuratorate and court, illustrated how these three relational agencies interact with each other in criminal proceedings. Division of duties means that agencies can neither exercise their authority beyond legal boundary nor replace each other. Coordination of works means that agencies need to adjust their activities accordingly under the common goal of attacking crimes and protecting the society. Furthermore, there are various joint committees of the procuratorate and judiciary, whose functions are to discuss and determine serious cases and other difficult issues. Mutual supervision means they can restrain each other, suggest their own opinions to other agencies, and take precautions against undesirable deviations by the other agencies, and require them to correct existing errors, no matter whether they are harmful or harmless. Notably, the final objective of mutual checks is to ensure the correct and effective enforcement of law. It can be seen in the following circumstances: 1 The police checks refusal to arrest by the procuratorate (CPL art. 90); 2 the police checks non-initiation of prosecution by the procuratorate (CPL art. 174); 3 the procuratorate checks the case filed for investigation by the police (CPL art. 109); 4 the procuratorate checks illegalities by the police in their investigatory activities (CPL art. 98); 5 the procuratorate checks salient errors in a judgment or order of first instance made by the court (CPL art. 216), and so on. The relationships amongst three agencies seem to be partly determined. However, the decentralized structural arrangement may imply a flexible network model of management of the case.

This principle originated from counter-revolutionary experience in the early Communist Regime. To a certain extent, this institution had already been predetermined by the political context. During the campaign, the court, the procuratorate, and the police served together as an "important weapon to establish people's democratic dictatorship" (Central Committee of CPC, 1992) against class enemies. After the PRC was founded, the threefold bureaucracy of police, court, and procuratorate, was embedded in the principle of division, coordination and supervision. Li Lin, the then secretary of the Council of Political and Legal Affairs, derived the expression of "coordination of work and mutual supervision among police, procuratorate, and court" (Wang, 2008) from the Marxist dialectical method that regarded nature as "a connected and integral whole, in which things, phenomena, are organically connected with, dependent on, and determined by each other" (Commission of the CC of the CPSU, 1939). This principle was accepted by the Party's Central Committee on March 12, 1954. After legal anarchy in the Anti-rightist Movement, the Great Leap Forward and the Cultural Revolution, this principle was resumed in the 1979 CPL.

This principle can be used to restrict the problems of the prevailing bureaucratic culture by multi-directional control. We will not deny the function of "mutual checking" amongst criminal justice agencies for motivating compliance with the rules. However, there is a significant possibility that the legislators tacitly evade stipulating procedural consequences in criminal procedure and therefore merely enact elastic communicative mechanisms to resolve procedural disputes. Under this circumstance, procedural deficiencies are not solved by a hierarchical legal process, but through compromising, creating a relatively autopoietic platform. The principle of division, coordination and supervision has shaped a relational structure of criminal authority that is different from its counterparts in continental law jurisdictions or the Soviet Union. Instead of focusing on a sole center like the court or prosecution service, judicial authority in China's criminal procedure is evenly distributed among the police, procuratorate and court, creating multiple power centers in a horizontal structure of authority. And this unique structure is deeply rooted in China's history of justice practice. This principle is rather solid and has been regarded as a genuine Chinese creation. Admittedly, we cannot ignore the context that all three agencies are led by the Party. Due to the unified leadership and hierarchical order of the Party, mutual checks must be prevailed by mutual cooperation in terms of network arrangement. The reality of intertextuality results in the fact that the principle needs to be reinterpreted according to the Party text and inner-Party institutions.

126 Chinese Criminal Procedure System in Contrast

6.6.2.2 Legal Supervision from the Procuratorate

In China, the general functions and duties of public procurators are: 1 To supervise the enforcement of laws according to law; 2 to mount a public prosecution on behalf of the state; 3 to investigate criminal cases directly accepted by the people's procuratorates as provided by law; and 4 other functions and duties as provided by the law. Beyond the context of criminal law, the procuratorate also has a wide range of responsibilities. "Remarkable" (Zweigert & Kötz, 1998, pp. 324–325) to western eyes is the procuratorate, which is empowered by general legal supervision rather than simply the prosecution function in criminal procedure (CPL art. 8). While the English Crown Prosecution Service and the PRC's procuratorate are all the same in terms of prosecuting criminal cases, the procuratorate in the PRC is also an organ of legal supervision.

The historical evolution of the procuratorate of China was built on the model of the Soviet version of the Prokuraturar, an institution that was created in 1722 in czarist Russia by Peter the Great to serve as "the eyes of the Czar" (Castellucci, 2007). On the basis of the czarist prosecutor, Lenin created hierarchical procuratorates to carry out legal supervision (Shi & Guo, 2003), by virtue of which the procurator can ensure adherence to socialist legality throughout the entire state administration, including the courts and investigatory agencies (Zweigert & Kötz, 1998). Under the Legal Supervision Theory of Leninism, the procuratorate was the supreme agency in Soviet criminal institutions that exercised direct leadership over the investigative body. Its Chinese counterpart, however, was primitive when compared to the integral and powerful police. Consequently, the following legal reform was guided by pragmatism. By intentionally misinterpreting the vertical leadership of the Soviet model as horizontal coordination and supervision, the reformers sought to lower the threshold of reform through compromise. This might have resulted from the fact that the transplanted text must adapt to the local environment.

Among its responsibilities, the procuratorate supervises the work of justice agencies to ensure that no errors are made in the administration of justice. In exercising the supervision of enforcement of laws, the procuratorates are given the right to supervise criminal proceedings, to supervise the investigatory activities of public security organs, to supervise the court's compliance with litigation procedure, to exercise judicial supervision, and to supervise the execution of criminal punishments. If the procuratorate establishes an illegality or irregularity, it may file a complaint against the relevant body which must immediately cease the unlawful act until the matter has been reconsidered. If the body ultimately rejects the complaint, the procurator may protest against the refusal to the superior authority of the body and, ultimately, the procurator may bring criminal or civil proceedings against an offender. As part of its function in judicial supervision, the procuratorate can protest against any illegal or unfounded judicial decisions and ultimately reverse the judgment. Thus in criminal procedure, the procuratorate is widely seen as possessing elements of what would be the judicial power in the west. Alongside this, it also serves as an ombudsman in the criminal justice system and beyond.

6.6.2.3 Justice Agencies' Independence

In the western world, judicial independence is always emphasized and interpreted as justice personnel's own independence. Westerners are accustomed to think that the legal system is primarily a social institution within which people can make claims against other persons and have these resolved by a neutral trier of fact and law (Jones, 1994, pp. 4–8). In the western legal tradition, the legal arena is clearly distinguishable from the political arena, and demonstrates more autopoietic characteristics. Criminal process turns out to be technical in nature. It is well-known that in England, at the time of Sir Edward Coke, the king was denied participation in the adjudication process of his court on the theory that he lacked professional legal training.

In China, however, independence is also referred to but as an independence of organization rather than the judge or prosecutor's personal independence. It is stipulated in article 5 of the CPL that people's courts shall exercise judicial powers independently in accordance with law, and people's procuratorates shall exercise procuratorial powers independently in accordance with law, without interference by any government authority, social organization, or individual. It is worth mentioning here that independence in China is different from the western version of judicial independence, as the latter is an important pillar of power separation, and a key element of political organization. In China, it is a working rule rather than a political principle. It emphasizes the performance of the courts and procuratorates to be free from illegal interference. If opinions differ when a collegial panel conducts its deliberations, a decision shall be made in accordance with the opinion of the majority, but the opinions of the minority shall be entered in the record. The record of the deliberations shall be signed by the members of the collegial panel (CPL art. 179). After the hearings and deliberations, the collegial panel shall render a judgment. With respect to a difficult, complex or major case, in which the collegial panel considers it difficult to make a decision, the collegial panel shall refer the case to the president of the court for him to decide whether to submit the case to the judicial committee for discussion and decision. The collegial panel shall execute the decision of the judicial committee (CPL art. 180).

The term "interference" refers to conduct amounting to illegal interference, such as replacing laws with personal orders, suppressing the authority of laws by personal powers, and demanding the submission of courts or procuratorates to personal orders. By contrast, suggestion or guidance within the scope of an official's responsibilities is not referred to as "interference" in this context. Judicial work is also under the legal supervision of the Supreme People's Procuracy.

128 Chinese Criminal Procedure System in Contrast

Procuracy is defined in the constitution as the legal supervisory organ of the state. Once a procuracy protests a decision, the court is bound to reconsider the case. Under the constitution, the so-called judicial independence refers to only the independence of the relevant people's court, not the individual judges. Hence, inside the people's court, a judge may be subordinated to his division head, the president and vice president of the court, and the Trial Supervision Committee as the supervising organ to review all the complicated or high-impact cases. As a result, the institutional design makes it difficult for the courts and judges to be truly independent from the influence of other organs and individuals.

This limitation of independence can be traced to the tradition which regards law and legal systems as subservient instruments of state policy. Historically, justice is not regarded as being independent. It was subordinated to the administrative power of the leader who can dispose all serious cases in his jurisdiction. A unified power was advocated so that counterrevolutionaries may be easily defeated. Even after the new-democratic period has passed, a unified direction for the whole society is still being advocated. Also, a collective culture constitutes dominant factors in shaping the structure of justice agencies. These factors result in this organizational independence. Constitutionally, the courts fall under the supervision of the People's Congress. Since the late 1990s, in response to increased judicial corruption, some congresses at the provincial level have instituted a mechanism to supervise the courts more directly. The involvement of the people's congresses in criminal justice is not directly prescribed by the CPL, insofar as it is a legislative body.

Under the constitutional principle of "Democratic Centralism," the People's Congress has a general authority of "supervising the government, court, and procuratorate at the corresponding level" pursuant to constitutional law and organic law. Consistent with the trait of legal pluralism of socialist law, the local people's congresses, since the 1980s, have been gradually strengthening and elaborating this authority in criminal justice by pioneering a series of creative supervisory measures. These sociopoietic systems created by local congresses include ping-yi (appraisal) of judicial activities, zhi-fa jian-cha (examination of law enforcement), ge-an jian-du (supervision of individual cases), cuo-an ze-ren zhui-jiu-zhi (the system of ascribing responsibility for misjudged case), and so on. While ping-yi and zhi-fa jian-cha are chiefly aimed at general work conducted by justice agencies, the other two measures focus on individual cases. Some of these efforts are partly institutionalized by the relevant article in the supervision law. Nowadays, most local congresses use these supervisory tools to force the criminal justice agencies to correct any misconduct and to punish the relevant personnel. The supervisory power of people's congresses has thus already considerably encroached on the administration of justice so that it is necessary to categorize this legislative body as one of the criminal justice agencies.

The methods they used can place a court's operations under the systematic scrutiny of legislative deputies. It cannot be denied that the Party can get involved in certain criminal justice issues. Criminal justice agencies, as segments of the socialist state, will work together in many cases under the leadership of the Party. To expand control of criminal justice agencies and judicial bureaus of government, zheng-fa-wei (the Political and Legislative Affairs Committee of the Party) was created in the 1980s (Lou, 1997). It is a crucial agency as final decision-makers or coordinators in resolving criminal disputes. It is clear that criminal procedure institutions may suffer various external influence, being hardly autonomous and independent.

6.6.2.4 Substantive Truth

Justice is impossible without truth. In Chinese criminal evidence institutions, as part of the criminal procedure, substantive truth is preferred rather than legal truth. This is indicated by materialism in Marx's theory. The doctrine of historical materialism creates a strong emphasis on discovering the objective truth in criminal proceedings. China's emphasis on substance far outweighed emphasis on procedure. Truth is regarded as being more important than other values in the Chinese context of criminal procedure. This results in certain peculiar phenomena compared with English and other western countries' criminal procedures. Unlike the passive empire for the judge, in China, the judiciary still have the right or responsibility to investigate and clarify the facts. Chinese criminal procedure does not provide the accused the right to advice or counsel at the time of his initial interrogation, and does not provide the accused person the right to remain silent, either during that interrogation or at the time of his trial.

Thus, for example, the doctrine of double jeopardy, or non bis in idem, is rejected. Consequently, finding the truth has been always the prevailing value pursued in criminal procedure with much less regard for finality. While the judgment of a court of second instance is announced to be final, nevertheless, there is a specific section of the CPL called "trial supervision," through which a judgment with the force of res judicata through a concluded appeal may yet be revised by higher courts. Moreover, a request to reconsider any final judgment, including those issued by the Supreme Court, may be made by the procuratorate, as explained above, or by the Supreme Court itself. Regarding criminal evidence, historical materialism results in the emphasis being on obtaining objective truth rather than satisfying rules of evidential discovery. All materials that may be used to prove the facts of a case are evidence (CPL art. 48). The CPL contains no features of substantial criminal evidence law, e.g. rules of admissibility, which constrains truth-finding. This demonstrates again the unconstrained pursuit of the truth in criminal procedure.

The presumption of innocence principle has not been adequately applied in China. The burden of proof is on the accused, who has the duty to cooperate with the state in the revelation of the truth if he is innocent. He does not enjoy the right of silence as the English accused may have. The accused is encouraged

130 Chinese Criminal Procedure System in Contrast

to truthfully confess to the investigators. An important criminal policy is that a criminal suspect who confessed his offences truthfully may be treated mercifully. Those who do not confess, reveal truthful information, or who want to conceal certain facts from the investigators, may be treated severely. The court, procuratorate and public security authority shall have the authority to gather or require the submission of evidence from the relevant entities and individuals. The relevant entities and individuals shall provide true evidence (CPL art. 52). Any person who has information regarding a case has the obligation to testify (CPL art. 60).

6.6.2.5 Relying on the Masses

The mass line has been an important policy in every aspect in China. In terms of criminal procedure, it has been implemented not only now but also during the legal anarchy period. It may be demonstrated in the different forms of institutions; the so-called "relying on the masses" refers to the people's courts, the people's procuratorates, and the public security organs for criminal proceedings, and should adhere to the mass line and the mass viewpoint, and should rely on the wisdom and strength of the masses. In order to complete the tasks stipulated in the criminal procedure law, "relying on the masses" is the expression of "citizen participation" in the context of China. It is stipulated in article 6 of the CPL that people's courts, people's procuratorates, and public security organs must rely on the masses for criminal proceedings. This provision can be referred to as the "relying on the masses" principle. The reasons for relying on the masses as the basic principle are as follows: 1 It is determined by the nature of the socialist country under the people's democratic dictatorship of our country; 2 it is a fine tradition maintained by our public security and judicial work for a long time; and 3 it can inform the people of the process of criminal activities through education, training, and experience, thus mobilizing the masses to actively fight against illegal and criminal acts. At the same time, this is to establish and maintain good social order fundamentally, preventing and reducing crime.

The criminal justice agencies in China seem peculiar to observers from common law and civil law jurisdictions. It almost goes without saying that the label "people" or "comrades" precedes the name of all organizations, such as People's Public Security Organ (police), People's Procuratorate and People's Court, and this of course demonstrates the ideological force of socialist legality. "Popular justice" conducted on a massive scale at the grass-roots level during the Cultural Revolution temporarily broke down even preliminary socialist legality. Though there might not be fixed institutions regulating popular justice, it has certain routinely pronounced features when it is put into practice. The recent uproar in the Yu Huan case is also a manifestation of the people's wishes: precisely because of the people's participation, Huan's sentence changed from the first trial of life imprisonment into a term of imprisonment for five years.[8] The participation of citizens, the process and results of litigation impact, because many citizens were of superposition and of individual power, can create strong public opinion and social pressure, rendering the public security and judicial organs unable to ignore the surging wishes of the people. Arguably, the context of popular democracy provides solid soil for practicing less institutionalized popular justice.

Nevertheless, in the Frame-c sense, the current criminal procedure law provides some provisions for citizens to participate in criminal proceedings. These institutions can be broadly divided into two general relational categories. One is assisted participation: some of this assistance is reflected in helping public security and judicial organs to advance criminal proceedings. For example, citizens rather than lawyers can be entrusted as defenders.[9] As a fugitive, escapee, or "wanted" person, any citizen can be immediately sent to the public security organs, people's procuratorate or the people's court; any unit or individual finding the facts of a crime or a criminal suspect has the right and obligation to report to the public security organs, people's procuratorate or the people's court. Some serve as the presence or witness: for example, at the time of the search, there should be a search party, or his family, neighbors or other witnesses present, while others are supervised by the presence.

Another is the participation of decision-making. In trying cases, people's courts shall apply the people's assessor system in accordance with this law (CPL art. 13). People's assessors are, by being seated with the professional judges, regarded as having equal importance with them. Trials of cases of first instance in the Primary and Intermediate People's Courts are conducted by a collegial panel composed of three judges, or of judges and people's assessors totaling three; this is called a collegial panel (Head, 2011; CPL art. 178). The Decision of the National People's Congress on People's Assessors sets out the qualifications for the people's assessors. They are granted equal rights with judges as collegial members, except that they cannot serve as presiding officers in trials. They can vote independently, request further discussion of the cases, and participate in the cases. The People's Assessor System in Chinese criminal procedure not only shows judicial democracy, and ensures judicial fairness, but also provides a good approach to strengthen the spread and education of legality. In order to strengthen the supervision of the people's procuratorate investigating crimes committed work, and to safeguard social fairness and justice, the Supreme People's Procuratorate instituted a system of people's supervisors. Generally speaking, the people's supervisor system also belongs to decision-making participation.

6.6.2.6 Death Penalty Review

China may have the largest figures for the death penalty, while the abolition of this capital punishment seems still to be a long way away, as it is embedded in the Chinese revenge culture context. By absorbing the merits of "Cautious Punishment" in ancient China[10] and "Autumn Trial" in the Ch'ing Dynasty,[11] China instituted the death penalty review procedure institution. It was used to reduce

132 Chinese Criminal Procedure System in Contrast

the wrongful killing and demonstrate the virtue of the monarchy. In the past, the provincial court could exercise this power, but on October 31, 2006, the death penalty review was retained by the Supreme People's Court. It demonstrates that China nowadays takes the death penalty more seriously. "Less killing" and "cautious killing" is the guiding principle for death penalty policy.

A case of first instance where the death sentence has been imposed by the intermediate people's court and the defendant does not appeal, shall be reviewed by the higher people's court and submitted to the Supreme People's Court for approval. If the higher people's court does not agree with the death sentence, it may bring the case up for trial or remand the case for retrial. Cases of first instance where the higher people's court has imposed the death sentence and the defendant does not appeal, and cases of second instance where the death sentence has been imposed shall all be submitted to the Supreme People's Court for approval (CPL art. 236). A case where the intermediate people's court has imposed a death sentence with a two-year suspension of execution, shall be subjected to approval by the higher people's court (CPL art. 237). Reviews by the Supreme People's Court of cases involving death sentences and reviews by the higher people's court of cases involving death sentences with a suspension of execution shall be conducted by collegial panels each composed of three judges (CPL art. 238). The panel shall approve or disapprove the decision. For those disapproved cases, the Supreme Court shall remand the case for retrial or change the decision directly (CPL art. 239).

In order to protect the right of life for the accused, the Supreme Court shall listen to opinions from the defense counsel if the latter put forward the request (CPL art. 240). When a judgment of the death penalty with immediate execution is pronounced or approved by the Supreme People's Court, the president of the Supreme People's Court shall sign and issue an order to execute the death sentence. If a criminal sentenced to death with a two-year suspension of execution commits no intentional offense during the period of suspension of the sentence, his punishment should therefore be commuted according to law on expiration of such period, and the executing organ shall submit a written recommendation to the higher people's court for an order. If there is verified evidence that the criminal has committed intentional offense, and his death sentence shall therefore be executed, the higher people's court shall submit the matter to the Supreme People's Court for examination and approval (CPL art. 250).

If it is discovered before the execution of the sentence that the judgment may contain an error or if, before the execution of the sentence, the criminal exposes major criminal factors rendering other significantly meritorious service, thus the sentence may need to be revised; or if the criminal is pregnant, the execution shall be suspended, and if it is a fact, the death penalty shall be altered (CPL art. 251). The people's court shall, before causing a death sentence to be executed, notify the people's procuratorate at the same level to send an officer to supervise the execution. If it is discovered before the execution that there may be an error, the execution shall be suspended and a report submitted to the Supreme People's Court for an order. The execution of the death sentence shall be announced but shall not be held in public. After a death sentence is executed, the court clerk on the scene shall prepare a written record of the execution. The people's court that caused the death sentence to be executed shall submit a report on the execution to the Supreme People's Court and notify the family members of the criminal (CPL art. 252). Due to the relative uniqueness of this subject, the related institutions, though being sociopoietic, demonstrate real Chinese characteristics in terms of text and context.

Being mindful of length, we have only listed a series of principles which underpin the specific systems. It shall be noted that there are many detailed innovations for criminal procedure institutions. For example, in terms of compulsory measures, custody is a normal practice while bail is an exception. This contrasts with English criminal procedure. Also, incidental civil action is quite continental, which is different from the separation between civil and criminal procedure. In terms of technical investigation measures, the formalities of approval in China might be easier than in the English case, though it is claimed that technical investigation measures must be implemented strictly according to the category, object of application and time limit approved (CPL art. 150). The method used for analyzing China's criminal procedure is primarily inductive. It is clear that our institutional work is still at the basic level. In any case, before evaluating a certain institution, it is at least necessary to work out how to describe it. A scanning approach is adopted to look at the rules and practice in a hermeneutic fashion.

6.7 Conclusion

There is a rationale to the institution of criminal law "with Chinese characteristics". Before analyzing the peculiarities of Chinese criminal procedure institutions, commonalities between Chinese criminal procedure and all other systems including the English ones must be considered. These commonalities include common phases for all criminal procedure and modern trends. In order to define the peculiarities, it is also necessary to understand the categories used in the criminal procedure area. Based on these concepts, debates regarding Confucius versus Weber, autopoietic versus sociopoietic, Frame-t versus Frame-c, and specification versus adaptation, were examined as they can be used to describe Chinese criminal procedure. The historical evolution of criminal procedure in China proves that these concepts do work and can be used to analyze the institution.

From a rather macroscopic perspective, Chinese criminal procedure institutions demonstrate a strong paternalism compared to the English ones. The traditional autocracy and socialist legality may jointly result in this institutional culture. Also, reform has been part and parcel of the history of Chinese criminal procedure. We may anticipate significant reform, no matter whether it has been

134 Chinese Criminal Procedure System in Contrast

scientifically and cautiously reviewed or not. In terms of principle, there are certain institutional innovations that may be distinct from other global legal systems. For example, division of powers, coordination and mutual restriction came from the combative ideology of the revolutionary period. It is quite different from the English checks-and-balances theory. Legal supervision from the procuratorate has a Soviet legacy but with Mao's own adaptations. The supervision is a peculiar but a real Chinese characteristic. Also criticized but still persistent is China's justice agencies' independence. Although China is sensitive to western criticism about the lack of judicial independence, it has its own explanation for the reason why China adapts its own collective responsibility institution. Reflecting the materialism advocated by Karl Marx, substantive truth rather than legal truth is the more widely applied standard in evidence law in China practice. As a socialist jurisdiction, relying on the masses rather than the legal elites is a demonstration of the people's democracy. People's assessors may be quite different from the English jurors, as they play a really symbolic and less important role in trying the case. Certainly, death penalty figures in China are as large as the sum of all other countries in the world, and the review process is also a unique institution across the world. All these innovations are analyzed in a broad institutional approach.

Notes

1 The original terms are "Common law family," "Romano-Germanic family," "family of Socialist laws" and "other systems" (David & Brierley, 1985).
2 The 36 Stratagems (in Chinese: *San-shiliu Ji*) are the representatives.
3 It means a dynamic procedure in order to achieve an aim without a strict adherence to a fixed sequence of steps planned in advance (Muhlemann, 2011).
4 CCP Central Committee Decision concerning Several Major Issues in Comprehensively Advancing Governance According to Law.
5 The same argument can be seen in western arguments (Verin, 1987).
6 For example, in northern China during the Liberalist War period, the principle of dividing powers and mutual checks amongst the public security agency and justice agencies was established (Xiong, 2006).
7 See art. 7 of CPL and art. 135 of Constitutional Law; the sentences in both articles are almost the same except that the conditions are slightly different in expression: the former is "in conducting criminal proceedings," but the latter is "in handling criminal cases."
8 *The South Weekend* reported in an article titled "stabbed the person who was affronting my mother," attracting the public's attention to the case of Yu Huan. The public could not be convinced that Yu Huan should be sentenced to life imprisonment for killing the person who was taking extremely harsh measures to affront Yu Huan's mother. After investing again carefully, the Senior People's Court of Shandong Province took the case to trial and made a final judgment. Yu Huan was finally sentenced to five years in prison. In this case, it is media supervision that promotes realization of justice and has a great effect on judicial credibility.
9 The defenders include lawyers; persons recommended by a public organization or the unit to which the criminal suspect or the defendant belongs; and guardians or relatives and friends of the criminal suspect or the defendant (CPL art. 32).

10 The ancient system of death penalty review began in the Han Dynasty. During the Northern Wei Dynasty, the emperor paid more attention to the death penalty. The system matured in the Sui and Tang Dynasties.
11 This system was inherited from the Ming Dynasty.

References

Berman, H.J., Cohen, S., & Russell, M. (1982). A comparison of the Chinese and Soviet Codes of Criminal Law and Procedure. *The Journal of Criminal Law and Criminology*, 73(1), 238–258.

Castellucci, I. (2007). Rule of law with Chinese characteristics. *Annual Survey of International & Comparative Law*, 13(1), 39–40.

Central Committee of CPC. (1992). Instruction on activities to suppress counter-revolutionaries. In Party Documents Research Center (Eds.), *Selected important documents since the founding of P. R. China*. Beijing: Zhongyang wenxian chubanshe.

Chen, A.H.Y. (1999). Confucian legal culture and its modern fate. In R. Wacks (Ed.), *The new legal order in Hong Kong* (pp. 505–533). Hong Kong: Hong Kong University Press.

Chen, J.H. (2012). A criminal justice system for a new millennium? In I. d'Hooghe & E.B. Vermeer (Eds.), *China's legal reforms and their political limits* (pp. 78–79). Hoboken: Taylor & Francis.

Chu, M. (2001). Criminal procedure reform in the People's Republic of China: The dilemma of crime control and regime legitimacy. *UCLA Pacific Basin Law Journal*, 18, 157.

Commission of the CC of the CPSU. (1939). *History of the Communist Party of the Soviet Union (Bolsheviks): Short course*. New York: International Publishers.

Damaška, M. (1973). Evidentiary barriers to conviction and two models of criminal procedure: A comparative study. *University of Pennsylvania Law Review*, 121, 3, 506–589.

Damaška, M. (1975). Structures of authority and comparative criminal procedure. *The Yale Law Journal*, 84(3), 480–544.

David, R., & Brierley, J.E.C. (1985). *Major legal systems in the world today: An introduction to the comparative study of law* (3rd Ed.). London: Stevens & Sons.

Garner, B.A., & Black, H.C. (2004). *Black's law dictionary* (8th Ed.). St. Paul, MN: Thomson West.

Head, J.W. (2011). *Great legal traditions: Civil law, common law and Chinese law in historical and operational perspective*. Durham, NC: Carolina Academic Press.

Hulsewé, A.F.P. (1955). *Remnants of Han law*. Leiden: E.J. Brill.

Ingraham, B.L. (1987). *The structure of criminal procedure: Laws and practice of France, the Soviet Union, China, and the United States*. New York: Greenwood Press.

Jones, W.C. (1994). *The great Qing code*. Oxford: Clarendon Press.

Lin, Y.H. (2005). *Criminal procedure law*. Beijing: China Renmin University Press.

Long, Z.Z. (1998). On form of criminal court trial in our country. *China Legal Science*, 4, 88–89.

Lou, Z. (1997). A study of the functions of the Party Committee and the Political and Legislative Affairs Committee of the Party. *Law Science Magazine*, 100, 28.

Lubman, S. (1991). Studying contemporary Chinese law: Limits, possibilities and strategy. *American Journal of Comparative Law*, 39, 299–300.

136 Chinese Criminal Procedure System in Contrast

Marsh, R.M. (2000). Weber's misunderstanding of traditional Chinese law. *The American Journal of Sociology*, 106, 281.

Mattei, U. (1997). Three patterns of law: Taxonomy and change in the world's legal systems. *American Journal of Comparative Law*, 45, 12.

McCabe, E.J. (1989). Structural elements of contemporary criminal justice in the People's Republic of China. In R.J. Troyer, J.P. Clark, & D.G. Rojek (Eds.), *Social control in the People's Republic of China*. New York: Praeger Publishers.

Muhlemann, G. (2011). China's multiple legal traditions: An overview. In M. Tomasek, & G. Muhlemann (Eds.), *Interpretation of law in China – Roots and perspectives*. Prague: Karolinum Press.

Packer, H.L. (1964). Two models of the criminal process. *University of Pennsylvania Law Review*, 113, 1–64.

Peerenboom, R. (2003). The X-Files: Past and present portrayals of China's alien "legal system." *Washington University Global Studies Law Review*, 2, 37.

Shi, S., & Guo, L. (2003). Lenin's thinking on legal supervision and China's prosecution system. *Law and Social Development*, 54, 3–11.

Verin, J. (1987). Foreword. In B.L. Ingraham (Ed.). *The structure of criminal procedure: Laws and practice of France, the Soviet Union, China, and the United States*. New York: Greenwood Press.

Wang, G.W. (2008). Wang Guiwu's lecture on procuratorate. *China Procuratorate Press*, 429.

Wei, X. (2000). Revision and location on the new Criminal Procedure Law. *Legal Forum*, 15, 87–94.

Xiong, Q. (2006), Criminal procedure law in Mainland China: Past, present and future. In D. Tang & P. Wang (Eds), *The legal development of the Mainland, Taiwan, Hong Kong, and Macau*. Taibei: New Xuelin Publishing Ltd.

Yin, B., & Duff, P. (2010). Criminal procedure in contemporary China: Socialist, civilian or traditional? *International and Comparative Law Quarterly*, 59, 1099.

Zweigert, K., & Kötz, H. (1998). *An introduction to comparative law* (3rd Ed.), trans. T. Weir. Oxford: Clarendon Press.

Legislation

Criminal Procedure Law of the People's Republic of China, art. 2, Jul. 1, 1979
Criminal Procedure Law of the People's Republic of China, art. 8, Jul. 1, 1979
Criminal Procedure Law of the People's Republic of China, art. 13, Jul. 1, 1979
Criminal Procedure Law of the People's Republic of China, art. 14, Jul. 1, 1979
Criminal Procedure Law of the People's Republic of China, art. 32, Jul. 1, 1979
Criminal Procedure Law of the People's Republic of China, art. 37, Jul. 1, 1979
Criminal Procedure Law of the People's Republic of China, art. 48, Jul. 1, 1979
Criminal Procedure Law of the People's Republic of China, art. 50, Jul. 1, 1979
Criminal Procedure Law of the People's Republic of China, art. 52, Jul. 1, 1979
Criminal Procedure Law of the People's Republic of China, art. 53, Jul. 1, 1979
Criminal Procedure Law of the People's Republic of China, art. 54, Jul. 1, 1979
Criminal Procedure Law of the People's Republic of China, art. 60, Jul. 1, 1979
Criminal Procedure Law of the People's Republic of China, art. 90, Jul. 1, 1979
Criminal Procedure Law of the People's Republic of China, art. 98, Jul. 1, 1979
Criminal Procedure Law of the People's Republic of China, art. 109, Jul. 1, 1979
Criminal Procedure Law of the People's Republic of China, art. 150, Jul. 1, 1979

Criminal Procedure Law of the People's Republic of China, art. 174, Jul. 1, 1979
Criminal Procedure Law of the People's Republic of China, art. 179, Jul. 1, 1979
Criminal Procedure Law of the People's Republic of China, art. 180, Jul. 1, 1979
Criminal Procedure Law of the People's Republic of China, art. 216, Jul. 1, 1979
Criminal Procedure Law of the People's Republic of China, art. 236, Jul. 1, 1979
Criminal Procedure Law of the People's Republic of China, art. 237, Jul. 1, 1979
Criminal Procedure Law of the People's Republic of China, art. 238, Jul. 1, 1979
Criminal Procedure Law of the People's Republic of China, art. 239, Jul. 1, 1979
Criminal Procedure Law of the People's Republic of China, art. 240, Jul. 1, 1979
Criminal Procedure Law of the People's Republic of China, art. 250, Jul. 1, 1979
Criminal Procedure Law of the People's Republic of China, art. 251, Jul. 1, 1979
Criminal Procedure Law of the People's Republic of China, art. 252, Jul. 1, 1979
Criminal Procedure Law of the People's Republic of China, art. 1, as amended through to
  Mar. 17, 1996.
Criminal Procedure Law of the People's Republic of China, art. 92, as amended through
  to Mar. 17, 1996.
Criminal Procedure Law of the People's Republic of China, art. 37, para. 2, as amended
  through to Mar. 14, 2012.
Criminal Procedure Law of the People's Republic of China, art. 37, para. 4, as amended
  through to Mar. 14, 2012.
Criminal Procedure Law of the People's Republic of China, art. 47, as amended through
  to Mar. 14, 2012.
Criminal Procedure Law of the People's Republic of China, art. 55, as amended through
  to Mar. 14, 2012.
Criminal Procedure Law of the People's Republic of China, art. 83, as amended through
  to Mar. 14, 2012.
Criminal Procedure Law of the People's Republic of China, art. 93, as amended through
  to Mar. 14, 2012.
Criminal Procedure Law of the People's Republic of China, art. 99, para. 1, as amended
  through to Mar. 14, 2012.
Criminal Procedure Law of the People's Republic of China, art. 100, as amended through
  to Mar. 14, 2012.
Criminal Procedure Law of the People's Republic of China, art. 101, as amended through
  to Mar. 14, 2012.
Criminal Procedure Law of the People's Republic of China, art. 116, as amended through
  to Mar. 14, 2012.
Criminal Procedure Law of the People's Republic of China, art. 121, as amended through
  to Mar. 14, 2012.
Criminal Procedure Law of the People's Republic of China, art. 223, as amended through
  to Mar. 14, 2012.
Criminal Procedure Law of the People's Republic of China, art. 225, para. 2, as amended
  through to Mar. 14, 2012.
Criminal Procedure Law of the People's Republic of China, art. 226, para. 2, as amended
  through to Mar. 14, 2012.
Criminal Procedure Law of the People's Republic of China, art. 239, as amended through
  to Mar. 14, 2012.
Criminal Procedure Law of the People's Republic of China, art. 240, as amended through
  to Mar. 14, 2012.

138 Chinese Criminal Procedure System in Contrast

Criminal Procedure Law of the People's Republic of China, art. 256, as amended through to Mar. 14, 2012.

Criminal Procedure Law of the People's Republic of China, art. 289, as amended through to Mar. 14, 2012.

7

CONCLUSION
China, the Looking-Glass

The primary motivation for the book was the opportunity provided by the vigorous scope and pace of institutional evolution occurring in China today. Intellectually, the central motivation was the gap in analytical concepts for describing these changes. The underlying premise of some commentary today is that the innovations underway in China are simply a movement from centralized, state-centered institutions to liberal, free market institutions championed in the same countries in which these writers work. Such a premise proves to be too limiting, and conclusions from these evaluations simply return, in circular fashion, to the initial set of assumptions – i.e., markets have to be more laissez-faire, there needs to be more democracy, the state needs to be more efficient. This is the problem of the a priori analytic which finds, upon analysis, simply what the analyst embedded into the analytical framework to begin with (Lejano, 2006, 2016). The goal of the book, then, was to try to turn "to the things themselves" and find descriptives that are more able to capture what is unique and innovative about institutional change in China.

But this does not mean that institutions evolve just for change's sake. While we maintained a purely descriptive stance throughout the preceding chapters, we can shift a little to a more normative discussion of these changes. Specifically, we discuss some fundamental conflicts or contradictions that these institutional changes have to respond to.

We also turn to contexts outside China and reflect on the utility of the descriptives developed herein in other countries (the US being the foremost example of choice).

7.1 Essential Tensions

Part of the discourse of governance in China is founded upon a critique of western-style capitalism. The critique builds on fundamental contradictions within

140 Conclusion: China, the Looking-Glass

capitalism that systems of governance have to deal with (if not remedy). These contradictions include the problem with declining profit margins for corporations, as production increases in scale around a new idea or product and the variable element of capital (entrepreneurship, innovation, etc.) diminishes relative to it. As the theory goes, this creates an ever-present tendency toward periodic crises and boom-and-bust economic cycles. The great recession of 2008 only gave provenance to such crisis theory. And there are other areas of tension that are perpetual within the capitalist system. The alienation of the worker, as her labor is reduced to its commodity or exchange value, works out in terms of poor or unreliable working conditions and work opportunities in practice. And there is the ever-increasing rate of inequality, as whatever profits are generated increasingly accrue to a smaller and smaller stratum of the population. As we have seen over the last decade or so, globalization has only served to dramatize these tensions (Castells, 2010).

But the Chinese model has to deal with a set of fundamental tensions, as well, and some of these are shared with the conventional capitalist system. There is the inherent tension between empowerment of the people and disempowerment of the person. While the liberal model might define the people as simply a collection of individuals, a socialist model is in danger of equating it with something apart from individuals (such as a group or the state). So how does one design an institution that understands the collective in this complex fashion? If a market institutionalizes the individual agent to the prejudice of the group, what kind of market design brings back collective life? It is possible that some of the experiments we are seeing (such as with rural property vouchers) are evolving some kind of balance between these tensions, or maybe not (time, and better descriptive analysis, will tell). Similarly, how will the state and the Party balance its need to maintain central control with the merits of decentralized governance? And these questions redound to the socio-cultural sphere as well – for example, how will the tension between the desire for a unified polity and the diversity of peoples, comprising more than fifty ethnic groups, existing in China, be managed?

And there is the question of continued development. It would seem that China, in creating an expectation of continually high growth rates, is in a position of having to run as fast as it can simply to stay in place (and, were it to wish to progress further, must run twice as fast as that, to borrow a phrase). The current catch phrase is innovation-led development, but what is that and, more to the point, what institutional environment is needed for that to happen?

The most immediate question, of course, is what exactly is a "socialist market economy," in the ideal and, as importantly, in practice? It is certainly not the idealized model of perfect competition. What kind of hybrid or complex system will eventually emerge? What is the meaning of price and value in such a market system? The ideal is no more the equilibrium at which consumer surplus is maximized, so what is it? What is a stock market if stock prices are not simply endogenous to supply and demand? Prior to questions of efficiency, the first question is, what is it? The experiments we have examined provide some insights into what outcomes might be forthcoming from this institutional experimentation, though it is too early to say (though perhaps it is always too early to say). Somehow, markets are being designed and operated within a network of policy actors, acting in concert to steer the market toward what seems satisfactory to decision-makers, and the logics behind this are never simple (e.g., never just profit maximization).

What is "socialism with Chinese characteristics"? The standard refrain is that it began with Marxist-Leninist principles, then grew with Mao Zhedong's principles and blossomed with what is known as Deng Xiaoping Theory, and is being furthered by the thought and practice of other leaders to follow. As this book is being written, there is a motion to amend the Constitution to formally include Xi Jinping theory. All of these bodies of thought deal with but the outlines of the Chinese model (of socialism, of the market). But the model escapes exact definition perhaps because it is best left malleable and adaptive (Heilmann & Perry, 2011). The rabbit has simply gone down into the rabbit hole, and it is unclear where it will lead to. It is, as best as we can define it, a work perpetually in progress.

And, so, defining a "Chinese model" of governance escapes us, at the moment, because it is still early in its formative stages. After all, the People's Republic of China came into being in 1949, a newcomer in the league of nations. Xi Jinping characterizes China's socialist system as an established "path, theory and system,"[1] but, perhaps, it is enlightening to also understand it as a series of questions that the leadership and the people constantly struggle to answer.

7.2 Landscapes of Institutional Change

So, where have the changes tended, thus far? Many of the experiments are transitioning into something altogether different from the idealized model of collectivization. The point of the book is that what it is transitioning to seems different, too, from the institutions of liberal politics. There is a sense, in some of the scholarship, that these changes naturally tend toward institutions in western society – i.e., the idealized laissez-faire market, pluralist politics, formal and substantive separation between state and nonstate actors. But our early assessment of these trends speaks to something different, that perhaps the changes are tending to something new. Whatever China's leaders have meant by the term "socialism with Chinese characteristics," and it is possible they were not so sure what it meant, perhaps this is what is coming to pass.

For the purpose of describing these transitions, we borrowed the notions of autopoiesis and sociopoiesis from systems theory and began using the concept to understand institutional design. Many of the transitions described in this book seem to be reasonably (though partially) described by the idea of sociopoiesis. If we define autopoiesis as a subsystem that exists on its own, then a perfectly competitive market,

142 Conclusion: China, the Looking-Glass

where prices are endogenous, would correspond to this idea. In contrast, a socio-poietic system involves sources of influence outside the subsystem. It is a flexible concept that we adjust as we apply to different contexts. In the area of rural property rights, we saw how decision-making around the transferable market instrument was not limited to buyers and sellers but also involved a network of other actors, including the village collective and various levels of state government. In such a system, prices are not simply the outcome of supply and demand but also influenced by decisions regarding the collective good and social stability.

The chapter on environmental nongovernmental organizations (ENGOs) spoke to the larger question of civil society in China. Again applying the idea of socio-poiesis, an autopoietic system might delineate clean boundaries between civil society, business, and government. But in a sociopoietic system, boundaries are blurred. ENGOs are a fitting example of this. We described how their composition (the leadership but also staff) often drew from government ranks, and their mode of action varied across the spectrum from a politics of protest to one of clientelism.

If the formal system boundaries (i.e., rules, lines of authority) do not describe the system well, what does? In these types of systems, we turn to the language of relationships to interpret the blur. That is, what the institution is in actuality emerges from the working and reworking of relationships among the various policy actors. The rules of the game are worked out as a result of these interactions. In the case of rural land vouchers, discussions take place among villagers, the collective, developers, and the municipality, and these discussions are set against the larger context of provincial and state government influence. And these interactions occur in a complex set of venues, none of them evoking the idealized Habermasian model (where stakeholders gather around a round table and argue in agonistic fashion). Relationality contrasts the informal with the informal but, more than this, contrasts the actualized, embodied institution with the textualized, codified one.

This brings us to another point of departure, which is the realization that policy texts can mean different things in different contexts. Whereas textualized systems contain policy prescriptions within them (at least in the ideal), contextualized systems do not rely solely on policy texts (which are codified rules, laws, and practices). Even when they rely on texts, a policy text draws from a universe of other texts – a condition referred to as intertextuality. In a contextualized system, intertextuality can be considerable. As an example, institutions in China are not simply governed by legal documents such as the constitution or regulations. They can also be influenced by speeches from leaders, present and past, aphorisms, and we presume by everyday speech, spoken and not written, by its party and leadership. The role of these, otherwise non-legal, utterances in policy are a sign of a sociopoietic system, where relational processes determine institutional design, not just formal policy texts.

Examining how policy texts work also provides insight into what makes China different. There is an interesting contextuality to policy in China, such that a policy text underspecifies an institutional design, leaving it to other elements to

Conclusion: China, the Looking-Glass **143**

provide the rest. The flip side of this is that texts can have a richer function than simply specifying policy. The interesting digression into the strategic use of metaphor, euphemism, and aphorism in political life is an indicator of the important role that context plays in policy formulation. They can work as master frames, within which a network of policy actors can improvise how a program or policy is to be.

The changes taking place occur within a political culture of experimentation. This is a mode of institutional development characterized by the new economic innovation program, wherein eight municipalities have been named as pilot project sites for rural land reform, where use of transferable market instruments are expanding beyond the initial two pilot sites. This makes a comparative approach particularly useful. As in the case study of rural land exchange quotas, comparing Chengdu's program against Chongqing's helps delineate the particularities of either one. Another useful comparative approach is to compare the actual program against the idealized template. Sometimes we describe a thing by differentiating it from another.

7.3 Looking Beyond China

But the preceding considerations bring us to an important question: Are these insights not true also of other nations? Are there not sociopoietic elements found in the US, as well, to cite just one example? Contrary to the formally autopoietic nature of the US Constitution, to where laws trace their basis, is it not also subject to intertextuality, to some degree? What a passage in the constitution means is not quite self-contained and, instead, can draw from centuries of legal interpretation (and, so, scores of other texts). Surely, its meaning is contextual, as well. Consider the meaning of the word "equality," which evidently meant something different in Jefferson's plantation era from what it means today (and, presumably, a century from now).

And this brings us to a fundamental point, which is that, yes, these modes of description are equally applicable to these other systems. While we have been developing these alternative analytics with an eye to China, in this conclusion we state our underlying motive, which is to produce new analytics that are applicable elsewhere.

Readers from other continents, or Asian countries outside China, will recognize many of the same difficult-to-describe institutional phenomena occurring in their own contexts, as well. To focus, again for example's sake, on the US for a moment, was there not sociopoiesis at play in the real estate market crash of 2008? Was the inflated property market not an outcome of a concerted effort of multiple players, beyond buyers and sellers, including government institutions, credit rating agencies, and the media? And was the resolution of the real estate crash not determined by a network of government and private interests who collaborated to intervene in the crisis and save a host of large financial corporations? Though conservatives may pay allegiance to the autopoietic notion of the

144 Conclusion: China, the Looking-Glass

free market, was the Troubled Asset Relief Program (or TARP) of 2008 not an indication of sociopoiesis at work? The answers are obvious.

But what did we learn from the great recession of 2008? First, that the systems of governance in the US approach nothing close to that idealized (again to repeat the obvious point). The second point is more subtle, and it is that, by and large, our scholarly communities seem to not have learned much from it. The standard neoclassical economic doctrine of Friedman and Hayek still seems hegemonic in economics. The liberal model of pluralist politics seems unchanged in political science. Urban planning theory seems not to have realized, or dealt with, its role in the real estate crisis. And, though we cannot prove it, there are probably distinguished academics in business schools who are, at this moment, dreaming up a new set of complex financial instruments destined to fail in some not-so-distant future. Theoretically, we seem to have oscillated back to the pre-2008 state of intellectual life. But, given the magnitude of the crisis, how is it that this system of thought seems not to have undergone any adjustment?

Part of the reason for conceptual stagnation, it seems to us, is a lack of new modes of description by which we can characterize institutional life. Many of the terms of description, such as those derived from the rational choice and collective action fields, or the sociology of structure versus agency, or organizational theory, have remained and become hegemonic in the world of research. Understanding of property regimes is aided, but also hindered, by the dominant conceptual lens of property rights as a bundle of goods. Institutions are a set of rules to be implemented by street-level bureaucrats and communities. In short, it is what Bourdieu (1977) called doxa in the different scholarly fields, the taken-for-granted sets of ideas that, when reflected upon, start to resemble full-fledged ideologies. Keynes once wrote: "The difficulty lies, not in the new ideas, but in escaping from the old ones" (Keynes, 1936, p. vii). Writing shortly after the great recession of 2008, Coyle observed, "The gap between the interesting questions or real-world problems being taught to students at all levels has become a chasm since the start of the crisis ... It is only a slight exaggeration to say that students are taught as if nothing had changed ..." (Coyle, 2012, blurb). If the understanding of an institution like the market has been too dogmatic, what more the conventional notions of its institutions for democracy, human rights, family, school, etc.? With the arrival of a new populism, perhaps even a new insularity, in politics in the US and the world over, what is left of its cherished ideal of democracy (except the criticism that there was never much there to begin with)?

This brings us to the overarching point of the book, which is that the study of institutions needs the intervention of new concepts. If one is to understand how institutions are evolving in a neo-populist US, post-Brexit UK, post-Nehruvian India, not to mention quasi-capitalist China, we will need to stray far from the institutional doxa. For example, Granovetter made the point that it is never the case that "a market is a market is a market," and that this institution varies richly from place to place (Granovetter, 1985). So being, we might begin to understand institutions as phenomena, describing them as they are and not according to a prefabricated template. Too often, programs that do not match the template are found wanting, which is a problem since, invariably, no real thing matches the abstract template. Program evaluators base their stock-in-trade on binary analyses, wherein a program either is a success (i.e., it matches the model) or not (i.e., it does not match the model). But the gains to be had will come from increasingly attempting to describe programs as they are, how their design evolved, and how they function in actuality.

What is an institution? Unlike definitions that emphasize its formal aspects, such as Douglass North's definition of an institution as the "rules of the game" (North, 1990), we take a more phenomenological perspective. A good part of our answer is, it is how established social systems and practices actually work and are experienced. Just as Argyris and Schon pointed out the divergence between the rules of an institution as designed, and rules-in-place or theories-in-practice (Argyris & Schon, 1974), so do we realize that what an institution is supposed to be and what it is in practice can be two very different things. But the problem with strong analytical concepts is that one is primed to find, in the field, only what is found in the theory. To the utilitarian, one only finds utilities, and even such a progressive ideal as participation can become hegemonic (Cooke & Kothari, 2001). This lends to the suggestion that one takes a view of institutions as phenomena that are best understood in place.

What is an institution, as experienced? Somehow, this includes everyday realities of how it works, looks, sounds, and feels. In this book, we reflect on the observations, feelings, and perceptions of the governed, but also of the analysts themselves, as they examine the everyday life of institutions in China. In some cases, we attempt fresh description of the phenomena and, in others, are guided by contrasting how the institution appears with how it is supposed to be.

How does an institution feel? There are two questions being asked. The first is that, how can a program or policy incorporate the affective, non-formalized aspects of governance? Taxation never feels right to the taxed, but there is a difference between feeling taxed and feeling victimized. Emotion is a register that is all-important and, yet, never described in institutional life, but it should be (e.g., Durnová, 2015; Friedland, 2017). Secondly, how does a program or policy intuit the needs, responses, and experiences of the governed? This has to do with going beyond understanding institutions as a set of rules or lines of authority, toward an understanding of it as a set of relationships, an interacting group of people, bodies, things, texts, sounds, and feelings.

In the end, what is unique to China? With regard to its quest to somehow blend capitalism with socialism, is this not something also being undertaken by nations in the former Soviet Union and even Western Europe? In its ongoing issue with dealing with ethnic diversity, is this not an issue also being taken up by almost every other country? In its looming issues with national debt, aging demographics, and ever-increasing health care expenditures, are these not issues shared with Japan,

146 Conclusion: China, the Looking-Glass

the US, and others? Are these systems themselves not perpetually in flux? Is not the need to perpetually defend individual (and collective) freedoms present in these other polities as well? Are fundamentalist ideologies not threatening to undermine progress everywhere? Are not all political systems, across the planet, coming up short vis-à-vis the challenge of global environmental change? The need to reform institutions to fit the world of the 21st century is a challenge shared by all.

Surely, it is not completely responsible to regard China as a looking-glass for the rest of the world. Each place is uniquely different, and there are things in China that are not found elsewhere in the world.. One has to admit, notwithstanding the tomes of recent scholarship on China, it continues to fascinate. In this book, we propose that it should be a rich source of insight into the evolution of institutional life.

It is a strange thing to say that we study China in order to better understand the rest of the world – Germany, Brazil, India, whichever contexts are of immediate interest to the reader. Each of the conceptual devices developed in this book should have some use in more richly capturing essential elements of institutional life in these different contexts. Sociopoiesis, relationality, and contextuality are all to be found in, and should better depict, each system. And, so, we admit that this is not, ultimately, a book about China, but about institutional innovation whenever and wherever it occurs. China just happens to be, among the grand experiments in nation-building, perhaps the biggest one of all, and some of the lessons to be learned can be seen in a more distinct light by looking at exemplars and limiting cases. China is a lens through which others can each see their own context, a portal through which we notice curiouser and curiouser things. It is a lesson for scholars that to better discern what lies at your feet, it sometimes helps to look at a distant horizon.

Note

1 Xi Jinping, Study, Disseminate and Implement the Guiding Principles of the 18th CPC National Congress, Speech given at the first group study session of the Political Bureau of 18th CPC Central Committee, Nov. 17, 2012.

References

Argyris, C., & Schon, D.A. (1974). *Theory in practice: Increasing professional effectiveness.* Jossey-Bass.

Bourdieu, P. (1977 [1972]). *Outline of a theory of practice*, trans. R. Nice, Vol. 16. Cambridge: Cambridge University Press.

Castells, M. (2010). *End of millennium: The information age: Economy, society, and culture*, Vol. 3. New York: John Wiley & Sons.

Cooke, B., & Kothari, U. (2001). The case for participation as tyranny. In B. Cooke & U. Kothari (Eds.), *Participation: The new tyranny?* (pp. 1–15). Zed Books.

Coyle, D. (Ed.). (2012). *What's the use of economics?: Teaching the dismal science after the crisis.* London Publishing Partnership.

Durnová, A. (2015). 12 Lost in translation: Expressing emotions in policy deliberation. *Handbook of critical policy studies*, 222.

Friedland, R. (2017). Moving institutional logics forward: Emotion and meaningful material practice. *Organization Studies*, doi:0170840617709307.

Granovetter, M. (1985). Economic action and social structure: The problem of embeddedness. *American journal of sociology*, 91(3), 481–510.

Heilmann, S., & Perry, E.J. (Eds.). (2011). *Mao's invisible hand: The political foundations of adaptive governance in China* (p. 320). Cambridge, MA: Harvard University Asia Center.

Keynes, J.M. (1936). *The general theory of employment, interest, and money.* London and New York: Macmillan.

Lejano, R.P. (2006). *Frameworks for policy analysis: Merging text and context.* New York: Routledge.

Lejano, R. (2016). 政策分析框架 融合文本与语境 (Frameworks for policy analysis: Merging text and context), Chinese translation. Beijing: Tsinghua University Press.

North, D.C. (1990). *Institutions, institutional change, and economic performance.* Cambridge: Cambridge University Press.

INDEX

adaptation 2, 6, 10, 22, 25, 30, 80, 97–99, 100, 120, 133
aphorism 6, 10, 35–39, 41–45, 49, 142, 143
autopoietic, autopoiesis 8, 14–17, 21–22, 29–34, 50, 63, 70, 84, 97–98, 102–103, 108–109, 123–127, 133, 141–143

Bourdieu, Pierre 15, 18, 27, 144

Changzhou 5, 80, 83, 86–91
Confucius, Confucian 7, 8, 36–37, 44, 48, 74, 96–97, 102, 113, 121, 133
construction land quota 48, 57–58, 60–63

Deng Xiaoping 2, 4, 10, 36, 42, 49, 120, 122, 141
dialectic 7, 9, 18, 20, 23–24, 42–43
di piao 63–64

ENGO, Environmental Non–Governmental Organization 78–85, 88–92, 142
epoché (bracketing) 4, 7, 14, 20, 27
euphemism 6, 10, 35–38, 40, 43–45, 143
experiment, experimentation 2–6, 10–11, 36, 39, 43, 48–49, 67, 72–75, 95, 124, 141–143, 146

Frame–c 16, 34, 97–99, 131–133
Frame–t 14, 16, 97–99, 112, 133

guanxi 5, 71–72

hermeneutic 7, 9, 13, 16–18, 23–24, 34, 36, 39–40, 45, 114, 124, 133
Husserl, Edmund 3–5, 7, 13, 27

ideal types 98–99, 109
Incrementalism, incremental 2, 10, 23, 41, 48–49, 55, 67, 98
innovation (institutional) 2, 4, 10, 23, 27, 35, 48, 60, 63, 91, 94, 98–99, 119–120, 146
institutional fit 23–25, 83, 97
intertextuality 18–19, 26, 34, 37, 114, 124–125, 142–143
isomorphism 22, 25, 54

Kristeva, Jula 18–19, 26, 37

land ticket 64, 71, 73
legal families 95–96, 98, 100, 102

Mao Zhedong 36, 41, 122–123, 141
metaphor 6, 10, 21–22, 34–42, 44–45, 49, 67, 70, 120, 143
multicorporality 20–21, 50, 69, 71

Index **149**

Nu River 78, 80, 82–86, 88, 91

phenomenology 3–7, 13–14,
 18–19, 22, 25, 35, 70, 78
plenary good 20–21, 30, 48, 69, 71
policy advocacy 81–82, 85–87,
 89–91
polymorphism 10, 22, 25,
 30, 54, 97
property rights 6, 48, 51–52,
 54, 57,
 59–61, 66–67, 71, 74, 142–144

rationalization 7, 15, 29, 74
relational, relationality 5, 8,
 20–22, 26–30, 48, 50,
 54, 70–72, 74–75, 79, 91,
 99, 107, 124, 125,
 131, 142, 146
Ricoeur, Paul 7, 13, 26, 39

socialist market 2–3, 6, 10–11, 41–42, 45,
 48, 67, 95, 140
sociopoietic, sociopoiesis 15–18, 21–22,
 29–30, 34, 63, 70, 79–84, 86, 91,
 97–98, 100, 102, 104, 108–114,
 122–123, 128, 133, 141–146
specification 5, 22, 25, 30, 41, 98, 114,
 119, 133
structures of care 27–30

textuality 16–19, 26, 34–37, 97, 110, 114,
 124–125, 142–143
Transferable development rights, TDR 49,
 51, 54, 61, 62
Transductive 9

urbanization 1, 48–49, 57

Weberian 5, 8, 26–29, 74–75,
 98–99, 102

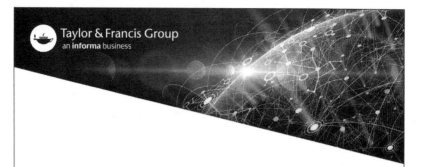

Taylor & Francis eBooks

www.taylorfrancis.com

A single destination for eBooks from Taylor & Francis with increased functionality and an improved user experience to meet the needs of our customers.

90,000+ eBooks of award-winning academic content in Humanities, Social Science, Science, Technology, Engineering, and Medical written by a global network of editors and authors.

TAYLOR & FRANCIS EBOOKS OFFERS:

A streamlined experience for our library customers

A single point of discovery for all of our eBook content

Improved search and discovery of content at both book and chapter level

REQUEST A FREE TRIAL
support@taylorfrancis.com